ESSAYS IN
AMERICAN AND ENGLISH
LITERATURE
PRESENTED TO
BRUCE ROBERT MC ELDERRY, JR.

Bruce Robert McElderry, Junior

Essays in
American and English
Literature

Presented to

Bruce Robert McElderry, Jr.

EDITED BY

Max F. Schulz

WITH

William D. Templeman

AND

Charles R. Metzger

OHIO UNIVERSITY PRESS
Athens, Ohio

*We wish to thank the Leo S. Bing Fund
for its generous financial assistance
in making this book possible.*

Contents

II. ENGLISH LITERATURE

Bruce Robert McElderry, Jr.

ஃ ஃ

Surely one of the happiest tasks is to praise a deserving man. The rare and privileged scholar like Bruce R. Mc-Elderry renews himself annually. With a capacity for endless growth, his taste continues to defy the constriction of literary presumption and to assimilate each new critical shift and literary feint. It is now more than forty years since he sat as a young Ph.D. candidate in Hardin Craig's class in Shakespeare at the University of Iowa. The breadth of his scholarly interests from then to the present is impressive. With significant results he early studied Spenser's use of poetic diction in *The Faerie Queene,* Coleridge's revision of *The Ancient Mariner,* Browning's structuring of *The Ring and the Book* as well as the Victorian reception of it, and later, Henry James's reasons for residing in Europe. It is this rich and continuing range of curiosity that the present volume of essays celebrates.

The years have been productive professionally as well for McElderry. He has served on the faculties of four universities. After leaving graduate school he taught for several years at the University of Wisconsin and Western Reserve University, then for a dozen fruitful years at Washington State University. Following three years of wartime service in the Air Corps, spent mostly in London, he came to the University of Southern California. Already established as a scholar in the English Renaissance and the Romantic Period, he moved with characteristic flexibility and enthusiasm into American literature, in which like most members of his generation he had never had formal training for the simple reason that in his student days courses in American literature were seldom taught. McElderry has also taught as visiting professor on summer faculties at New York University, Columbia University, the University of North Carolina, and the University of Iowa. In addition to steady participation in west coast scholarly meetings and organizations, he is a past chairman of the English II Section of the Modern Language Association. And in 1965 he was selected, the sixth professor in the history of the university to be so honored, to receive the University of Southern California Associates Award for Creative Scholarship and Research.

McElderry's humanity matches his scholarship and professional élan. With unflagging zeal, he will put his time and professionalism at the disposal of the beginning scholar. Many remember with deep appreciation and affection the kind words he offered them year after year when they crossed paths with him at the annual meetings of the Modern Language Association as well as the thoughtful notes he wrote in response to offprints of articles sent to him. In recent years he has been known to help a new member of the English department by baby-sitting children while the harried newcomer to Los Angeles canvassed sixty square miles of residential area to find a place to live. There are those who can testify that he changes diapers as well as any man. *Hier ist ein guter Mensch.*

At sixty-seven McElderry still carries himself like a military officer. Delightfully nicknamed by some of his friends "Robert the Bruce," he will battle for principles with the abandon of the happy warrior, but his policy is without calculation, his contention without meanness. As his midwestern Scots' background suggests, he follows unswervingly the path of duty. People who help to build universities have to make sacrifices in order to do so. For years his own literary projects languished while he turned his attention as a senior professor to the para-scholarly problems of administration, to service as president of the university senate, to service on the committee which designed and executed the university's first Mast Plan, to designing and putting into effect the university's American Studies Program, to founding the Southern California Chapter of the American Studies Association. As director of the project which catalogued the Hamlin Garland manuscripts at the University of Southern California, he also gave generous aid (as one contributor to this volume will testify) to young scholars come to explore these holdings.

Even as we now celebrate his past achievement, he continues vigorously at work. Although he officially retired in 1964, he still teaches as a visiting professor one regular semester and one summer session a year. He has also resumed projects that the press of academic responsibilities had forced him to set aside for years. He has completed in the past three years biographies of Thomas Wolfe and Henry James, an anthology of American Realism, and a book-length consideration of Shelley's prose. He is currently working on a biography of Max Beerbohm as well as a book-length study, in depth, of the year 1798, both near completion. At this rate he bids fair to pace us all for years to come. His friends and admirers honor him with this book accordingly, not at the end of his career but with it still traveling the high road.

M.F.S.
W.D.T.
C.R.M.

AMERICAN
LITERATURE

Merton M. Sealts, Jr.

❧ ☙

Melville's "Geniality"

When completion of the Northwestern-Newberry edition of the writings of Herman Melville makes possible a full concordance of his "talismanic language," [1] it will be found that the word "genial" and its cognates—"ungenial," "genially," "genialness," "genialization," and especially "geniality"—appear in some one hundred instances. Like other words he made peculiarly his own, such as the complementary pair studied in 1945 by R. E. Watters, "sociality" and "isolatoes," [2] Melville's term "geniality" deserves careful attention, for it reveals one persistent strain of sensibility linking his years at sea, his career as an author, and the retrospective musings of his late private writing. "Despite the mythic identification of Melville with the tragic 'iso-

MERTON M. SEALTS, JR., is Professor of English at the University of Wisconsin.

latoes' he created," as Edward Rosenberry has said, "he had a life-long passion for the comforts of friendship and conviviality, founded about equally on a love of talk and a love of sharing his animal enthusiasms for food and drink." [3] Among his books it is *Mardi* (1849) that most fully expresses Melville's fondness for genial conviviality; it is *The Confidence-Man* (1857) that most caustically exposes its weaknesses and dangers. Even in his last years, when nostalgia for the idealized companions of earlier days marked much of his writing, he had praise for geniality as "the flower of life springing from some sense of joy in it, more or less," as he put it in his sketch of John Marr (1888).[4]

Because *The Confidence-Man,* of all Melville's works, has the most frequent references to "genial" characters, "genial" wine, and "genial" talk, including a long conversation on the subject of geniality itself,[5] it is the one book to receive closest examination here. First, however, a glance at Melville's use of "genial" in his earlier writings will be helpful in bringing out the principal associations and connotations that geniality evidently held for him. "The Paradise of Bachelors" (1855), written not long before *The Confidence-Man,* is an appropriate place to begin. This composition recalls the "genial hospitalities" Melville enjoyed at the Temple in London during 1849—in particular a "good, genial dinner." The modern Templar he salutes as "best of comrades, most affable of hosts, capital diner. . . . His wit and wine are both of sparkling brands." During the dinner,

> as the wine ran apace, the spirits of the company grew more and more to perfect genialness and unconstraint. . . . It was the very perfection of quiet absorption of good living, good drinking, good feeling, and good talk. We were a band of brothers. Comfort—fraternal, housefold comfort, was the grand trait of the affair.[6]

To be genial for Melville was thus to be affable, comradely, even fraternal, enjoying the good drinking and good living that foster good feeling and good talk. Letters to his friends, especially Duyckinck and Hawthorne, express the same sentiments; in his books, eating, drinking, and smoking, as Rosenberry has effectively shown, repeatedly constitute "the thematic handmaidens of social intercourse." [7] *Mardi* in particular is filled with Rabelaisian feastings, its interpolated songs celebrating the "genial glow" of wine and the comfort brought by tobacco.

Except for *White-Jacket* (1850), with its admiring portrait of Jack Chase as a companionable man of "good sense and good feeling" (Chapter 4) and its enthusiastic praise of fraternal smoking (Chapter 91),[8] the nature of Melville's writing after the exuberance of *Mardi* required relatively few passages in the convivial vein until "The Paradise of Bachelors." In *Moby Dick* (1851), Ahab is made to abandon his symbolic pipe, "this thing that is meant for sereneness," in the realization that on such a revengeful quest as his, "smoking no longer soothes" (Chapter 30); he lacks "the low, enjoying power" (Chapter 37). Save for Pip, who radiates "that pleasant, genial, jolly brightness peculiar to his tribe" (Chapter 93),[9] there is little geniality in the book, though occasionally Ishmael voices his "free and easy sort of genial, desperado philosophy," born of "that odd sort of wayward mood" in which a man "takes this whole universe for a vast practical joke," when "nothing dispirits, and nothing seems worth while disputing" (Chapter 49).[10] The despairing young hero of *Pierre,* another Melville dark book (1852) which particularly anticipates *The Confidence-Man,* comes to know this same mood—in sharp contrast with the optimism, cheerful good-will, companionableness, and sterling charity that we are told marked him in the days of his boyhood.[11]

There are scattered references to geniality in several of

the magazine pieces that Melville wrote between *Pierre* and *The Confidence-Man,* but most of the stories are of a predominantly somber cast. Occasional touches of human kindliness and warmth are present, but the prevailing themes are poverty and sickness, failure and rejection, withdrawal and isolation—even naïveté and deception, as in *The Confidence-Man* itself. The poverty-stricken narrator of "The Two Temples," finished in 1854, longs to become part of some "genial humane assembly of my kind; such as, at its best and highest, is to be found in the unified multitude of a devout congregation," but is rebuffed by the sexton of a fashionable New York church; Melville's satire seemed so pointed in its application that *Putnam's Magazine* declined to risk publishing the sketch. Following "The Paradise of Bachelors," with its celebration of wit, wine, and genial hospitality, "Jimmy Rose" (1855) describes a bachelor's unhappy downfall. Jimmy is "a great ladies' man" who never marries; his cheeks bloom with health and "the joy of life." But after his misfortunes, few of his friends except the narrator remember his cheeriness and sparkling wit in the old days of his great dinners, suppers, and balls, when his noble graces and glorious wine marked his "bounteous heart and board." [12] "Old wine" and a "comfortable pipe" provide part of the warmth in "I and My Chimney" (1856), while in "The Apple-Tree Table" (1856) Melville deals with the eventful re-emergence of a "sad little hermit of a table, . . . long banished from genial neighborhood, with all the kindly influences of warm urns, warm fires, and warm hearts." [13] If bounteous hospitality, conviviality, and fraternal unity are outward signs of true geniality, humane warmth and kindliness are clearly its motivating spirit.

But there is another aspect of geniality, a negative one—and Melville never lets his readers overlook it. In "The Paradise of Bachelors," immediately following the "band

of brothers" passage quoted above, comes the following observation:

> Also, you could plainly see that these easy-hearted men had no
> wives or children to give an anxious thought. Almost all of
> them were travelers, too; for bachelors alone can travel freely,
> and without any twinges of their consciences touching deser-
> tion of the fireside.
> The thing called pain, the bugbear styled trouble—those two
> legends seemed preposterous to their bachelor imaginations.
> How could men of liberal sense, ripe scholarship in the world,
> and capacious philosophical and convivial understandings—how
> could they suffer themselves to be imposed upon by such
> monkish fables? [14]

From at least the time of *Mardi,* undertaken not long after
his own marriage, Melville had repeatedly used bachelors
—bachelors and sophomores—as his favorite examples of
pleasure-loving immaturity and naïveté, as yet untouched
by misfortune. It is so in Chapter 115 of *Moby Dick,* for
example, where the "moody" *Pequod,* outward bound,
meets the *Bachelor,* a "glad ship of good luck" returning
from a prosperous voyage.

> "Come aboard, come aboard!" cried the gay Bachelor's com-
> mander, lifting a glass and a bottle in the air.
> "Hast seen the White Whale?" gritted Ahab in reply.
> "No; only heard of him; but don't believe in him at all," said
> the other good-humoredly. "Come aboard!" [15]

As for "The Paradise of Bachelors," the earlier part of the
sketch expresses honestly Melville's genuine love of "good
living, good drinking, good feeling, and good talk." But its
later paragraphs show his equally clear recognition that the
genial way of living he describes, for all its fraternal comfort and warm attractiveness, implies a denial of the responsibilities and grimmer realities of mature life. This
double evaluation carries over into *The Confidence-Man,*

where spurious geniality is a peculiarly enticing bait for trapping the young or unwary among passengers of the *Fidèle*, the Mississippi steamboat evidently to be taken as a microcosm of contemporary society.

Geniality in *The Confidence-Man* is a principal element in those episodes involving two particular manifestations of the masquerading title-character—"this apostle of geniality," as a reviewer at the time aptly described him, who beneath his affable manner is indeed what the same critic suspected: "an arch-imposter of the deepest dye." [16] These are the bogus stock salesmen of Chapters 9–15, named as "Mr. Truman" by the herb-doctor in Chapter 20, and the "cosmopolitan" calling himself Frank Goodman who dominates the entire second half of the book, from Chapter 23 to Chapter 45. The seemingly open, warm, convivial manner of these two figures has an irresistible attraction for their fellow-passengers of a like disposition, though not for other characters less genially warm than suspicious, cold, and even misanthropic.

A quick résumé of the operations of the stock salesman will develop this point and set a pattern for studying the more important figure of the cosmopolitan. Entering the story with "genial jauntiness" (p. 51) as "president and transfer-agent" of "the Black Rapids Coal Company," the salesman successfully peddles his stock to three of his potential victims, though with a fourth he apparently meets defeat. In Chapter 9 a gullible young college student—appropriately, a sophomore, one fond of champagne dinners, cigars, and "fellows that talk comfortably and prosperously," falls easy prey to the salesman and his flattering remarks about the young man's caution and "genial humor" (pp. 51–56). In Chapters 10–13 a warm-hearted, genuinely charitable merchant is just as unwary—and unintentionally alerts the salesman to the presence aboard of his third victim, the miser of Chapter 15. But early in Chapter 10 the confidence-game does not work. In the ship's cabin the "ruddy-cheeked" salesman first encounters "a little, dried-up man, who looked as if he never dined," engaged in reading verses on a handbill thrown about the cabin:

> *Alas for man, he hath small sense*
> *Of genial trust and confidence.*

Though feeling momentarily "trustful and genial" after reading these lines ("not unlike a sermon," he says of them), the little man rebuffs each advance as the salesman invites him to enjoy a game of "genial cards" ("Somehow I distrust cards"), a bottle of wine, cigars, or story-telling, for all of these appurtenances of geniality are really foreign to his habits and disposition (pp. 57–59).[17] Thus Melville establishes his reader's association of geniality with mutual "trust and confidence," its absence with mistrust and suspicion.

In the later episodes involving the cosmopolitan, where Melville treats geniality at greater length and on a more philosophical level, this same general pattern also applies. The cosmopolitan makes his first appearance at the end of Chapter 23, which opens with the rifle-carrying Missourian called "Pitch"—a mature man of skeptical outlook but still one of Melville's extensive gallery of bachelors—meditating ruefully upon a bargain he has just concluded: a certain "man with a brass plate," agent of a "Philosophical Intelligence Office," has somehow managed to persuade him, against his previous experience and firm resolution, to hire a fifteen-year-old boy, sight unseen, and to advance money for his passage to Missouri. As the reader knows, the employment agent was really the masquerading confidence-man in another disguise. The Missourian, though now too late, correctly "begins to suspect him" and "half divines, too, that he, the philosopher, had unwittingly been betrayed into being an unphilosophical dupe" (p. 147). This man is obviously shrewder than the collegian and more suspicious than the merchant. How, exactly, had he been tricked?

> Philosophy, knowledge, experience—were those trusty knights of the castle recreant? No, but unbeknown to them, the enemy stole on the castle's south side, its genial one, where Suspicion, the warder, parleyed. In fine, his too indulgent, too artless and companionable nature betrayed him. Admonished by which, he thinks he must be a little splenetic in his intercourse henceforth (p. 148).

As the Missourian "revolves the crafty process of sociable chat" by which he fancies he had been duped (p. 148), he is roused by a "genial hand" laid on his "ungenial shoulder." It is the rosy-cheeked cosmopolitan, "king of traveled good-fellows, evidently," with his Nuremburgh pipe in hand, symbolically wreathed in tobacco smoke. Identifying himself not by name but as "a true citizen of the world," the "warm and confiding" cosmopolitan, in Chapter 24,[18] takes direct issue with the "unrosy" Missourian's "unprofitable philosophy of disesteem for man," charging that it springs from "a certain lowness, if not sourness, of spirits inseparable from sequestration." His remedy is conviviality. One should "mix in," he says, have a good time, and cure "sober sottishness" with a little judicious tippling, as a sick old woman was once cured by her doctor's prescription of "a jug of Santa Cruz" (pp. 149–152). The Missourian, surprised into interest by the anecdote, nevertheless prefers his customary jug of cold water to a jug of wine, thinking even "the too-sober view of life" to be "nearer true than the too-drunken" and finding "Rabelais's pro-wine Koran no more trustworthy than Mahomet's anti-wine one." The cosmopolitan, shifting his tactics, then proposes a walk among the other passengers, arguing that by natural law "men are social as sheep gregarious. . . . I say, mix with man, now, immediately, and be your end a more genial philosophy" (pp. 153–156).

At this point the irritated Missourian flings off the other's "fraternal arm," gestures with his own symbolic rifle, and cries out roundly against "any sly, smooth, philandering rat" (i.e., insincere man-lover) which may be plundering the *Fidèle*'s "human grain-bin." But when the cosmopolitan counters by ambiguously praising the "humor" of Diogenes the Cynic above that of the openly man-hating Timon, the Missourian suddenly seizes his hand, squeezes it vigorously, and hails his companion as a brother misanthrope! "You are Diogenes," he exclaims, "Diogenes in disguise. I say— Diogenes masquerading as a cosmopolitan." The confidence-man professes amazement. Quickly retaliating, he labels the Missourian "an Ishmael" whom he had earnestly hoped to reclaim for the human race, and promptly moves away "less lightsome than he had come, leaving the discomfited misanthrope to the solitude he held so sapient" (pp. 156–157). In the prickly Missourian, once burned and now twice shy, he has met his match, and their encounter thus ends in a virtual draw.

The next episode, which also ends with the shrewd penetration—this time by the cosmopolitan—of another's disguise, introduces one more seemingly genial passenger: Charles Arnold Noble,[19] himself a Mississippi sharper in search of a victim, whose revealing countenance betokens "a kind of bilious habit" (p. 158). Here too occurs a discussion in which convivial geniality is proposed as counterweight to misanthropy. Passing over Chapters 26 and 27, where Noble expounds "the metaphysics of Indian-hating" and relates in some detail the borrowed story of Colonel John Moredock, we find him concluding the latter account with the suggestion that the Missourian is an Indian-hater like Moredock. In such men Noble detects "something apparently self-contradicting," however, for "nearly all In-

11

dian-haters have at bottom loving hearts; at any rate, hearts, if anything, more generous than the average." Thus Moredock himself was "not without humane feelings. . . . He could be very convivial; told a good story . . . , and sung a capital song" (p. 175)—in short, he had the very attributes Melville associates with geniality.[20] But the cosmopolitan is dubious. Though ready to grant that the Missourian is not what he seems ("His outside is but put on"), and to assert that Pitch really loves men even while "snapping at them all the time," such a man is still no Indian-hater. As for the story of Moredock himself, its seeming contradictions strike the cosmopolitan as incredible.

> "To me some parts don't hang together. If the man of hate, how could John Moredock be also the man of love? Either his lone campaigns are fabulous as Hercules'; or else, those being true, what was thrown in about his geniality is but garnish. In short, if ever there was such a man as Moredock, he, in my way of thinking, was either misanthrope or nothing; and his misanthropy the more intense from being focused on one race of men" (p. 177).

As the cosmopolitan goes on to develop this line of thought, he brings sharply into focus the central issues of the book. For him, it is all or nothing: one must either love man or hate him, as in religion one must either believe or disbelieve. Misanthropy and infidelity are in fact co-ordinates; they spring

> "from the same root, I say; for, set aside materialism, and what is an atheist, but one who does not, or will not, see in the universe a ruling principle of love; and what a misanthrope, but one who does not, or will not, see in man a ruling principle of kindness? Don't you see? In either case the vice consists in a want of confidence" (p. 178).

In the conduct of social life it is the same alternative of either/or: a man must be altogether genial or else turn not merely suspicious but a thoroughgoing misanthrope:

"Can a misanthrope feel warm, I ask myself; take ease? be companionable with himself? Can a misanthrope smoke a cigar and muse? . . . Has the misanthrope such a thing as an appetite? Shall a peach refresh him? The effervescence of champagne, with what eye does he behold it?" (pp. 178–179).

With these sharply phrased views Charlie Noble readily agrees; indeed, as the cosmopolitan observes pointedly, were their sentiments "written in a book, whose was whose, few but the nicest critics might determine." Still, when Noble proposes celebrating their new friendship over a bottle of wine the cosmopolitan at first demurs, on the ground that he has already drunk so much with "so many old friends, all free-hearted, convivial gentlemen," that he finds "his head of less capacity than his heart" (pp. 179–180). Grateful for this lead, Noble endeavors to make his intended victim tipsy by plying him convivially with wine while abstaining himself, but the wily cosmopolitan shows himself thoroughly equal to this old game. Noble's fulsome praise of wine (he is not drinking) and tobacco (he is not smoking) sets the tone of their wide-ranging conversation: as given in Chapters 29–35 it is filled with "genial" thoughts and punctuated with "genial" gestures. Noble ultimately steers the talking back to the subject of conviviality, which for him "signifies the highest pitch of geniality" and "implies, as indispensable auxiliary, the cheery benediction of the bottle" (he is still not drinking). His conclusion is that the man who "loves not wine" should be hanged for an "ungenial soul" (pp. 198–199). The wine-drinking cosmopolitan, hearing from Noble much the same one-sided argument he himself had offered the water-loving Missourian, now raises an objection: "Conviviality," he asserts, "is one good thing, and sobriety is another good thing." Noble concedes the point, blaming the wine for his one-sidedness: "Indeed, indeed, I have indulged too genially" (p. 199).

Now the scene is properly set, and Noble's remark becomes the cue touching off an extravaganza of comedy. The dialogue which follows toward the close of Chapter 30 (pp. 199–201) brings to a head the whole complex of interrelated themes we have been examining: warm geniality, trust and confidence, philanthropy *versus* ungenial coldness, doubt and suspicion, misanthropy. The exchange is both comic and dramatic; the speeches will be given here as though Melville had written them for a play, with each speaker duly labeled for the reader's convenience. Noble is still holding forth. "By the way," he continues, "talking of geniality, it is much on the increase in these days, ain't it?"

GOODMAN "It is, and I hail the fact. Nothing better attests the advance of the humanitarian spirit. In former and less humanitarian ages . . . geniality was mostly confined to the fireside and table. But in our age . . . it is with this precious quality as with precious gold in old Peru, which Pizarro found making up the scullion's sauce-pot as the Inca's crown. Yes, we golden boys, the moderns, have geniality everywhere—a bounty broadcast like noonlight."

NOBLE "True, true; my sentiments again. Geniality has invaded each department and profession. We have genial senators, genial authors, genial lecturers, genial doctors, genial clergymen, genial surgeons, and the next thing we shall have genial hangmen."

GOODMAN "As to the last-named sort of person, I trust that the advancing spirit of geniality will at last enable us to dispense with him. No murderers—no hangmen. And surely, when the whole world shall have been genialized, it will be as out of place to talk of murderers, as in a Christianized world to talk of sinners."

NOBLE "To pursue the thought, every blessing is attended with some evil, and—"

GOODMAN "Stay, that may be better let pass for a loose saying, than for hopeful doctrine."

NOBLE "Well, assuming the saying's truth, it would apply to the future supremacy of the genial spirit, since then it will fare

with the hangman as it did with the weaver when the spinning-
jenny whizzed into the ascendant. Thrown out of employment,
what could Jack Ketch turn his hand to? Butchering?"

To the cosmopolitan's sly suggestion that the hangman
may "turn valet," in view of his "familiar dexterity about
the person," Noble asks, "Are you . . . really in earnest?"
Goodman's "mildly earnest" reply brings the whole discussion to its designed climax:

> "I trust I am never otherwise; but talking of the advance of
> geniality, I am not without hopes that it will eventually exert
> its influence even upon so difficult a subject as the misan-
> thrope."

> NOBLE "A genial misanthrope! I thought I had stretched the rope
> pretty hard in talking of genial hangmen. A genial misanthrope
> is no more conceivable than a surly philanthropist."

The cosmopolitan insists that there *is* such a being as "a
surly philanthropist"; indeed, the Missourian is a perfect
example:

> "Does he not . . . hide under a surly air a philanthropic heart?
> Now, the genial misanthrope, when, in the process of eras, he
> shall turn up, will be the converse of this; under an affable air,
> he will hide a misanthropical heart. In short, the genial mis-
> anthrope will be a new kind of monster, but still no small im-
> provement upon the original one, since, instead of making faces
> and throwing stones at people, like that poor old crazy man,
> Timon, he will take steps, fiddle in hand, and set the tickled
> world a' dancing. In a word, as the progress of Christianization
> mellows those in manner whom it cannot mend in mind, much
> the same will it prove with the progress of genialization. And so,
> thanks to geniality, the misanthrope, reclaimed from his boorish
> address, will take on refinement and softness—to so genial a de-
> gree, indeed, that it may possibly fall out that the misanthrope
> of the coming century will be almost as popular as, I am
> sincerely sorry to say, some philanthropists of the present time
> would seem not to be, as witness my eccentric friend named
> before" (pp. 200–201).

A look at the movement of Melville's skillful rhetoric through these tightly structured speeches discloses the intensely serious thrust behind the humorous extravagance. When the comic Noble makes his increasingly fatuous remarks about the forward march of geniality, the witty Goodman, pretending to agree, not only caps each successive point on Noble's own level but at the same time transforms their verbal exchange into a series of increasingly serious jabs at prevalent contemporary assumptions about "the advance of the humanitarian spirit" and "the progress of Christianization." His inference, obvious to the clear-eyed reader, is that "the whole world" is just about as likely to turn genuinely Christian as it is to become truly "genialized": "In a word, as the progress of Christianization *mellows those in manner whom it cannot mend in mind,* much the same will it prove with the progress of genialization" (emphasis added). "Geniality" in this immediate context is actually Melville's rhetorical stalking-horse for an exposure of the pretensions of humanitarianism and religion, conceived in terms of the prevailing nineteenth-century faith in inevitable "progress" that so frequently drew his fire.[21] This point once established, the function of "geniality" in *The Confidence-Man* as a whole is further illuminated. When the dealer in "confidence" assumes geniality as his mask, it becomes the exact equivalent of such other humbugs as the superficial piety and charity he displays elsewhere in the book. And when passengers aboard the *Fidèle* cannot resist playing the confidence-game, both its operators and their gullible victims get out of it about what they both deserve.

Beside the consummate performance of the cosmopolitan throughout every episode in which he appears, the forced geniality of the bilious Charlie Noble during their long conversation seems ridiculous and crude: Noble is but an ordinary journeyman sharper while Goodman is the confidence-man *par excellence.* But in Chapter 24, we recall, the Missourian Pitch, a shrewder observer than Noble, had seen in Goodman a misanthrope "masquerading as a cosmopolitan"—and conversely, in Chapter 28, the cosmopolitan had spoken of Pitch himself as really a philanthropist in disguise. Goodman's intriguing distinction in Chapter 30 between the "surly philanthropist" and "genial misanthrope" is of a piece with these earlier identifications: indeed his double picture here "so resembles the Missourian and himself respectively," in Miss Foster's words, "as to amount to confession." [22] But again what the careful reader detects is lost on Charlie Noble, who, "a little weary, perhaps, of a speculation so abstract," breaks off the discussion of the genial misanthrope by repeating that one "must be genial or he is nothing. So fill up, fill up, and be genial!" (p. 201). The wily cosmopolitan, observing accurately that "I do about all the drinking, and you do about all—the genial" (p. 202), is now ready to put his "boon companion" to the test: "I am in want, urgent want, of money," he declares, and Charlie is going to loan him fifty dollars. But the "noble kindliness" of Charlie has undergone a predictable metamorphosis, and Noble promptly invites Goodman to "go to the devil, sir! Beggar, impostor!—never so deceived in a man in my life" (pp. 202–203).

There are two sequels to this exposure of the falsely genial. One of them follows immediately, when in Chapter 32, by producing "ten half-eagles" from his pocket, the cosmopolitan as if by magic "restores" his former friend (p. 204). The other comes in the play-acting of Chapter 39, when with a man called Egbert taking the part of "Charlie" the cosmopolitan again requests a loan of his "bosom-friend" and once more is met with a flat refusal. In practical terms the results are the same, though the original Charlie is transparently a sharper while Egbert is a professed exponent of the mystical philosophy of one Mark

Winsome—a distinctly Emersonian figure who makes a brief appearance in Chapter 36, ungenially declines to finish what remains of Noble's bottle of wine, and enjoys instead a goblet of ice-water (pp. 212–218). Beneath their unlike masks the ungenial mystics and falsely genial operators are thus presented as equally cold and equally nonbenevolent.

Faced with the task of evaluating this book of variations on the theme of confidence, more than one critic has responded by writing it off as the despairing outcry of a confirmed misanthrope—thus ascribing to Melville himself the all-or-none philosophy put forth in turn by such dubious speakers as Frank Goodman and Charlie Noble. But it is clear from Melville's writing after *The Confidence-Man* that he neither renounced mankind nor forswore geniality, despite the obvious reservations he had expressed there about both. Before going on to the later writings, it will be well to examine one more passage in *The Confidence-Man* itself, again linking wine with confidence and trust, which affords a clue to his own mature view of the issues. It occurs in Chapter 29, as the talkative cosmopolitan is commenting on Noble's observation that good wine is "the peculiar bond of good feeling," even though some "gloomy skeptics . . . maintain that now-a-days pure wine is unpurchasable" (p. 182). Though ostensibly horrified at so painful an example of "want of confidence," and lamenting the consequences to "convivial geniality" if "wine be false, while men are true," the cosmopolitan is nevertheless reminded of certain reports he has heard (pp. 182–183). There exists, it is claimed,

> "a kind of man who, while convinced that on this continent most wines are shams, yet still drinks away at them; accounting wine so fine a thing, that even the sham article is better than none at all. And if the temperance people urge that, by this course, he will sooner or later be undermined in health, he answers, 'And do you think I don't know that? But health with-

out cheer I hold a bore; and cheer, even of the spurious sort,
has its price, which I am willing to pay' " (p. 183).

"Such a man, Frank," responds Noble to these words, "must
have a disposition ungovernably bacchanalian." "Yes," replies Goodman, "if such a man there be, which I don't
credit." After offering still further disclaimers of his "fable,"
he then goes on to say that from this very story "I once
heard a person of less genius than grotesqueness draw a
moral even more extravagant than the fable itself." According to him,

> "it illustrated, as in a parable, how that a man of a disposition
> ungovernably good-natured might still familiarly associate with
> men, though, at the same time, he believed the greater part of
> men false-hearted—accounting society so sweet a thing that even
> the spurious sort was better than none at all. And if the Roche-
> foucaultites urge that, by this course, he will sooner or later be
> undermined in security, he answers, 'And do you think I don't
> know that? But security without society I hold a bore; and
> society, even of the spurious sort, has its price, which I am will-
> ing to pay' " (p. 184).

What is said in these carefully balanced passages does not
represent the attitude of the cosmopolitan himself—that
genial man-hater who by the end of the book is revealed as
probable surrogate for Satan. Indeed, he repeatedly dis-
claims the "fable" and impugns the freak who draws from
it his "extravagant" moral. That anonymous "person of less
genius than grotesqueness" bears a distinct family resemblance to other Melvilleian characters, however: minor figures often described as eccentric who turn up in works from
Mardi to *Billy Budd* as spokesmen for points of view Melville preferred not to espouse directly through flat authorial
comment.[23] Indeed he is very much like that "rare bird"
introduced as "Hilary" in the "Inscription Epistolary" to
John Marr and Other Sailors (1888): a "companionable"

man "at once genial and acute. Genial, I mean, without sharing much in mere gregariousness, which, with some, passes for a sort of geniality. . . ." [24] This thumbnail sketch exactly hits the outline of Melville's own figure as it emerges from the shadows of his later years through the medium of his occasional writing.

Following completion of *The Confidence-Man* in 1856, Melville set out for Europe and the Near East in search of rest and restored health. He looked up Hawthorne in Liverpool, but with the old spirit of adventure gone out of him, he confessed during their conversation, he anticipated little real pleasure from the trip. ("Bachelors alone can travel freely," he had written in recalling his previous voyage of 1849.) "To be a good traveler, and derive from travel real enjoyment," he said in the lecture of 1859 called "Traveling," one "must be young, care-free, and gifted with geniality and imagination, for if without these last he may as well stay at home." [25] Geniality is a quality repeatedly celebrated, even in correspondence, throughout Melville's so-called "silent years." A verse-letter to one of his New York friends, Daniel Shepherd, extending an invitation for a Berkshire visit in 1859, promises that though Shepherd might miss his accustomed otard and claret while at Arrowhead, the "guest *unwined*" there could still count on plenty of bourbon, cold water, and "genial Friendship." Melville himself praised the "genial hospitality" of his favorite "Cousin Kate" and her husband, Abraham Lansing, in Albany during his visits there from New York, where he resumed residence in 1863. And to a sympathetic brother-in-law, John Hoadley, he voiced in 1877 the hope that his letter expressed "good-fellowship," for "at my years, and with my disposition, or rather, constitution, one gets to care less and less for everything except downright good feeling." [26]

Nor is the genial spirit banished from Melville's poetry,

serious though much of it is in subject and tone. Even in *Clarel* (1876), where the mood is prevailingly subdued, there is considerable talk of wine. The word "genial" itself occurs nearly a dozen times in the poem, always with familiar connotations [27]—notably in the characterization of Rolfe, a partial self-portrait of the author, who possesses both a "genial heart" and "a brain austere" (I, xxxi, 14) much as Hilary in the later *John Marr* volume combines his geniality with acuteness. The old association of conviviality with a genial temper is also renewed in the *John Marr* poems such as "Bridegroom Dick," with its celebration of the pipe and "the wine's genial cup" and its recollections of Melville's cousin Guert Gansevoort, a wine-bibbing naval officer:

> *O Tom, but he knew a blue-jacket's ways,*
> *And how a lieutenant may genially haze;*
> *Only a sailor sailors heartily praise.*

Among other sailors so praised is Jack Chase, this time as "Jack Roy":

> *Never relishing the knave, though allowing for the menial,*
> *Nor overmuch the king, Jack, nor prodigally genial.*[28]

In prose, the Burgundy Club sketches, begun about 1875 as Melville was finishing *Clarel*, feature a "genial foreigner," the Marquis de Grandvin, a personification of wine, and that "genial spirit" Jack Gentian; in his adoption of the Marquis' "genial philosophy" Gentian "may not improperly be regarded as his disciple." Thinking of the symbolic character of the Marquis, Melville specifically observed in "The Marquis de Grandvin" that "a person of genial temper is not only very likely to be a popular man's man, but also, and beyond that, a favorite with the ladies." [29] Writers as different as Shakespeare and the poet James Thomson attracted Melville as "genial"; [30] so too did a figure of his own imagination, Billy Budd, whom he conceived from the first as "genial in temper, and sparklingly so." In *Billy Budd* itself, the culminating work of the late years, rosy-cheeked Billy is "happily endowed with the gaiety of high health, youth, and a free heart" that Melville still treasured so much, and likeable for his "genial happy-go-lucky air" [31]— but with Melville's earlier innocents, he proves all too trusting of mankind in a world that produces both Billy Budds and John Claggarts.

These later works, major and minor, are not the writings of an embittered misanthrope—not even of a "genial" one. Their author, one infers, was a man neither "confident" nor even gregarious, but one who never ceased to value good fellowship and good feeling, in the company of a few convivial intimates or else in memories of the past. Like Melville's "Hilary," such a man could be termed both genial and acute—perhaps more genial in later years than in the 1850's when *The Confidence-Man* was being written. In 1851 he had frankly confessed to Hawthorne, while asserting his "ruthless" and "unconditional" democracy, his "dislike to all mankind—in the mass"; [32] in 1855 he concluded "I and My Chimney"—so brightly magazinish on the surface and so dark beneath—with the narrator's wry acknowledgment that his "city friends" think he is "getting sour and unsocial. Some say that I have become a sort of mossy old misanthrope. . . ." [33] But Melville himself was at bottom no more a misanthrope than a philanthropist, or no less; he was plainly something of both. In mankind, to adapt Hawthorne's much-quoted words about him in 1856, he could apparently neither quite "believe" nor be comfortable in his unbelief. Hawthorne thought him "too honest and courageous not to try to do one or the other," but "one or the other" was exactly the rub—witness the all-or-none reasoning of "Goodman" and "Noble"! There is nothing in *The Confidence-Man* to align Melville himself with these spurious figures or with their dubious propositions on either side of the argument.

On the contrary, human nature impressed Melville, like the tortoise of "The Encantadas," as both black and bright: "Enjoy the bright, keep it turned up perpetually if you can," he admonishes in Sketch Second, "but be honest, and don't deny the black." [34] His work of the fifties and after illustrates his honest and courageous acknowledgment of both—even when the darker side seems more in the ascendant. "That which we seek and shun is there." [35] But skepticism is not cynicism, and a nonbeliever in "confidence" and "progress" who disliked mankind in the mass could nevertheless remain a realist, a democrat, and a confirmed lover of "good living, good drinking, good feeling, and good talk." Like the essentially good-natured, wine-drinking, but still clear-eyed man in the fable, though all too aware that wines may be sham and humanity false-hearted, Melville would settle for neither "health without cheer" nor "security without society." Geniality, even of the spurious sort, has its price—and he was never unwilling to pay.

NOTES

1. The phrase is Newton Arvin's, applied to Melville in his Introduction to *Hawthorne's Short Stories* (New York, 1946), p. xv.

2. R. E. Watters, "Melville's 'Sociality,'" *American Literature*, XVII (March 1945), 33–49; "Melville's 'Isolatoes,'" *PMLA*, LX (December 1945), 1138–1148.

3. Edward H. Rosenberry, *Melville and the Comic Spirit* (Cambridge, Mass., 1955), p. 3.

4. *Collected Poems of Herman Melville*, ed. Howard P. Vincent (Chicago, 1947), p. 161.

5. In this book alone are more than seventy occurrences of "genial" and its cognates, concentrated in thirteen of the forty-six chapters: 9–11, 13, 23–24, 27–31, 34, 36. For still other instances, see the related fragment "The River" and Melville's draft of projected chapter titles, both printed in *The Confidence-Man*, ed. Elizabeth S. Foster (New York, 1954), pp. 380, 381. Page references to this edition are given

parenthetically in the discussion below, along with inclusive chapter numbers applicable to any edition of the work.

6. "The Paradise of Bachelors," in *The Complete Stories of Herman Melville*, ed. Jay Leyda (New York, 1949), pp. 187, 189, 191, 192–193.

7. *Melville and the Comic Spirit*, p. 53. I am particularly indebted to Mr. Rosenberry's treatment of the "gastronomic" comedy in *Mardi* and its predecessors, which goes far beyond the necessarily limited discussion here.

8. *White-Jacket* (New York, 1892), pp. 16, 361–366.

9. In "Benito Cereno" (1855) Captain Delano, "like most men of a good, blithe heart, . . . took to negroes, not philanthropically, but genially, just as other men to Newfoundland dogs" (*Complete Stories*, p. 307). In *The Confidence-Man*, Chapter 11, the bogus stock salesman holds Negroes to be "by nature a singularly cheerful race" who "even from religion" dismiss "all gloom" (p. 64).

10. *Moby Dick* (New York, 1952), pp. 126, 165, 225–226, 410.

11. *Pierre* (New York, 1949), p. 324 (Book 20, Chapter 1).

12. Jimmy's misfortunes are somewhat like those of Charlemont in Chapter 34 of *The Confidence-Man*, except that the latter is ultimately restored to "genial friendships" (p. 209).

13. *Complete Stories*, pp. 160, 244, 385–386, 412.

14. *Ibid.*, p. 193.

15. *Moby Dick*, p. 489.

16. *The Critic*, as quoted by Miss Foster in the invaluable Introduction to her edition, p. xxxv.

17. There is possibly a coda to this encounter. The stock salesman, taking a hint from the merchant's reference in Chapter 11 to "a shrunken old miser . . . stretched out, an invalid, on a bare plank in the emigrants' quarters" (p. 63), later visits this man, succors him with a glass of water, and before leaving his side extracts from him "ten hoarded eagles" for an unspecified investment (Chapter 15). The miser's flesh is described as "dry as combustibles" (p. 82); when he reappears, tottering, in Chapter 20, he is seen as "dried-up . . . , with the stature of a boy of twelve" (p. 114). Except for the implication that the miser has not previously left the emigrants' cabin, one might infer from this studied phrasing that he is to be identified with the "little, dried-up man" seated in the cabin (p. 58) who had resisted the salesman's proffered wine and other blandishments. It is possible that at one point Melville intended some connection between the two figures.

18. Entitled "A Philanthropist Undertakes to Convert a Misanthrope, but Does Not Get Beyond Confuting Him." An earlier version of this title had called overt attention to their emblematic pipe and rifle: "The Philanthropist & Misanthrope. *The Rifle* & Pipe [*The Pipe* & Rifle?]." See Miss Foster's edition, p. 381.

19. The name he gives in Chapter 29, where the cosmopolitan identifies himself as Francis Goodman; both names are palpably false. Miss

24

Foster, in her edition, terms Noble's middle name, "Arnold," a "visible tag of treachery" (p. lxxiii); "Charlie Noble," as Melville surely
knew, is a sailor's term for the smoke-pipe of a ship's galley: see
Leland P. Lovette, *Naval Customs, Traditions, and Usage* (Annapolis,
1939), p. 222.

20. Compare what Melville had said of Jack Chase in *White-Jacket:*
"No one could be better company . . . ; no man told such stories,
sang such songs . . ." (Chapter 4, p. 16).

21. Melville's scornful rejection of the notion of "progress" runs
through his correspondence of the mid-fifties and his subsequent lectures on "Statues in Rome" and "The South Seas." The latter embraces his familiar animadversions against his old target the mission-
aries; compare the satirical thrust at missionary "progress" in Chapter 7 of *The Confidence-Man,* where the man in the gray coat proposes to "quicken" Christian missions with the modern "Wall street
spirit" and so convert the Chinese *"en masse* within six months" (pp.
45–46)! Elsewhere, the repeated linking of geniality with tippling,
particularly in the cosmopolitan's story of the deacon's wife and her
"jug of Santa Cruz" (p. 152), may involve hits at religious enthusiasts.

22. In the Introduction to her edition, p. lxxii.

23. Like the "honest scholar" and "writer whom few know" of *Billy
Budd, Sailor* (Chicago, 1962), pp. 74, 114; other examples in Melville
are cited in editorial discussion elsewhere within the volume (note,
p. 161). John C. Cawelti, "Some Notes on the Structure of *The Confidence-Man,*" *American Literature,* XXIX (November 1957), 278–288,
also finds in the "parable of the wine-drinker" a clue to Melville's
own position, with its characteristic recognition that "there are at
least two opposing sides to everything" (p. 287). I am indebted here
to this provocative discussion. But I do not concur in Mr. Cawelti's
specific identification of the wine-drinker with the "genial misanthrope" of Chapter 30, since like Miss Foster I believe that Melville
intended the phrase "genial misanthrope" to apply particularly to
the cosmopolitan just as "surly philanthropist" in the same context
clearly applies to his opposite number the Missourian.

24. *Complete Poems,* p. 468.

25. Sealts, *Melville as Lecturer* (Cambridge, Mass., 1957), p. 182.

26. *The Letters of Herman Melville,* ed. Merrell R. Davis and William
H. Gilman (New Haven, 1960), pp. 196–197, 260, 263.

27. "Genial" in the sense of pleasant, warm, gay is applied variously
to the Greek climate and people (III, vi, 87–88 and 111; compare
"The Parthenon" in *Collected Poems,* p. 247), to Rolfe's heart (I,
xxxi, 14), to the spirits and heart of the liberal churchman Derwent
(II, xxxix, 43; III, xvi, 189–190), to the gestures of the wine-loving
Arnaut (III, xi, 150–151), and to the faith that Rolfe would instill in
Clarel (IV, xxiii, 76–77). Conversely, it is said that the apostate
Margoth fixes "no genial glance" (II, xxix, 103); and that events
"overrode the genial part" of Ungar (IV, v, 138–140), making him
misanthropic. Modern religion, for Rolfe, has lost its "deity/So

genial" (II, xxi, 65–66); to Ungar, modern democracy lacks "free/And genial catholicity" (IV, xix, 151–152).

28. *Collected Poems*, pp. 167, 173, 175, 185.

29. See my "Melville's Burgundy Club Sketches," *Harvard Library Bulletin*, XII (Spring 1958), 253–267, which explores the relation of these pieces to the aspects of Melville under discussion here.

30. In, respectively, a manuscript fragment on Shakespeare among the Melville papers in the Harvard College Library and a letter of 1886 (*Letters*, p. 283).

31. *Billy Budd, Sailor*, pp. 49, 275. Elsewhere, Melville characterizes the surgeon's manner as "less genial than polite" (p. 124).

32. *Letters*, p. 127.

33. *Complete Stories*, pp. 407–408.

34. *Ibid.*, p. 56.

35. *Collected Poems*, p. 94. Melville applied his line to Shakespeare; of himself he once said that though "neither pessimist nor optimist [*sic*]," he "relished" pessimism in the poetry of Thomson "if for nothing else than as a counterpoise to the exorbitant hopefulness, juvenile and shallow," of the times (*Letters*, p. 277).

John C. Gerber

Mark Twain's Search for Identity

Mark Twain was born in November 1835, two weeks before the perihelion of Halley's comet. He died in 1910, the year of the comet's next return, and this time within twenty-four hours of its perihelion. He himself had predicted the second event. "I came in with Halley's comet in 1835," he told his biographer, A. B. Paine, the year before. "It is coming again next year, and I expect to go out with it. It will be the greatest disappointment of my life if I don't go out with Halley's comet. The Almighty has said, no doubt: 'Now here are these two unaccountable freaks; they came in together, they must go out together.' Oh! I am looking forward to that." [1]

JOHN C. GERBER is Professor of English at the University of Iowa.

If we wished, we could find an almost wondrous symbolism here. The fates did seem to single out Samuel L. Clemens for their special attention: they raised him, they tossed him about, and they dropped him—and always with what Tom Sawyer called "style." Clearly a star is not appropriate to signal Mark Twain's birth and death. It had to be something flashier. And freakish though the comet may seem to be, it calls attention to the presence and nature of the more conventional celestial bodies. That is precisely what Mark Twain did. Picturesque, eccentric, and even neurotic, he dramatized for all of us the abiding predicaments of modern man.

Looking back over his life, one feels that Twain never had even the slimmest hope of finding inner harmony. His father was an austere freethinker; his mother was an amiable Calvinist. He was brought up in Hannibal where pious New Englanders lived side by side with easygoing Southerners. To the rationalities he learned in school were added the superstitions of his Negro friends. The manners of the middle-class in Hannibal were countered by the violence of the poor who lived in the shanties near the river. The precepts of the faith taught him in Sunday School were soon contradicted by the precepts of the skeptics whose works he began reading in his late teens. It was inevitable in later life that he should politically become a Mugwump, a political phenomenon that both Democrats and Republicans loved to refer to as a fence-sitter with his mug on the one side and his wump on the other. Unhappily for him Twain was a mugwump *whatever* the subject. As one of his friends once said, if he couldn't find a fence to sit on, he would create one.

Even his name was a force for *dis*integration. Some friends called him Clemens, others called him Twain or Mark. In letters to his family he signed himself *Sam,* to many close friends *Mark,* to those he knew less well *Mark*

Twain, to business associates *Mark Twain* or *SLC,* and on formal documents *Samuel L. Clemens.* Psychologically it might have been better for him if his pseudonym had identified him with a role or fictional character, as "Artemus Ward" did for Charles Farrar Browne or "Petroleum Vesuvius Nasby" did for David Ross Locke. Then he would have been Clemens as the real man and Twain as the fictional character, and the distinction would have been clear. But who was to say which was Clemens and which was Twain, or what either represented? Certainly not Twain himself. By adopting the pseudonym he capitalized on his fame of the moment in Western newspapers. But he robbed himself of a psychological prop, the effects of which should not be underestimated. Having done this, he could not say to himself: "Whatever else may be, this I know. My name is Samuel L. Clemens." For his name was also Mark Twain.

To many, his inner contradictions were apparent in his looks and behavior. Partly because of his shock of hair he looked tall but really wasn't. His eyes, however, were what his friends remarked about. He was all there for you, one friend said, but you weren't all there for him. There was something shabby and yet suitable about his clothes; something intimate and yet distant about his demeanor; something gay and yet melancholy about his spirit.

He was almost childlike—his wife called him Youth—in his love for games, charades, parades, and splashy effects. He had his billiard cloth changed from green to red to make it brighter. The ceiling of his billiard room in Hartford was decorated with designs showing billiard balls and cues and crossed cigars. He could be almost feminine in the gentle way he had with his wife and children. And he was thoroughly masculine in his temper and in the way he argued and joked with his male companions. He was a man of many moods. Noises bothered him. His daughter Clara said she never recalled him wearing a watch because the ticking annoyed him. He had fearful dreams and some inclination toward paranoia. Yet there was a gentle pixie quality in him. He would skip down a hotel corridor if he felt like it and thought no one was looking. Once in Florence to amuse his ailing wife he pinned notes on the trees asking the birds not to sing so loud.

We must study his writings, however, if we would realize the full extent of Twain's inner complexity. T. S. Eliot has pointed out that Tom Sawyer and Huckleberry Finn are projections of the two sides of Twain, the gregarious part that was willing to accept society as it was and to make use of it to his own advantage, and the lonely part that was detached and critical.[2] Even in its oversimplicity the observation is a shrewd one. For there *were* two Twains: the one who wanted to make out and the one who wanted to be right, the Twain of expedience and the Twain of principle. On reflection it seems almost as though there were two consciousnesses at work in Twain, one constantly sensing personal opportunity, the other constantly sensing human need and aspiration. Behind this disparateness one finds it difficult to detect any basic self, a central and responsible unity.

If there *is* a central self to be found in Twain, it will not be found in great moments of epiphany when it emerges from behind the welter of contradictions, and asserts itself in ringing tones of harmony and conviction. Twain seems to have no such moments, at least none of any great significance. On certain issues and at certain times he may have been less ambivalent than at others, but the difference was one of degree and not of kind. And if he did assert himself confidently on an issue today, he would have misgivings about his confidence tomorrow or the next day.

If we are to discern any centrality in him, then, it must be through the process of inference. We must review his countless comments upon the contradictions of life, many of these comments contradicting one another, and see what emerges. The task is made harder because he was willing to say almost anything for a joke, and thus we must deal with deliberate distortion as well as with the confusions of an unsystematic mind and the disturbing urges of the subconscious.

What finally does emerge, it seems to me, is not even a reasonable facsimile of a self such as the one Whitman boasted of when he wrote that his "foothold was tenon'd and mortis'd in granite," but a self constantly in search of a foothold. Herein, I would submit, lay such centrality as Mark Twain had: a persisting and driving desire to learn his own identity, to be able to define himself in terms of the contexts in which he existed. Like Melville he wanted to pierce the mask of life and find what lay behind it—for the mask itself seemed merely an absurd enigma.

In religion he found little with which he could identify. Yet his failure in this regard was a source of uneasiness, for the religious training of his youth became so much a part of him that he was never able to accept a secular philosophy without a sense of guilt. Possibly the basic difficulty was that the religious teaching he received dwelt too strongly on God's vengeance and much too little on God's grace. Certainly Twain seemed never to have any sense of the security possible in the belief that through Christ's intervention man can anticipate divine grace and hence eternal happiness. That the doctrine of grace was strongly preached from the Presbyterian pulpit in Hannibal in the 1840's is not clear. If it was, it failed to be effective with at least one of the young parishioners.

The aspects of his early religious teachings that did affect Twain were those that most vividly appealed to his youthful imagination: the stories of the Old Testament, and the concepts of sin, the conscience, the last judgment, and eternal damnation. What he learned of these in the little Presbyterian Sunday School and church to which his mother dragged him as a boy must have been strongly fortified by the terrifying stories told him by the Negroes and the hellfire shouted forth from the pulpits of the Campbellite campmeetings. To an impressionable young boy this material became for a while a part of the reality of life, and seeped so deeply into his subconscious that the later man, who ridiculed and resented a good part of it, was never able to forget it.

The material wells up from his subconscious and onto his printed pages with a persistence that is astonishing. No important American writer of fiction ever made so much use of the Bible stories. Twain's narratives abound with references to Adam and Eve, Noah and Methuselah, Gabriel and Michael and, of course, Satan. Allusions to the last judgment occur in the most surprising places, and so do references to hell-fire and damnation. He can deal humorously and gently with the Biblical material as he does in *Tom Sawyer*. Or he can treat it blasphemously as he does in "Letters from the Earth" where he castigates men as being arrogant and presumptuous in thinking God cares about what happens to them, and thoroughly perverse in imagining a heaven in which what they like most (intercourse) is left out and what they like almost least (hymn-singing) is put in.

Western humor, which helped to formulate Twain's literary forms and attitudes, reveled in irreverence. But Twain's irreverence seems to cut deeper and come from a more basic resentment of the inhibitions he felt fostered by religion. He swore with unusual animation and color, and took an unusual delight in it. "If I cannot swear in heaven," he confided to his Notebook, "I shall not stay there." [3] To his biographer he added "in certain trying circumstances, urgent circumstances, desperate circumstances, profanity furnishes a relief denied even to prayer." [4]

It is no accident, it seems to me, that his favorite Biblical character was Satan, for here was the character that stood in opposition to the God of the Old Testament that Twain himself opposed. In his bitter late years when he wanted especially to castigate what presumed to be a Christian society it was Satan to whom he turned for a mouthpiece. It was through Satan, the damned, that Twain hurled his invective at man and thereby made man seem like the double damned.

Yet Twain found little lasting satisfaction in such irreverence because always it was accompanied by a sense of guilt—and even fear. Once he said that he could find no shred of evidence for the existence of hell; yet it might exist and that possibility made him afraid to die. There were Christians he knew and admired and loved, people like his mother and his wife and the Reverend Joseph Twichell, his warmest friend in Hartford. He so loved Negro spirituals that the message of these minor-keyed expressions of faith seemed at times to him to be almost convincing.

In this welter of contradiction one thing is clear: Twain was never able to find a secure identity in religious terms. Though he might carry through life the Biblical stories and the threats of damnation and even the doctrines of predestination and of the elect, they never led him to faith in God's grace. He was too much of a skeptic and, later, the determinist, really to surrender himself to what, one suspects, he really wanted to believe.

Nor could he define himself satisfactorily in terms of the Christian *ethic,* or any other strong and sustaining *code of morality.* In such a code he might have found a context that would have provided him with a meaning and a sense of purpose such as were found by his contemporaries Edward Bellamy and William Dean Howells.

As a matter of fact, he did find a kind of satisfaction in thinking of himself as a moralist. Nothing so delighted him when he was a young man on the West Coast as to be called "the Moralist of the Main." Later he referred to his humor as preaching—meaning that it was essentially moralistic.

> Humorists of the "mere" sort cannot survive. Humor is only a fragrance, a decoration . . . Humor must not professedly teach, and it must not professedly preach, but it must do both if it would live forever. By forever, I mean thirty years . . . I have always preached. That is the reason I have lasted thirty years. If the humor came of its own accord and uninvited, I have allowed it to have a place in my sermon, but I was not writing the sermon for the sake of the humor.[5]

Such a statement is not wholly true, but it is certainly partly so. Just about every one of Twain's major works had a moral purpose. In *Innocents Abroad* he lashed out at the greed and hypocrisy of contemporary Europe; in *The Gilded Age* he did the same thing for America. In *The Prince and the Pauper* and *A Connecticut Yankee* he attacked man's cruelty to man in the long past, in *Huckleberry Finn* he did the same for the near past, and in all of these plus others he belabored his own times. In *Joan of Arc* he held up as a human saint one whose actions, as he believed, corresponded with her ideals. And even in *Tom Sawyer* he gently exposed the hypocrisy inherent in what passed for respectability.

He was a satirist and reformer, then, and hence a moralist. And he found considerable satisfaction in being one. What is more, at the time of writing *Huckleberry Finn* he believed that each of us possesses an innate moral sense of value beyond price. He had been reading W. E. H. Lecky's *History of European Morals* and had quickly come to agree with Lecky that we have two sets of values, one innate and the other acquired. Since the one grows out of an absolute sense of goodness and the other comes to us from our environment, the two are most of the time fiercely at war.

Such a war Twain magnificently dramatizes in Huck's struggle to decide whether to help Jim go free as his intuition dictates, or return him to Miss Watson as society dictates. To the reader, Huck's decision to help Jim seems like a moral triumph, but for Huck it is a lonely triumph—if a triumph at all. He knows that he has done "wrong" so far as his society is concerned and may, therefore, as society sees things, end up in hell. Part of the greatness of this book is that here for possibly the only time Twain finds a stable and dependable source of moral value. The result is a clarity of vision and a sureness of perspective that Twain achieved neither before nor afterwards. For once he seems to have believed, however briefly, in a source of strength and certainty.

Most of the time, however, he conceived of morals as simply an acquirement—"like music, like a foreign language, like piety, poker, paralysis." [6] As such he found them almost invariably accompanied by fraud, duplicity, and even brutality. The more virtuous a man pretended to be, the worse his vices. The Sunday School superintendent was the vainest of men. Congressmen who were forever mouthing moral platitudes were simply thieves. "It could probably be shown by facts and figures," Twain wrote, "that there is no distinctly native American criminal class except Congress." [7] And the so-called Christian nations were for Twain the most bloodthirsty. He was infuriated by the hypocrisy of the United States in the Spanish-American War. Under the guise of wanting to carry Christian principles to the Philippines, he felt that we annexed them really for our selfish commercial purposes. In the New York *Tribune* for January 1, 1901, he wrote a sardonic welcome to the twentieth century.

I bring you the stately maiden named Christendom, returning bedraggled, besmirched, and dishonored, from pirate raids in

Kiao-Chou, Manchuria, South Africa, and the Philippines, with her soul full of meanness, her pocket full of boodle, and her mouth full of pious hypocrisies. Give her soap and towel but hide the looking-glass.[8]

It was not only the hypocrisy of the so-called moral people that led him finally to distrust morality: it was also that he came to feel that our so-called Moral Sense instead of ennobling us actually vitiates us. In a lighter moment on the subject he wrote that "the Moral Sense teaches us what is right, and how to avoid it when unpopular." [9] More seriously, he argues in *The Mysterious Stranger* that the moral sense degrades us below the animals. They kill simply to stay alive. Because of our moral sense we inflict pain and death for the pleasure of it. Without the Moral Sense, even the bullock is angelic. So Twain found in morality little more psychological support than he did in religious faith.

Nor did he find much in *manners*. Twain was not born into a stratum of society where there was a strong code of decorum, and he never became part of such a society until he married Olivia Langdon and moved to Hartford. From then on, few were so eager to establish social status as he. His house was easily one of the finest in Hartford. His carriage was excellent. He kept three servants and a coachman. He dressed well and entertained lavishly with the most expensive wines and best cigars. When his wife was not feeling well and had to travel, he hired a private railroad car. He cultivated the society of literary men and came to dislike being called a humorist. He was among the very first to buy a telephone and a typewriter.

Yet there was always a perverse rebellion implicit in all this. His house had a porch and dormer in it reminiscent of the deck and pilot house of a Mississippi River steamboat. Startling designs in orange slate and brick traced themselves across the roof and outside walls. Instead of being traditionally elegant, his clothes were spectacular, especially the white suits that he affected in the last twenty years or so of his life. He attacked in his writing the kinds of business tycoons and royalty that he was delighted to meet. All of this was more than the *gaucherie* of the *nouveau riche.* More profoundly it was the ambivalence of a Westerner who sought the protection of decorum against the violence and uncertainty of life but who was too much of a rebel really to accept the protection he sought.

More than this, Twain was too intimately aware of the violence in life to be able really to feel that it could be brought under control by manners.

In this sense, as in most others, he was quite the opposite of Henry James. Except in the *Princess Casamassima,* as Frederick Hoffman has shown in *The Mortal No,* James was able in his books to show how violence can be brought within the range of manners and thus be contained. Except in this one instance James's heroes renounce their purposes or ends in order to preserve the decorum of means. Not one's private and selfish goal, but the preservation of the social code becomes the ultimate end. As hero, one may not get what he specifically wants, as Christopher Newman does not get Claire de Cintré. But he does not create a ruckus, and he finds that there is great satisfaction in renouncing his private aim. For the Jamesian hero, such renunciation is at once being right with one's self and behaving like a gentleman. Good manners in short are almost indistinguishable from high moral action—and the combination leads to inner satisfaction of the highest order.

Twain's work makes clear, however, that he did not believe that men are really willing to surrender their private goals for social decorum. At least his heroes, with the possible exception of Tom Sawyer, never do so. Man for Twain was too selfish, and violence was too much a part of his nature. In *The Gilded Age* his characters lie, rob, and murder; in *Huckleberry Finn* they lie, cheat, rob, swindle, enslave, and murder. And in *Pudd'nhead Wilson* they do the same.

Possibly *A Connecticut Yankee* is his most interesting book in this regard. In it he sends his Yankee craftsman off to sixth-century England to set up a perfect society based on nineteenth-century craftsmanship and know-how. Presumably it is to be a peaceful society where because of nineteenth-century comforts and a knowledge of economics and political economy men will be able to live a mannerly and peaceful life. Edward Bellamy had pictured such a life in *Looking Backward* and W. D. Howells would shortly do so in *The Traveler from Altruria*. In each of these works society is marked by a decorum that precludes violence. But no such society develops in Twain's Camelot. From the beginning there is wrangling, jealousy, and fighting, and instead of getting better the situation ultimately becomes worse. Even the Yankee gets desensitized to brutality. At the beginning of the story he views the derelicts in Morgan le Fay's dungeons with sympathy and horror; at the end of the book he electrocutes and drowns 25,000 knights and considers the act his grandest effect. Consciously or unconsciously, Twain is arguing that given the nature of man decorum is weak security. Furthermore, he seems to be sensing, as many of his contemporaries did not, that science and technology would serve only to increase our violence and thus make the possibility of its being contained by manners considerably less.

So though he sought the satisfaction of being one of the social Establishment, there is no evidence that manners provided him with profound peace of spirit. He was too much of a Westerner really to take great stock in manners, and he was too perceptive to think that decorum could really contain the growing violence of his time.

Nowhere is his characteristic ambivalence so dramatic as it is on the subject of *wealth* and material things generally. He was the creature of his age and wanted to make all the money he could; yet he was also the critic of his age and deplored its materiality.

He feared poverty. He had known it as a boy, and that knowledge undoubtedly was partly responsible for his desire to be rich. He was more than joking when at about the age of thirty he wrote:

> Honest poverty is a gem that even a King might feel proud to call his own, but I wish to sell out. I have sported that kind of jewelry long enough. I want some variety. I wish to become rich, so that I can instruct the people and glorify honest poverty a little, like those good, kind-hearted, fat, benevolent people do.[10]

When only nineteen he made plans to go fortune-hunting in the Amazon country but settled for being a Mississippi river pilot instead. The pilots were the best-paid artisans in the whole valley. He almost starved to death mining for silver and gold in Nevada. He turned to lecturing when he found there was money in it and not too much work. He became an author when he was assured there was "a fortune in it." Later, feeling that he was not being paid handsomely enough by his publishers, he started his own publishing house.

He was an inveterate speculator—and one of the unluckiest. In addition to the publishing firm just mentioned he invested in such items as a typesetting machine, a magazine, an accordion letter file, a watch firm, a steam pulley, a carpet pattern machine, an insurance scheme, a steam generator, an easy-open notebook, an engraving process, a self-pasting scrapbook, a food for invalids, spiral hatpins, marine telegraphy, a system of memory training, a children's theater, and an automatically adjusting vest-strap. One afternoon he came home to tell his wife proudly that he had been accosted by a stock salesman and had stoutly resisted the salesman's rhetoric. His wife was inordinately proud of him. It was only some time later they discovered that the salesman was peddling stock in a new firm called the Bell Telephone Co. Nevertheless, at the height of his success, about 1890, Twain was probably worth well over a half million.

Yet even during his period of success he could not be completely happy. After all, he had been brought up on the Christian ethic and had early read the works of such products of the Enlightenment as Rousseau, Tom Paine, and Thomas Jefferson. There is an abundance of evidence that his speculation nurtured within him a keen sense of guilt. It was a foolish thing to do, and it was an evil thing to do. "There are two times in a man's life when he should not speculate," he wrote, "when he can't afford it, and when he can." [11] The real yellow peril, he averred, is gold. As the title indicates *The Gilded Age* (or at least the part of it Twain wrote) is a sustained attack on the shoddy materialism of the time. And *A Connecticut Yankee* mounts an even broader and more devastating attack.

It was not until Twain lost his fortune in the Panic of 1893, however, that he became really disillusioned about the power of wealth to bring security and satisfaction. Everything he had was wiped out and with it went part of his wife's fortune. There followed those bitter years in which he became more and more contemptuous of the human species. "Some men worship rank," he wrote, "some worship heroes, some worship power, some worship God, and over these ideals they dispute—but they all worship money." [12] At times he hated the rich: "Prosperity is the surest breeder of insolence I know of." [13] Once in an open letter to Cornelius Vanderbilt in *Packard's Monthly* he told the financier: "Go and surprise the whole country and do something right."

Sardonic about individuals who sought only wealth, he raged about the nation when he thought it was motivated by greed. The imperialism of the McKinley administration he greeted with writing about as bitter as has ever been penned by an American. In our exploitation of the Philippines, he suggested with blistering sarcasm, we had repaired the slave chains that Lincoln had broken. He suggested that a few minor changes be made in the flag: the white stripes should be painted black, and the stars replaced by the skull and crossbones.

It was a short step from his attack on national greed to an attack on man in general. "Man is the Only Animal that Blushes," he declared. "Or needs to." [14] "Man was made at the end of the week's work when God was tired." [15] "Concerning the difference between man and the jackass: some observers hold that there isn't any. But this wrongs the jackass." [16] "I have been reading the morning paper," he once wrote to W. D. Howells. "I do it every morning—well knowing that I shall find in it the usual depravities and basenesses and hypocrisies and cruelties that make up civilization, and cause me to put in the rest of the day pleading for the damnation of the human race." [17] Wealth offered small comfort to one like Twain who was also a reformer and moralist.

It was primarily to *science* that Twain turned in the last twenty years of his life. As early as the late seventies he had delivered a paper to his Monday Evening Club in Hartford in which he suggested that our life is mechanically determined and that we therefore have no choice, only the illusion of choice. His friends were horrified. Later in *A Connecticut Yankee* he suggested that the only thing original about us is what can be put on the end of a cambric needle. But of course so long as he held that there is *anything* original about us he was qualifying his determinism. After his misfortunes in the early and middle nineties he eliminated the reservation. All that we do, he asserted in *What Is Man?*, we do for self-gratification. Our desires are built into us and over them we have no control.

Twain attributed his determinism to Lecky, but many of the ideas were his before he had read Lecky. He might more properly have attributed it to the science of the second half of the nineteenth century, especially to the popular physical theory that we are composed of myriads of molecules in motion. Eons ago, so the theory went, two of these molecules hit each other and bounced off into other molecules and they in turn bounced into other molecules, and since that time everything has been predetermined by the bounce of the molecules. In *The Mysterious Stranger* Twain compares life to a row of upended bricks. Knock the first into the second, and the whole row will go down. By an evolutionary process this endless operation of the molecules has produced a man who will *always* do the thing which will bring him the most mental comfort. And what invariably brings him the most mental comfort, according to Twain, is public opinion. The desire for public approval will make men go to war, will make a right-principled man do a wrong thing, will make a kind man do a cruel thing. Though we sometimes think we are making sacrifices for others, we are simply seeking public approval. And there is nothing in the world we can do about this. Man is a machine that differs from the animals only in efficiency and not in kind.

There is no doubt that this philosophy of determinism gave Twain, if not security, at least occasional defense against his own conscience. He spells this out in *The Mysterious Stranger* where he has his spokesman say:

> It shows how foolish people are when they blame themselves for anything they have done . . . nothing happens that your first act hasn't arranged to happen and made inevitable; and so, of your own motion you can't alter the scheme or do a thing that will break a link.[18]

But we already know enough about Twain to know that he could not really believe in a philosophy which permitted him neither to praise nor to blame. He was too much the moralist. And in theory a man cannot be a moralist and a determinist at the same time, for the moralist assumes that man is responsible for his acts and the determinist assumes that he is not. Twain saw something of his dilemma though he never confronted it fully or fairly. His spokesman in *What Is Man?* says,

> Having found the Truth; perceiving that beyond question man has but one moving impulse—the contenting of his own spirit—and is merely a machine and entitled to no personal merit for anything he does, it is not humanly possible for me to seek further. The rest of my days will be spent in patching and painting and puttying and caulking my priceless possession and *in looking the other way when an imploring argument or a damaging fact approaches.*[19]

And in a letter to Joe Twichell in 1904 he wrote almost plaintively,

> I wish I could learn to remember that it is unjust and dishonorable to put blame upon the human race for any of its acts. For it did not make itself, it did not make its nature, it is merely a machine, it is moved wholly by outside influences, it has no hand in creating the outside influences nor in choosing which of them it will welcome or reject, its performance is wholly automatic. . . . I wish I could learn to pity the human race instead of censuring it and laughing at it; and I could, if the outside influences of old habit were not so strong upon my machine. It vexes me to catch myself praising the clean private citizen Roosevelt, and blaming the soiled President Roosevelt, when I know that neither blame nor praise is due to him for any thought or word or deed of his, he being merely a helpless and irresponsible coffee-mill ground by the hand of God.[20]

What comes out so poignantly in such passages is that Twain couldn't really believe what he said he believed.

What he liked to call his philosophy permitted him to define the self as a "homeless thought . . . wandering forlorn among the empty eternities." There was comfort of a sort in feeling that as a homeless thought he could not have been responsible for the misfortunes that struck down his family. Ironically, however, having intellectually accepted determinism he experienced a new sense of guilt, for such a belief required him to deny the existence of the purposeful Creator in whom he deeply wanted to believe. So what he insisted clarified the nature of the self and thereby gave him peace, in the end simply added to his vexations.

Whether Twain found spiritual integration in his *art* we can perhaps only speculate about. There were many times, certainly, when he found writing at least an escape. Frequently he wrote to Howells about how well his work was going, that he was turning out thirty or fifty or even seventy pages a day, and there is evident delight in such remarks. He records the happy experience of writing on *Joan of Arc* in the morning and early afternoon and each day reading the results of the day's work to his wife and girls. After the death of Susy, his favorite daughter, he turned to *Following the Equator.* He was writing to forget, he said, and spending twelve hours a day at it.

One suspects, however, that writing was more than simply escape for Twain. It takes no great schooling in psychiatry to see that Twain turned to his writing to rid himself of guilt. Time and again one can see him striking out at himself, witness his attacks on love of show, the desire for popularity, speculation, and the general irresponsibility of man. His sense of guilt became sheer torture in the nineties after he had lost his fortune, after his mother and oldest daughter had died and his wife had declined into permanent invalidism. He held himself responsible for all of these and other misfortunes. It seems no accident, therefore, that

44

among his incomplete manuscripts are several from this period in which he attempts to describe a man with a wife and daughters who is somehow lost. In the best known of these manuscripts, "The Great Dark," the man dreams he is on a mystery ship sailing through darkness filled with storms of ice and snow—no one knows where they are going or for what purpose.

But did Twain find in his writing an integration of his torn spirit? I think the answer must be only occasionally, and then only under special circumstances. He himself said that "one can't write a book unless he can banish perplexities and put his whole mind on it." This is what he was ordinarily not able to do. He became too emotionally engaged with his material. He would burlesque it, satirize it, sentimentalize over it, rage at it. Ordinarily, in short, he was incapable of achieving the aesthetic distance which is so necessary if any kind of unified tone and view are to be achieved.

Twain seemed able to achieve aesthetic distance only when he adopted a mask or persona to which he was willing to surrender himself. This happened on the lecture platform when he played, for example, the role of a Negro or a befuddled old codger trying to remember something about a ram. In writing it happened in short pieces such as the "Jumping Frog" in which he played a clear-cut role that he understood and enjoyed. Only once did it happen in a longer work, and that of course was in *Huckleberry Finn*. In it he adopted a persona that he knew and liked and was willing to surrender himself to. The result was a clarity of perception, a consistency in point of view, and a tonal unity that he never achieved in a long work before or after. It may be important to note that as a young, unschooled boy Huck ruled out the perplexities that dogged the adult Twain—or at least made it very difficult for Twain to drag them in.

The restricted point of view of the persona simplified life for Twain, and thus made it tolerable. From the thousands of conflicting ways of seeing and judging life, the persona isolated one. Furthermore, it pushed life to a distance and made it less disturbing. How profoundly the persona of Huck served Twain as a psychic prop is, of course, a matter for speculation. We *can* say, though, that for a person of Twain's temperament it seemed to offer the ideal therapy: simplification, detachment, minimization. We must remind ourselves again that *Huckleberry Finn* was the only book in which he achieved such healing detachment. And even here he almost lost it by making Tom Sawyer the focal center in the last fourth of the book.

In conclusion I want to make clear that I have not been arguing that Twain's life was one of unremitting agony. In love and horseplay he found escape. In his eagerness to establish status—to belong, so to speak—he could find a modicum of satisfaction in every context: religion, morals, manners, wealth, science, and art. And in his perceptions of the absurdity of life he was just as quick to sense the comic as the melancholic. Despite such sources of satisfaction, however, he came to the end of his life feeling that it had been a failure. In a light moment he would say that he wished the Creator had asked his advice when fashioning the world; he could have suggested several improvements. In a black moment he would long for death. After Jean, his youngest daughter, died the day before Christmas in 1909, Twain wrote that if he had the power to bring her back to life he would not use it. For only in death could any peace be found. His attempt to define himself in the contexts in which he lived had failed, and he found rest nowhere.

In comparing himself to Halley's comet, Twain had called himself a freak. He was a freak only in that he was especially picturesque—and talented. His search for identity was the search of every thoughtful man, and his failures were those of his age—and ours. In his life and his works he dramatized the abiding predicament of modern man.

NOTES

1. A. B. Paine, *Mark Twain, a Biography* (New York, 1912), III, 1511.
2. In his introduction to *The Adventures of Huckleberry Finn* (London, 1950), viii.
3. *Mark Twain's Notebooks* (New York, 1935), p. 345.
4. Paine, I, 214.
5. *Mark Twain in Eruption,* ed. Bernard De Voto (New York, 1922), p. 202.
6. *Mark Twain's Speeches,* Definitive Edition (New York, 1923), p. 260.
7. "Pudd'nhead Wilson's New Calendar," *Following the Equator,* Definitive Edition (New York, 1923), I, 80.
8. Paine, III, 1127.
9. "The United States of Lyncherdom," *Europe and Elsewhere,* Definitive Edition (New York, 1923), p. 244.
10. *Mark Twain's Travels with Mr. Brown,* eds. Franklin Walker and G. Ezra Dane (New York, 1940), p. 236.
11. "Pudd'nhead Wilson's New Calendar," *Following the Equator,* II, 215.
12. *Mark Twain's Notebooks,* p. 343.
13. *Mark Twain's Travels with Mr. Brown,* p. 110.
14. "Pudd'nhead Wilson's New Calendar," *Following the Equator,* I, 238.
15. *Mark Twain's Notebooks,* p. 381.
16. *Ibid.,* p. 347.
17. *Mark Twain's Letters* (New York, 1917), II, 678.
18. *The Mysterious Stranger,* Definitive Edition (New York, 1923), p. 100.
19. *What Is Man? and Other Essays,* Definitive Edition (New York, 1923), p. 75.
20. *Mark Twain's Letters,* II, 763–764.

Oscar Cargill

☙ ❧

Walt Whitman and
Civil Rights

I have chosen the topic, "Walt Whitman and Civil Rights,"
with deep misgivings, for anyone who has even half-digested
Whitman's poems, his autobiographical writings, his letters,
his journalistic pieces, and his conversations with Traubel
and others knows that on practically any issue Whitman
can be found on both sides of the fence. He could declare,
for example, that "The dirtiest book in the world is an
expurgated book," yet permit William Rossetti to bowdlerize
his poems. He could persist against Emerson's advice in
retaining offensive sexual passages in *Leaves of Grass*, but
quietly over the years adumbrate many of them himself.
While most daring in testing his own right for free expres-

OSCAR CARGILL is McGuffey visiting Professor of English at Ohio University.

sion, we do not find him rushing to the defense of others under attack. Comstockery was born in 1872 and raged throughout Whitman's latter years. A public statement from Whitman might have had some slight effect in checking it, but none was issued. Contradictions of this sort abound in his career and make positive statements about his thinking very hazardous. Our only recourse in trying to fix a conviction on Whitman is to discover whether there was a permanent sway or trend in his utterances in one direction, particularly at crucial or testing times. The result of such an examination may be somewhat less reliable than determining next Saturday's weather from wetting one's finger and holding it to the wind; nevertheless the difficulty of determination is a bold and prickly challenge to method and the topic timely enough to allow some charity for error.

"I am a radical of radicals," Traubel reports Whitman as saying, "but I don't belong to any school." This is a sufficiently puzzling statement to one who remembers that as editor of the Brooklyn *Daily Times* Whitman upheld the death penalty, opposed the free education of women, advocated making the situation of paupers so "unpleasant" that the lazy would not accept it, found that the loosening of marriage ties and divorce were the result of the evil influence of "the novels of Balzac, Sand, and Bulwer," and equated abortion with murder. Whitman teed off editorially, in April and June, 1858, both against the reformers and radicals who met in council in Rutland, Vermont:

> Here all the uneasy spirits of the day seem to have met to
> enter a protest against conventionalisms and to find a safety-
> valve for erratic ideas with which they are boiling over. There
> are free-lovers, ultra-abolitionists, trance media, finale atheists,
> vegetarians, phrenologists, people in short possessed of all the
> 'isms of the day, and eager to participate in the feast of reason
> (?) and flow of soul.

49

In so comprehensive a group, representing "all the 'isms of the day," one would suppose a "radical of radicals" would have found some one or some 'ism to identify with, rather than choosing to lump the lot for the amusement of his readers.

A radical who belongs to no school is, perhaps, hardly a radical, but a bemused sampler of the radical smorgasbord, yet if Whitman was of no left-wing school, he was somewhat consistently a Democrat in politics down to the Free-Soil campaign of Frémont in 1856, when his position is regarded as ambiguous. Too much should not be made of Whitman's dismissal in 1848 from the Brooklyn *Eagle* because his stand was that of a Barnburner while that of the *Eagle's* proprietor was Hunker. These, as everyone knows, were factions in the Democratic party in New York State, and insomuch as the Barnburner faction supported the Wilmot Proviso, it was the more liberal from a national point of view. But Whitman, who had supported Silas Wright for Governor in the previous election, had become identified with what was to become the Free-Soil faction before the Proviso was offered in Congress. Whitman's earlier activities were those of a man who hoped sometime for political preferment. He had declared that editorial work was the easiest road to politics, and his editorial position may have been determined fully as much by his political ambitions and commitments as by idealism. One doesn't desert without cost political allegiances to which one has committed one's self. While Whitman boasted that the *Eagle* was the first newspaper to take the Free-Soil position and although Wright was silent on the issue, the word was around that Wright favored Free Soil. What I'm trying to say is that Whitman came out for Free Soil when that was the side to stick with, trusting that this faction would win out, particularly since labor in New York City favored it.

After Whitman's dismissal, the *Tribune,* in mentioning

that the Brooklyn *Eagle* had returned "to Old Hunkerism again" and repeating a rumor that the Barnburners were about to start a new daily with Mr. Walter Whitman as editor, adds a very interesting sentence: "The split in the Locofoco party rages with all bitterness in King's County— a place where a clique of office-loving Locos has for years bidden defiance to principle and public interest, too, for the sake of the drippings." The Locos were the radical labor wing of the Democratic party.[1] Henry Sutton of the *Eagle* says that Whitman's visitors at that time were "mostly politicians," and one wonders if they did not belong to the Loco clique. The *Tribune* appears to associate Whitman with a corrupt, demagogic faction in his party, which diminishes, if true, his stand on Free Soil. It seems strange that a paper in the deep South, in New Orleans, should have invited Whitman to become its editor in 1848 unless the proprietor recognized that his Free-Soil stand was a matter of local expediency.

A letter written to John Parker Hale in 1852, when the latter was an early candidate of the Free Soilers, seems to shed some light on Whitman's motivation. Whitman had returned from the South to find Locofoco faction in disarray, lacking leadership, and he sought to get the rapidly rising Hale to transfer his allegiance. Describing himself as a "true Democrat," he urges Hale "to take the nomination of the Democracy at Pittsburgh," for "Out of the Pittsburgh movement and platform it may be that a real Democratic Party is destined to come forth. . . ." He urges upon Hale an appeal to the young working people whom he declares that he himself knows very well:

> . . . behind the bosh of the politicians, there burns almost with fierceness, the divine fire, which more or less, during all ages, has only waited a chance to leap forth and confound the calculations of tyrants, hunkers, and all their tribe. At this moment New York is the most radical city in America. It would be the

most anti-slavery city, if that cause hadn't been made ridiculous by the freaks of the local leaders here.

The last appeal was made because of Hale's pronounced anti-slavery views. But Whitman failed to convert Hale to the Democratic party, and he, himself, having failed to strengthen his faction, slid back into the party ranks, as we shall see.

On another issue Whitman was a consistent party-liner—the issue of States' Rights. Even in the editorial which brought about his dismissal from the *Eagle* in 1848 he was a States' Rights advocate: "With the present Slave States," he declared, ". . . no human being anywhere out from themselves has the least shadow of a right to interfere." But in 1850 Whitman published in the New York *Evening Post* a poem entitled "Song for Certain Congressmen," later called "Dough-Face Song," in which he attacked the compromisers, both Whig and Democratic, but especially chastised the members of his own party who were for the compromise by lampooning them:

> *To put down "agitation" now,*
> *We think the most judicious;*
> *To damn all "northern fanatics,"*
> *Those "traitors" black and vicious;*
> *The "reg'lar party usages"*
> *For us, and no "new issues."*

The famous jeremiad of 1856, "The Eighteenth Presidency," which was never published and was found only in 1928 by Clifton Furness, attacks with withering scorn the Presidencies of Fillmore (a Whig) and Pierce (a Democrat) and heaps coals of fire on the head of James Buchanan, the nominee of the Democratic party. But it does not declare for Frémont, the Republican candidate whose Free-Soil and Abolitionist views were hardly concealed. Furness says, however, that "whatever may have been his [Whitman's] . . .

party affiliation at that time . . . , it [the jeremiad] grew
out of his active interest and effort to aid the cause of the
Republican candidate Frémont." But this is pure conjec-
ture. "The Eighteenth Presidency" renounces parties and
politicians and prays for a President who will be a simple
man of the people. This prescription excludes Frémont.
The Locofocoism of '48 infects the whole jeremiad—the
West belongs to the white American masses. "Workmen!
Workwomen! Those universal National American tracts belong to you . . . !" There is even a special appeal to
foreign-born workmen—the Presidency shall not exclude
them. And finally, there is a reaffirmation of States' Rights
—"Any one of These States is perfect mistress of itself." But
the doctrine is extended: "When States organize themselves
the Federal government withdraws. . . . The National ob-
ligation is passed over to the States. Then if they are false
to it and impose upon certain persons, can the National
government interfere? It cannot under any circumstances
whatever." The reference is probably to the Fugitive Slave
law which permitted Federal marshals to seize and return
runaway slaves. Whitman held that, under the Constitution,
the individual States were obligated to seize and to return
the fugitives, and faith in their willingness to do this should
be restored.

Ostensibly Whitman has utilized the States' Rights position, hitherto a shibboleth of the Democratic party and the
basis shortly for Secession and War, as a ground for resistance to the enforcement of Federal law in the North. In
line with this assumption is a thundered warning:

> To butchers, sailors, stevedores, and drivers of horses—to
> ploughmen, wood-cutters, marketmen, carpenters, masons, and
> laborers—to workmen in factories—to all in These States who
> live by their daily toil—Mechanics! A parcel of windy northern
> liars are bawling in your ears the easily spoken words of Democ-
> racy and the Democratic Party.

On the face of it, this looks as if Whitman were taking his leave of the Democratic party. But the direct address to all who live by their daily toil indicates that he was still trying to create a faction in that party. It may be that he never issued his jeremiad because he realized that he could not achieve his aim and was lost without the party. The lack of declaration for Frémont may be taken, then, of an unwillingness to cut bait and run. He choked over his jeremiad, but he swallowed it and went along with the Democrats.

Perhaps, then, we should be cautious in assuming that the poem "To the States" in the "Inscriptions" section of *Leaves of Grass* refers to anything more than Whitman's steady support of the independence of the individual States, though it is not incompatible with his stand on the Fugitive Slave law:

> *To the States or any one of them, or any City of the States,*
> Resist much, obey little,
> *Once unquestioning obedience, once fully enslaved,*
> *Once fully enslaved, no nation, state, city of this earth, ever*
>   *afterwards resumes its liberty.*

But since this is addressed to *all* of the States, it quite possibly does not have any special reference to the Fugitive Slave law. The poem was first published in 1860 but may have been written earlier. Nevertheless as late as 1858, as Professor Holloway pointed out, Whitman was more impressed by Douglas than by Lincoln. I will venture that he voted for him in 1860. It looks as if only Secession and the War divorced Whitman from the party. Or from his political ambitions.

The New York Democratic party disdained involvement in the abolition issue for fear it would split the party, North and South. Tammany Hall, of which Whitman was a sometime member, was a pro-slavery outfit and made no bones

54

of it. Was this Whitman's position? In the wave of indignation which swept the North after Webster's fourth of March speech in 1850 in support of compromise and the Fugitive Slave law, Whitman wrote "Blood Money," one of his earliest free verse poems. When he was asked about this piece much later, he was somewhat apologetic about it. "In those days I fell in mostly with abolitionists—noble big fellows, many of them, but all consumed by the notion, which I never would admit, that slavery—slavery alone—was evil, and the universe contained no other. There will always be this objection to including those poems with the others." That is, "Blood Money" and "Dough-Face Song," both of 1850, are pieces in which Whitman, in his own later view, was unduly swayed by abolitionist friends, and the pieces, as unrepresentative of himself, do not belong in *Leaves of Grass.*

I have conned the indexes of various Whitman volumes to find and list the radical abolitionist friends with whom Whitman was associated without great success. Surely Mrs. Tydale and Thoreau were not close enough. Did his sister Helen bring back regularly Beecher's ideas in her sewing basket? Whitman did, however, attend addresses on abolition at the Broadway Tabernacle where he heard Wendell Phillips, Emerson, Cassius Clay, John P. Hale, Beecher, Fred Douglass, William Lloyd Garrison, and others, but only half the list were interested in anti-slavery solely, and Whitman was not an intimate of these. It was Wendell Phillips whom Whitman characterized as "one-eyed, saw nothing, absolutely nothing, but the single blot of slavery." It seems likely that "Blood Money" and "Dough-Face Song," poems that made the Whigs prime targets, may be associated with Whitman's appeal to Hale to join the Democrats, the passions of 1850 convincing him that the moderate abolitionists could be used.

"The mad fanaticism or ranting of ultra-'abolitionists,' "

he had declared in the *Eagle,* "has done more harm than good to the very cause it proffered aid." In the Brooklyn *Daily Times* he alleged that the figures of the slave trade had been exaggerated. He assumed that Cuba (which he thought would one day be annexed to the United States) would be "so stocked with blacks that a confidence in their own strength and numbers will suggest an insurrection, as in Santo Domingo." Commenting on an abolitionist convention editorially, he wrote, "it should be remembered that the institution of slavery is not at all without its redeeming points, and also that there are just as great reforms needed in the Northern States." His emotions on the execution of John Brown, he declared, were "not enough to take away my appetite." On May 6, 1858, he applauded the infamous new Constitution of Oregon which "prohibits colored persons, either slave or free, from entering the State —making an exclusively white Population":

> Who believes the Whites and Blacks can ever be amalgamated in America? Or wishes it to happen? Nature has set an impassable seal against it. Besides is not America for the Whites? As long as the Blacks remain here how can they ever become anything like an independent and heroic race? There is no chance of it.

Long afterward, when anti-Negro sentiments like these were called to his attention, Whitman sheepishly defended himself: "After all I may have been tainted a bit, just a little bit, with the New York feeling with regard to anti-slavery." What does appear is that Whitman in his public utterances consistently supported the pro-slavery, pro-States' Rights, and Free Soil position of that Locofoco wing of the Democratic party within New York State whose primary appeal was to the laboring man's vote, so long as he had political ambitions, which was down to the Civil War. Beside this public record such things as notes he made for an anti-slavery speech (never written) pale in significance.

But what about the passages sympathetic to the Negro in "Poem of Salutation" and in "Song of Myself"? Here, in total contradiction to his stand on Oregon, Whitman admits the Negro into Spiritual equality with himself. One of these passages contains the finest egalitarian statement that I know of anywhere:

> *To the cotton field drudge or cleaner of privies I lean,*
> *On his right cheek I put the family kiss*
> *And in my soul I swear I will never deny him. . . .*
> *I seize the descending man and raise him with resistless will,*
> *O despairer, here is my neck,*
> *By God, you shall not go down! hang your whole weight upon*
> *me.*

Despite that contradictory passage of 1872 in "Ethiopia Saluting the Colors" in which a dusky turban'd Negro woman seems to Whitman as "hardly human," it would appear that he harbored a hope for the elevation of the race, at least did not want recorders ages hence to think that he did not harbor a hope. If he could have persuaded a majority faction of his party to favor abolition, seemingly he might have endorsed it. But the poet is sharply divorced from the expedient politician. After the Civil War, he showed no inclination to lift a hand, as did Wendell Phillips, to secure practical advantages for the Negro. Indeed, if a main line may be indicated, he was decidedly more dedicated to reconciling the Southerner than in pursuing justice for the emancipated race. In 1884 he was still a partisan Democrat in his thinking:

"I felt that the election of Blaine would be a slap in the face of the South: we had already conquered, subdued, subjugated the South—got it right under our heel"—bringing his foot down for emphasis—"and why should we rub it in?" As to the Negro question—"a confounded serious question: but who can say that the negro is more likely to get his due from the Republican than from the Democratic party? . . . The negro will get his due from the negro—from no one else."

It looks as if conscience were a thing that Whitman kept in a closet in the office where he schemed with dubious political associates, but that, when he opened the door a crack, it escaped and forced him to serve it. While free it dictated some immortal lines of American poetry. He was, however, able to recapture it and lock it up once more— tighter than ever.

NOTE

1. Both Arthur M. Schlesinger, Jr., in *The Age of Jackson* (New York, 1945, pp. 190–200) and Philip Foner in *History of the Labor Movement in the United States* (New York, 1947, pp. 149–162) maintain the strong influence of labor in the councils of the Equal Rights party, derisively labeled the Locofocos by the regular Democrats. Only Leo Hershkowitz has dissented from this view ("Loco-Foco Party of New York," *New York Historical Society Quarterly*, XLVI, July, 1962, pp. 304–329), who cites Trimble as supporting him. But his reading of William Trimble's "The Social Philosophy of the Loco-Foco Democracy" (*The American Journal of Sociology*, XXVI, May, 1921, pp. 705–715) has surely been hasty. Trimble writes, "Its philosophy, in truth, was that of a nascent proletarianism. . . ." He points out that it upheld the right of labor to organize, advocated the reduction of penalties for crimes in the penal code, and attacked monopoly in the ferry business—points particularly appealing to Whitman who was probably a member of Ely Moore's Typographical Association and certainly a Brooklynite and ferry-user. Hershkowitz's argument that there were only three labor leaders in the councils hasn't much force. How many were there in other parties and factions? Trimble maintains the permanent effect of the Locos on the national Democratic Party. The epithet hurled at Whitman, coupled with the inference of a split in the Locos themselves in Brooklyn, would put Whitman in the labor faction as do his "Carol of the Occupations" and "The Broad Axe Song." "Without yielding an inch the working-man and the working-woman were to be in my pages from first to last," Whitman says in "A Backward Glance O'er Travel'd Roads." All commentators refer to the apathy of the Locos in regard to slavery. Whitman was a Loco in this regard also. See ". . . the unscrupulous and energetic are Locofocos," said Emerson in 1846. Contrast Whitman's attitude toward the Fugitive Slave Law with Emerson's: "By God, I will not obey it."

Ernest Samuels

❧ ❧

Henry Adams and
the Gossip Mills

One March day, more than twenty years ago, I walked up
Boylston Street near the Fenway in Boston and entered the
Massachusetts Historical Society to lay siege to the Adams
Papers on closed deposit there since 1905. "Siege" is not
too strong a word, for Henry Adams II, the nephew of *my*
Henry Adams, regularly mounted guard within the storage
room where he would sit patiently sorting the family papers. The old man greeted me without marked enthusiasm.
Clearly I was not the first to appear on the scene eager to
know all and a little self-righteously impatient of the obstacles to research. "All you scholars are hunting for is
scandal," he observed somewhat testily. The not-so-soft im-

ERNEST SAMUELS is Professor of English at Northwestern University.

peachment took me aback. I was still fresh from the pages of Langlois and Seignobos and filled with that sense of mission that only the researcher dedicated to the pursuit of historical truth can know. Of course I stammered in embarrassment that my motives were of the purest, and I tried manfully to forget the rumors that had whetted my curiosity and the lively surmises that abetted them. I am sure that the canny old gentleman was not mollified, and our interviews went on under a grudging flag of truce. He answered my specific inquiries but balked at the fishing expeditions which are the life of research. I did not get access to the precious archives until 1954. Then, while reconnoitering the heaped up terrain of letters and memorabilia I chanced upon an anxious notation which the nephew had made alongside of a particularly cruel gibe at Henry Cabot Lodge, with whom the earlier Henry was recurrently out of sympathy. He feared that publishing the sentence would reopen old wounds. "Poor Uncle Henry," he protested, had suffered enough from "unjust allegations."

This Boston episode and the question of "unjust allegations" sprang to my mind not long ago when a British reviewer of my third volume scored my timidity in withholding the appellation "mistress" from my characterization of Adams's long and close intimacy with Elizabeth Cameron, the wife of Senator James Donald Cameron of Pennsylvania. People who knew them in Washington, he said, "were convinced that he was in fact Mrs. Cameron's lover and some of them were convinced that he was the father of Martha Cameron." It was evident, he went on, that I preferred to turn away my eye from "the possibility that Mrs. Cameron was Adams's mistress." He also charged that I neglected to allude to the theory that Adams was the "father of Martha Cameron."

The reviewer's authority, I subsequently learned from him, was gossip that he had received from the late Lloyd

Griscom, a former diplomat and newspaper publisher who died in 1959 at the age of eighty-six. In the eighties and early nineties Griscom's father had been an ally of Senator Cameron and through this connection he had become one of the youthful political protégés of Mrs. Cameron's Washington salon. When he published his autobiography, *Diplomatically Speaking,* in 1940 he looked back nostalgically across a half century to his fortunate initiation as a lad of sixteen or seventeen into Mrs. Cameron's brilliant circle. He was then a junior at the Wharton School of Finance where the students were given periodic leaves of absence to go to Washington to visit Congress. During these leaves Griscom would put up at the Camerons'. He recalled that "hardly an afternoon went by without the appearance of a small man with a small gray beard and an intellectual face. It was Henry Adams . . . [He] had a collection of nephews and nieces, some real, but most adopted. As one of this group, I frequently went to his breakfasts, served at twelve-thirty according to the French custom. When his colored major-domo answered your ring, you never inquired, 'Is Mr. Adams in?' He was always in, and the right number of seats were ready. Uncle Henry presided and discoursed in his dry ironical manner on everything under the sun, from the daily movement of gold to the evolution of furniture at the French court. . . ."

This was in the fall and winter of 1889 when Adams was hard at work winding up his nine volume *History of the United States during the Administrations of Jefferson and Madison.* Four years had passed since his wife's tragic suicide. By this time he had become chief courtier in the little group made up of Adams, John Hay, and young Cecil Spring Rice of the British embassy that flattered Mrs. Cameron with their sonnets and gallantries. The middle-aged Adams had fallen quite hopelessly in love with her and had come to dote on her infant daughter Martha, for his own marriage had been childless. Sensing danger, Mrs. Cameron urged him to set out on his long-meditated voyage to the South Seas. He departed with John LaFarge and remained away for more than a year and a half. Griscom, in spite of his youth, may have surmised some of this tension, but his autobiography gives no slightest hint of it.

Griscom saw Adams again in London in June, 1893. He had been recently appointed private secretary to Ambassador Bayard through the intercession of Mrs. Cameron. Adams took him to the opera where they occupied Mrs. Cameron's box. Adams glanced about at the bejeweled occupants of the other boxes and then, as Griscom recalled, philosophically gestured to the stalls below. "Do you see all those bald-headed men? . . . Those doddering old boys were dashing young blades about town when I was here first." He spoke of the time when he was serving as private secretary to his father and then "he lapsed from his usual cynical manner to give me a piece of advice which I never forgot. 'You've every opportunity to make friends that will influence your entire career. Be sure to keep your head and get the most you can out of it.' "

That anecdote is Griscom's second and last allusion to Adams. Adams's letters indicate that their acquaintance continued in a very desultory fashion on the few occasions when Griscom returned from his foreign posts to report to the State Department. The last of the few scattered allusions was made in 1906 when Adams reported to Mrs. Cameron, who was then absent from Washington, that Lloyd Griscom had brought him a tale of Theodore Roosevelt's latest political vendettas. Griscom never became an intimate of the Adams circle and his name drops out completely from the voluminous and gossipy correspondence. If in the forties or fifties Griscom was "convinced" of the truth of the rumors which he had picked up nearly a half century earlier and now chose to retail, that conviction evidently rested on no fresher evidence than an old man's afterthoughts or echoes of the gossip which he had heard. Perhaps he was recalling Adams's frequent visits to the Cameron salon in 1889 and finally concluded that the shortest explanation was the best. If that was the course of his speculation it overlooked the fact that the varieties, vagaries, and gradations of the relations that subsist between men and women passeth both numbering and understanding. Nor have the explorations of Freud and his followers done anything to simplify that interesting calculus. That Griscom may have in his old age yielded to the perfectly natural tendency to describe the love affairs of others in summary terms is understandable. The careful historian does not have that privilege.

The allegations against Henry Adams did credit to the reviewer's ear for long-lived gossip but it also raised the disquieting question of what explicit notice a biographer should take of floating gossip. Putting aside the question of the type of biography that is involved, the researcher would certainly be negligent if he did not pursue rumors in the hope that they might lead to a cache of useable evidence. But what if the rumor proves unfounded or distorts the fact and the pursuit turns out to be a wild goose chase? Should the biographer record the missed geese or the fish that got away? Possibly so, if he wishes to demonstrate his diligence. But if the evidence is inconclusive or in fact contradicts the rumor, he runs the risk of himself giving currency to the rumor by his emphasis. It was such false and misleading emphasis that I had determined to avoid. Whether a rumor deserved a page, a line, a footnote, or charitable oblivion would depend on the credible evidence for it and not on its piquancy. I am convinced that that is a sound principle of the biographer's art and though it discourages sensationalism it provides the more lasting nourishment of truth. Such at any rate was the principle

I finally adopted as appropriate to a scholarly biography. How I applied it in the case of the two allegations against Henry Adams is the subject of the following pages.

In limited space it is not possible to review in extenso the evidence dispersed through two volumes and various notes nor to supply the family and social ambiance in which that evidence must be felt, but the key data may be suggested which negatived the gossip and made its theories untenable.

Henry Adams had a keen sense of his social position and his special responsibility as a member of the highly conspicuous Adams family. Generations of political criticism of the dynasty had bred circumspection into the bone. Though he deplored the provinciality of Boston he never gave up its proprieties nor its pruderies. In fact he was a little proud of what he called his Boston "finickingness," turning away in disgust not only from physical untidiness but from sexual and social irregularities. He was admittedly, as Henry James depicted him, a fastidious snob. In the eighties he and his wife kept their door closed against Sarah Bernhardt, Oscar Wilde, and similar irregulars. The divine Sarah is unpleasantly hinted at in the figure of the repulsive and temperamental adventuress in his novel *Esther*.

He was as intolerant of untidy marriages as of adultery. Hearing that an English friend had married again and this time a much younger woman, he wrote censoriously to Mrs. Cameron that he never forgave a man marrying at sixty. "The sexual period in men and women is well defined. It is even a scientific distinction like infancy and senility." He thought it disgusting for an "elderly man" to flaunt a young bride in public. At the time he wrote this he was himself sixty-four. It was not an observation that a lover in possession would make to a handsome mistress of forty-five. He at least, if not Mrs. Cameron, had reached the decent age of sexual retirement. Three years earlier he had written to Mrs. Cameron that he had heard a "story," a piece of gossip about the two of them. "I am so damn respectable," he twitted her, "that the story would improve the social position of both of us, and I wanted no better than to figure in that immoral role. Unfortunately no one will ever believe it, and the more I struggle for a reputation of vice, the more I am conspicuous as a pattern of sexagenarian respectability. It's disgusting." Obviously it was a matter on which at sixty-one he could be safely facetious, sure that Elizabeth Cameron would know that his "vice" at least would not shock a Boston clergyman.

The stories did persist, for Adams availed himself of the prerogatives of harmless age to make himself at home in her salon whether in Washington or in Paris, accepted by their circle as the most favored of family friends and a kind of "uncle-in-residence" not only to her but to her stepchildren and all the young women whom she drew into her circle to please her aging cavalier. As he grew older he gladly submitted to her motherly management, at least of his regular Paris sojourns, and in return he served as her distinguished-looking escort. To his intimates there was of course no need for apology. Edith Wharton, whose deep involvement with Walter Berry was perhaps a different matter, felt free to twit him about his various "wives" whom he shepherded about Paris. As for the clack of the outside world, he protected himself with the fantasy of a "posthumous existence" (which had begun with the death of his wife) and it succeeded so well that in 1905 when he was sixty-seven the New York *Times* alluded to him as "the late Henry Adams."

Adams had begun to feel and act like an old man long before his sixties. After the death of his wife in 1885 he had written to an English friend that he had "become an old man in twelvemonth." At sixty in spite of his energy and capacity for hard work he protested that he felt like a hundred and constantly complained of real and imaginary illness. Even in his forties he had begun to be obsessed with the idea that he would become prematurely senile like his father and he figured that he could count only "on twenty years more brain, if the physical machine holds out." When in 1895 he and his brother Charles read their father's diary in preparation for the American Statesman volume, he found disagreeable confirmation of his theory. His father had begun to feel himself growing old at forty-eight and had begun to watch for signs of mental decay. The morbid introspectiveness of such passages with their reminders of the sternly repressed emotions of the household and the habits of Puritanical self-denial and propriety, caused Charles to write to Henry: "Great Heavens! Why wasn't I as a boy sent to boarding school!—Why didn't I as a young man go to Hell!" After a lifetime of rigid self-control for both of them, the time for such travel was patently gone.

When Henry Adams reached seventy all his neurotic fears of imminent senility seemed about to be realized when he experienced a short attack of amnesia. This was in 1908. His dependence on Mrs. Cameron's management increased. The effect of appearances on an impressionable younger man can be judged from Bernard Berenson's recollections at the age of ninety. By 1909 he was on a familiar footing with Adams. Seeing Adams so at his ease in Mrs. Cameron's apartment he took, as Adams would say, a "French view" of the case. Had he known Adams's status as a family friend of the Camerons for nearly thirty years and more of the history of Adams's romantic and hopeless devotion he might have made a less simple deduction.

Henry Adams and his wife Marian first met Mrs. Cameron in 1881 in Washington. Elizabeth Cameron was the daughter of Judge Charles Sherman and the niece of General William Tecumseh Sherman and Senator John Sherman. In 1878 at the age of twenty-one she married Senator James Donald Cameron whose first wife had died four years before. Senator Cameron was then forty-five, five years older than Adams. The gossip columnists described her as the most beautiful woman in Washington. Adams's wife, then thirty-three, made up for her want of beauty by the brilliance of her sharp wit. Both Marian and her husband were quickly drawn to the titian-haired and vivacious beauty. Adams soon became, as he wrote John Hay, a "tame cat" about the Cameron house and he and the senator strolled about with "our arms around our necks." In recommending her and her husband to Ambassador Lowell in London in 1883 Adams wrote, "Both my wife and I are very fond of her. . . . You will fall in love with her, as I have." About the same time he was writing Hay, "I adore her and respect the way she has kept out of scandal and mud, and done her duty by the lump of clay she promised to love and respect." The senator's social limitations were a frequent source of raillery among their little coterie of friends who called themselves the Five of Hearts. Mrs. Adams wrote her father that Mrs. Cameron had drawn "a blank" in Don. Marian Adams was herself enchanted by the dazzling young woman. When Mrs. Cameron and the senator were traveling in Europe, Mrs. Adams wrote to the absent "Perdita": "We miss you, miss you, miss you."

In April, 1885, Marian's father died after several months of agonizing illness. She had been extraordinarily close to him and helped nurse him through the final month of his illness. The strain of the loss affected her in much the way Adams had described his heroine's experience in the novel *Esther* which he had written the year before. It did not wear off and during the summer at Beverly Farms Marian sank deeper into mental depression. Adams had always known of the lurking danger. In fact, shortly before his engagement he had been reminded by his brother Charles of the mental illness that ran in her family. Charles had blurted out, "She'll kill herself, just like her aunt!" In mid-October he and Marian returned to Washington. Either on that journey or one taken shortly thereafter, Henry's brother Charles remembered going to where Marian and Henry were sitting and trying to talk with her. "It was painful to the last degree. . . . Her mind dwelt on nothing but self-destruction. . . . She was engaged the whole time in introspection and self-accusation." Charles's prophecy was fulfilled on Sunday morning, December 6, 1885, at the hour when she used to sit down to write her weekly letter to her father. Since still another malicious piece of gossip attributed her act to jealousy of Mrs. Cameron it is important to note that in the letter which was found on her desk, addressed to her sister, she wrote, "If I had one single point of character or goodness I would stand on that and grow back to life. Henry is more patient and loving than words can express. God might envy him— he bears and hopes and despairs hour after hour. . . . Henry is beyond all words tenderer and better than all of you even."

According to one of the allegations of gossip it was during this period of acute anxiety that Henry Adams begot Martha Cameron. Indeed I had myself entertained that possibility almost from the beginning of my research and before I picked up the old rumor. It was a perfectly natural speculation that a reader of the second volume of letters might venture when reading of Adams's devotion to Martha. The unpublished letters to Martha seemed to strengthen that impression. The gossip I had heard from Berenson seemed to confirm it. But when I hunted for evidence that might lend a degree of probability to the story I found that the likelihood of its truth steadily diminished until it seemed unworthy even of the emphasis of a footnote. In omitting this footnote I now see that I committed a tactical error.

Martha was born in Washington, June 25, 1886, in the Cameron home at 21 Lafayette Square. There is no hint in the many references to her that she was a premature infant requiring special attention. Making the allowance for the normal variation in the period of gestation, the latest date for conception would have been October 21, 1885, though the more probable date would be closer to September 26. Adams and his ailing wife arrived in Washington from Beverly Farms on October 17 and went into seclusion. Their handsome new house on Lafayette Square was at last nearing completion and the unpredictable architect, H. H. Richardson, managed to keep Adams in a state of worry about the finishing touches. Since Congress did not convene until December 7 there was no reason for the Camerons to come on from Donegal in Pennsylvania and reopen their establishment for the Washington season until November. One thing is quite clear: the senator and his wife were on good terms with each other and living together. There is no doubt that he had free access to his wife and one cannot question his virility; he had fathered six children by his first wife. Adams after thirteen years of marriage was childless.

Still further light is thrown upon the relations between the two households by a letter which Adams wrote to Mrs. Cameron immediately after receiving a letter of condolence from Senator Cameron.

Thursday [Dec., 1885]

Dear Mrs. Cameron

Nothing in the course of my troubles has touched me more than your husband's note and your own illness. To have been able to ask for help would have been a pleasure to me, but there are moments in life when one is beyond all help and I was almost relieved to know that you were not in a condition to think of doing anything for me or for my poor wife. All I can now ask is that you will take care of yourself and get well. All Clovers' friends have now infinite value for me. I have got to live henceforward on what I can save from the wreck of her life and it is lucky for me that she had no friends but the best and truest.

Please tell your husband that I love him. I am not given to many such declarations, but a note like his deserves it.

This note is confidential. Please keep it quite to yourself, or show it to no one but Mr. Cameron. I shall write soon to McVeagh [Mrs. Cameron's brother-in-law] when I get a little steadier in the head. Just now I am afraid of saying more—or less—than I should wish at a calmer time.

Ever your friend,
Henry Adams

Adams sailed for Japan with John LaFarge a few weeks before the birth of Martha Cameron. There is nothing in his voluminous letters to John Hay or Mrs. Cameron which even remotely reveals an interest in the new infant. The brilliant descriptions of his travels and the diverting accounts of their daily adventures and misadventures show him avid of new experience, self-assured, and carefree. It was only after his return that he became attached to the child and chiefly because she brought him closer to her mother. It seems a reasonable surmise that it was his subsequent devotion to Elizabeth Cameron and her daughter as the Madonna and child of his idealizing fancy that led some acquaintances to read back a darker explanation of his interest in the child.

As to the second allegation of gossip, that Elizabeth Cameron was the mistress of Henry Adams, the evidence is inconclusive. From what has already been shown it would seem safe to say that it was highly unlikely that they were lovers in the technical sense after 1900, which also happened to be the period when gossip appears to have been most active. Conceivably at some earlier period in their long intimacy, possibly after his return from England in 1892 and Mrs. Cameron's nervous breakdown in 1897, the inhibited courtier played the role of Lancelot. In that rather unlikely event the episode must have been a fleeting

interlude in their enduring attachment. Neither the published nor the unpublished letters change tone in the
slightest. The more dashing John Hay might salute her in
his letters as "Dearest Lizzie" and pelt her with adoring
endearments but Adams regularly hewed to the line of
"Dear Mrs. Cameron." The infrequent brief personal references which Worthington Ford edited out of Adams's
published letters, presumably at the behest of Henry Adams
II, turned out to be no more ardent or compromising than
"I wish you were here," or "I wish I were with you," or as
in a letter written from the Yellowstone in 1894 the concluding phrase "I am at least contented to be here . . ."
was docked of the following: "there or elsewhere I shall be
ever yours." Similarly, in a letter of 1895 explaining that
Adams's return to the United States might be delayed a
month, the editor silently dropped the addition: "Should
you mind?" Parenthetically, it should be noted that the
editor deleted with a similar delicacy every reference to
Mrs. Adams as if to conform to the self-imposed silence of
Adams's own *Education.* Mrs. Cameron was for years as
formally proper as Adams in her letters and only later
tended to drop the formal "Dear Mr. Adams" for the
affectionate "Dear Dor" or "Dordy," the nickname which
her daughter gave him.

The significant turning point in their romance came in
1892 when Adams returned to France from his year-long
travels in the South Seas. The separation of a year and a
half had not cured him of his infatuation. His brief reunion with Elizabeth and her six-year-old daughter in Paris
and London unsettled him much more than it did her.
Once more she held him off. His long, moody, and introspective journal-letters followed her across the ocean for
three months until, resigned to his fate, he returned to
America. Unfortunately this remarkable series of letters,
among the best that he wrote and the most personal, was

omitted from the published collection. Mrs. Cameron, concerned by the despairing and misogynist tone of his letters, bluntly told him that he ought to find a suitable companion and marry her, advice which he was receiving as he complained from all of his women friends. He protested to her that he had met only one woman he ever cared to marry and that was his dead wife. One passage of his self-examination is particularly relevant to their affair:

> More than once today I have reflected seriously whether I ought not to turn round and get back to Ceylon. As I am much the older and presumably the one of us two who is responsible for whatever mischief can happen, I feel as though I have led you into the mistake of bringing me here, and am about to lead you into the worse mistake of bringing me home. Not that I take a French view of the matter, or imagine you to be in the least peril of falling into the conventional dilemmas of the French heroines; but because no matter how much I may efface myself or how little I may ask, I must always make more demand on you than you can gratify, and you must always have the consciousness that whatever I may profess, I want more than I can have. Sooner or later the end of such a situation is estrangement, with more or less disappointment and bitterness.

Fortunately for the work which was to derive much of its inspiration from his affection for Elizabeth and her daughter, the *Mont-Saint-Michel and Chartres,* the estrangement did not materialize. Indeed he had already begun to think of them in symbolic terms. "Progress has much to answer for in depriving weary and broken men and women of their natural end and happiness," he wrote from Wenlock Abbey. "But even now I can fancy myself contented in the cloister, and happy in the daily round of duties, if only I still knew a God to pray to, or better yet, a Goddess; for as I grow older I see that all the human interest and power that religion ever had, was in the mother and child, and I would have nothing to do with a church that did not offer both.

There you are again! You see how the thought always turns back to you."

Thereafter, Adams settled down to his role once more as "tame cat," as he sometimes referred to it, or, in another one of his figures, as the aged Chateaubriand to her infinitely forbearing Madame Récamier. The desperate note of these letters was never to recur. In their subsequent correspondence there is no hint that he ever stepped out of his role. By the turn of the century, as we have seen from his censorious comment on the scientific limits of sexual activity, all passion was spent. As the much-envied hostess of one of the most important political salons in Washington and the wife of a very rich senator, Elizabeth had a well-developed sense of Victorian propriety at least as keen as that of the shy and circumspect Adams. The innumerable letters that passed between her and Adams show her in the character of a beneficent confidante, alter ego, and "safety valve," as he gratefully called her, who drew out his genius in thousands of pages of brilliant ruminations on politics, people, and all the intellectual hobbies of his restless mind. His love was channeled into efforts to form her taste and improve her mind. One is struck by the arresting contrast between the prosaic domestic details of his letters to his wife and the wide-ranging literary imaginativeness of those to his romantic idol. The contrast suggests the potent alchemy of unfulfilled love.

One ought not to leave the story of this romance without quoting from the letter that Elizabeth Cameron wrote to Henry Adams from war-ravaged France in 1915. She had stayed on to help in relief work among the hapless refugees on the northern front. She was then fifty-eight and he seventy-seven. He had suggested that the time was ripe for her to publish her correspondence with the remarkable men she had known. She protested that the magnitude of the task staggered her. Besides, she said, "I have no knowledge of *métier,* no literary training, no starting point even. But such records as I possess of you—such wonderful records cannot be lost. . . . I think of my reckless wasted life with you as the only redeeming thing running through it, always giving the sustaining power to keep going, always keeping me from withering up. Whatever I have or am is due to you, to that never failing, never ending, never impatient nor exhausted friendship. I wish I were more credit to you."

It is now more than thirty years since the noted literary critic Ernest Boyd remarked that an obsessive preoccupation with sex was a distinctive mark of modern biography, whether sex actual or sex sublimated. Now that the Kinsey Report has supplied the statistics that Freud lacked, the subject has grown even more engrossing, especially with the passing of the simple categories of male and female. What Boyd had to say, however, about the place of sex in a biography is still relevant. If we exaggerate the importance of sex, said Boyd, we give a pathological coloring to our interpretation of a man's achievement, and his work becomes a kind of function of his glands. This approach may gratify the reader's submerged pruriencies and frustrated fancies but it will certainly distort the biographical record. Boyd then quoted Shaw's very apt comment to a writer: "You can learn nothing about your sitter (or biographee) from a mere record of his gallantries. . . . In permanence and seriousness my consummated love affairs count for nothing beside the ones that were either unconsummated or ended by discarding the relation." In a similar vein, Leon Edel in his *Art of Biography* gives a passage from Geoffrey Scott's brilliant *Portrait of Zélide* whose candor goes to the heart of the matter. Scott arrives in his narrative at the point, says Edel, where a fervid reader would ask, "Were they then [Benjamin Constant and Madame de Charrière] lovers?" Scott answers, " 'The subject has its pedantries like any other. I will not explore them. Psychologically, the character of their relation is abundantly clear; technically the inquiry would be inconclusive.' " In my own researches, after fitting together the psychological pieces of the puzzling relationship between Henry Adams and Elizabeth Cameron, I concluded that the term "mistress" belonged among the pedantries of the subject.*

NOTE

* Grateful acknowledgment for the use of copyrighted materials in this essay is hereby made to The Adams Manuscript Trust and The President and Fellows of Harvard University.

Donald Pizer

❧ ❧

Hamlin Garland's
A Son of the Middle Border:
Autobiography as Art*

Hamlin Garland's *A Son of the Middle Border*, first published in 1917, has always been considered a major American autobiography. Its narrative of prairie life in the 1870's
and eighties is frequently drawn upon by historians, as is its
account of radical literary and political movements in the
eighties and nineties. It has been edited for use in the schools,
and at one time many Midwestern children were as familiar
with it as with Franklin's autobiography. The principal
approach to the work has been that it is a useful social and
personal record, that it informs us about a vanished phase
of American life and about the early life of an important
literary figure. Although most readers of the book have

DONALD PIZER is Professor of English at Newcomb College, Tulane University.

recognized its holding power as a narrative, the undeniable value of the autobiography as a cultural document has hindered consideration of its themes and form. It is along these lines, however, that I would like to discuss *A Son of the Middle Border*. Granting its historical relevance, I wish to demonstrate that the book gains an additional permanent interest from its own powerful inner life.

A Son of the Middle Border, like many literary works, has a dual character. To the general reader it appears coherent and unified, the work of an author writing out of one spirit at one moment. To the scholar aware of Garland's career it is a patchwork of material written or published by him over a thirty-year period. The account of the growth of *A Son of the Middle Border* which follows, and which precedes the discussion of its themes and form, has, therefore, a twofold purpose. It will clarify the complex history of an important work. And it will suggest the ways in which Garland gradually formed his reminiscences of his early life into a book which reflected an interpretation of his life rather than a memory of it. Or, in more literary terms, it will indicate the ways in which Garland profited from his thirty-year career as a professional writer of fiction to select, arrange, and emphasize the details of his life in order to impose design and meaning on his experiences and so transform personal history into art.[1]

All artists speak through a temperament, and in this sense all artists are autobiographical. But Garland was also more explicitly and more extensively autobiographical than most writers. From his early career in the 1880's to his death in 1940 he wrote continuously about himself and his family, first of his parents and then of his wife and children. He thought of his autobiographical writings in a Whitman-esque sense, that he wrote about himself in order to present some of the central experiences and themes of American life. But he also increasingly found that autobiography was the most compelling and satisfactory way of releasing his creative energy. He eventually found his own life not only his best theme but also his best means of expressing his theme.

Born near West Salem, Wisconsin, in 1860, Garland was raised on farms in Wisconsin, Minnesota, and Iowa. He was graduated from the Cedar Valley Seminary at Osage, Iowa, in 1881, and after several years of miscellaneous jobs and wandering (including over a year with his parents in South Dakota), he moved to Boston in 1884. There he established himself as a teacher, lecturer, and free-lance author. By 1887 he was writing fiction and poetry about his life on the prairie. His first major work, as well as his first important autobiographical effort, was a series of six articles, "Boy-Life on the Prairie," published in the *American Magazine* in 1888.[2] The articles describe a year's cycle of farm life, from corn husking in the late fall to "melons and early frosts" the following year. As his principal rhetorical strategy, Garland adopted the role of a Westerner anxious to inform eastern readers about the realities of western farm life. But he also wanted to dwell nostalgically on the lost world of his boyhood. The result is a frequently labored and effusive mixture of informative detail and nostalgic lyricism. The articles are best in Garland's ability to evoke the reality of particular moments and moods of boy-life on a farm—the despair and pain of husking corn in the fields on a cold, dreary October day, the exhilaration of wild horseback rides over the unfenced prairie. The series benefits, too, from its clear-cut form—a year's cycle of farm activities serving as the basis for a recollection of a boy's world. Some hints of two of Garland's later autobiographical themes appear in brief passages on the hard lot of farm wives and in longer passages on the changing conditions of western farm life. But for the most part Garland preserved the integrity of his "boy-life" angle of recall.

78

During the next decade Garland wrote a number of auto-biographical sketches, but he was primarily absorbed in achieving success as a writer of fiction.[3] His stories and novels during these years, however, were heavily autobio-graphical both in theme and incident. He drew upon such autobiographical material for his fiction as the return of his father from the Civil War ("The Return of a Private" in *Main-Travelled Roads* [1891] and Chapter I of *A Son*); a fight at a country dance ("The Sociable at Dudley's" in *Prairie Folks* [1893] and Chapter XVI of *A Son*); and his experiences at the Cedar Valley Seminary (*A Spoil of Office* [1892] and Chapters XVII–XIX of *A Son*). The significance of Garland's autobiographical fiction and sketches is that the effort of dramatizing a wide range of his own experi-ences in fictional or semi-fictional form kept alive his aware-ness of these moments as well as sharpened his ability to render memory into scene and dialogue. "Boy-Life" is lim-ited to the early 1870's in Iowa, and is primarily authorial summary rather than dramatic scene. Such stories and sketches as "The Return of a Private" (1890) and "Holding Down a Claim in a Blizzard" (1888) go beyond "Boy-Life" both in chronology and in technique. The first is set in 1865, the second in Dakota during the winter of 1883–1884. And both recreate event rather than recall it.

Early in 1898 Garland planned a long and difficult pack horse trip to the Klondike. The journey was dangerous enough for him to think about leaving a record of his life. He did so by dictating to a secretary in Washington an autobiographical narrative called "The Story of Grant Mc-Lane."[4] He not unnaturally included in this work much of his adulthood, but more surprisingly he cast the account in the third person. His ten years as a professional writer had apparently not only broadened his idea of the kind of autobiographical experience he could call upon but had also encouraged him to write of himself in semi-fictional or fictional forms in which he used the third person or a fictionalized first person. When he returned unharmed from Alaska and read "The Story of Grant McLane," he was attracted by the idea of publishing it. But after some consideration he decided that at thirty-eight he was "too young to have the air of writing my autobiography," [5] and put the book aside. The effort at full scale recall, however, followed by the stimulation of reading his account, led him to attempt a less pretentious autobiographical work, a much revised and expanded version of his 1888 "Boy-Life" series —*Boy Life on the Prairie,* published in 1899.[6]

Garland's autobiographical sketches and fiction of 1888–1898 and "The Story of Grant McLane" influenced *Boy Life on the Prairie* in several important ways. First, although he kept *Boy Life* a book about a boy's world, he increased the range and depth of that world. *Boy Life* begins with the young boy's arrival in Iowa with his family, an opening which suggests a greater emphasis on chronological sequence and social setting than exists in "Boy-Life." Garland preserved much of the cyclic structure of "Boy-Life," but he now (as in *A Son*) included this cyclic narrative of farm activities in a larger time scheme which begins with the family's arrival in Iowa and ends with the boy's departure for school in town (1869–1876, in effect). His greater use of what can be called plot and setting also led him to shift certain events and details. For example, in "Boy-Life" the incident of the boy's wonder at his first sight of wild horses occurs in a general account of prairie animal life. In *Boy Life* it appears at a more appropriately dramatic moment, the morning after the family's arrival on their Iowa farm.

Garland was influenced in another way by his autobiographical fiction of the previous decade and by "Grant McLane." He wrote *Boy Life* as fiction, telling the story of Lincoln Stewart in the third person. He decided on a fictional central figure, he explained in his preface, because he wanted to include experiences not strictly autobiographical yet characteristic of the time and place. Garland's emphasis on time and place, on the general truth of a boy's experiences on the Iowa prairies in the 1870's, indicates that despite his expansion of his "Boy-Life" material and despite his greater dramatic facility, his intent was the same in both works. He wished in both to represent the feelings and experiences of a typical prairie youth rather than to center on the particular, and more complex and provocative, characteristics of his own youth.

Boy Life on the Prairie is divided into two parts. The first, though it begins with a chapter narrating the trip to Iowa, is an expanded version of the "Boy-Life" material and pattern of a year's cycle of farm life. The second part consists of a non-chronological account of various prairie experiences and adventures, such as a chapter devoted to game hunting. As B. R. McElderry has noted, *Boy Life* is an unjustly neglected work.[7] It is a lively narrative of a pervasive American experience of the nineteenth century, growing up on a farm. Yet the work is essentially a boy's book in the sense that *Huckleberry Finn* is not. That is, its themes do not extend far beyond a boy's vision or an adult's nostalgia.

Although Garland continued to produce an occasional autobiographical sketch during the next ten or twelve years,[8] he devoted himself principally to novels about the mountain West. Toward the end of this period his interest in fiction declined and he also began to feel the need to deal more directly and fully with the major events of his life. He undertook *A Son of the Middle Border* in late 1911 both to put his scattered autobiographical writings into more ordered and permanent form and to give his career a new direction. Despite his enthusiasm for the project, Garland was again troubled by the "egotism" of the autobiographical form.[9] His doubts were confirmed when a number of leading magazines rejected the work during 1912–13 because of its limited interest. It was with these comments in mind that Garland in late 1913 set to work to produce a book which would still be his life story but which would attempt to give the impression that the story was not autobiographical.[10]

Garland completed this revision in January, 1914, and immediately took it to New York in a last effort to place the book. To his joy Mark Sullivan of *Collier's* accepted six chapters for early publication. Five installments, from March to August, 1914, appeared before war news crowded it out of the magazine.[11] The 1914 *Collier's* version of *A Son of the Middle Border* was still far from being a major work, though it was a notable advance over Garland's earlier autobiographical efforts. It began far back in his memory—indeed, at the beginning of memory when he was a child of four or five—and was intended to bring him to young adulthood in the early 1890's. Throughout the narrative Garland adopted the pose of a historian who has discovered "An Abandoned Autobiography" by one Lincoln Stewart (his *Boy Life* hero). The narrative consists of first person accounts by Stewart (in quotation marks) and third person editorial comment and continuity by Garland. This combined first-third person narrative supplied Garland with an easy solution to a difficult technical problem. With this method he was able to combine the vividness of first person narration with the commentary, thematic control, and authorial distance of a third person editor. He wished to create a sense of "truth" (hence first person) but he also wished to select and arrange the events of his life toward an interpretation of his life, without appearing egotistical, just as he had depicted other lives in his fiction (hence third person). The product of these not necessarily conflicting, but in this instance unreconciled, motives was an awkward and stumbling combination of first and third person narration.

But despite its failure, Garland's experimentation with autobiographical narrative technique in his 1914 *Collier's* version of *A Son* represents a step toward his successful narrative form in his final version of the book. For when he rewrote his autobiography in 1914–1917, he not only shaped his material with the force and freedom of the novelist (the "historian" of 1914) but also incorporated into a first person narrative those smoothly alternating passages of vivid recall and reflective comment which are one of the principal aesthetic strengths of the work.

The 1914 *Collier's* version of *A Son* is significant for other reasons than its technical experiment. Particularly important are its omissions and compressions. The five published chapters or parts bring Garland to his early years at the Cedar Valley Seminary. Yet the fourth chapter is the only one which deals with the 1869–1876 period to which Garland had devoted all of *Boy Life*. The first three parts are on Garland's boyhood in Wisconsin and on his move to Iowa, the fifth is on his experiences in Osage and at the seminary. Perhaps Garland did not want to repeat too literally or fully his *Boy Life* material, for that work was still in print. But whatever the reason for the compression, his ability to summarize these vital years and still tell his life story indicates the new direction his autobiography was taking. Unlike *Boy Life*, it was now unnecessary either to explain in detail the intricacies of threshing and husking or to present fully a boy's response to these activities. Now it was more vital to make these events and impressions part of the young Garland's expanding consciousness, and, more particularly, part of a complex of themes involving his growing antagonism to farm life, his emerging rebellion against his father's ideals, and his gradual division of his experience into that which he rejects and that which he seeks. The account of haying in the 1888 "Boy-Life" ("Meadow Memories") had been expanded into a full chapter in *Boy Life* ("The Wild Meadows—Haying Time") in order to dramatize this major event of a farm year. In the 1917 *Son*, which is similar to the 1914 *Collier's* version in this respect, haying is summarized in less than two pages (pp. 137–138). Although the beauty of haying time is preserved as a motif in this summary, its beauty plays a new and now ironic role in a larger theme. Haying in *A Son* is a brief interlude of glorious weather and of work in the open fields during which "even the toiling hay-maker, dulled and deadened with never ending drudgery, caught something of the superabundant glow and throb of nature's life." [12] And even this "glow and throb" is limited in range. Garland noted that farm wives are confined to their kitchens by the added work of haying time and therefore experience little of this exhilaration. Now, in short, haying is not merely the art of stacking or a boy's wonder and excitement. Its depiction also contributes to the expanded theme of the drudgery of farm life and to the new theme of Garland's response to drudgery in terms of sympathy for his overworked mother and rebellion against his stern, disciplinarian father.

Late in 1915, Mark Sullivan decided to resume publication of *A Son of the Middle Border* in *Collier's*. Garland had already, in August, 1914, begun to revise the work back into the first person,[13] and now, with Sullivan's encouragement, he undertook the tasks of preparing a number of revised installments for *Collier's* and of revising the entire work for book publication. Three installments of this revision into the first person appeared in *Collier's* from March to May, 1917, before publication was again interrupted, this time by America's entry into the war.[14] The first installment contained a laudatory preface by Theodore Roosevelt but there was no explanation of the change in form between the 1914 and 1917 serializations. These installments take Garland through his seminary and wandering years to the eve of his departure for Boston in October, 1884. The 1917 *Collier's* serialization is for the most part a heavily cut and condensed version of similar sections in the final version of the book.

This final version of *A Son of the Middle Border,* published by Macmillan in August, 1917, draws heavily on almost all of Garland's earlier autobiographical writing, yet the book is a new work. Garland had expanded his 1888 "Boy-Life" into his 1899 *Boy Life,* but he now omitted almost all of the second part of *Boy Life* and condensed its first part (the year's cycle) into approximately eighty pages (Chapters VIII–XIV of *A Son*). The third person indirectness of *Boy Life* and "The Story of Grant McLane," and the awkwardness of the first-third person narration in the 1914 *Collier's* serialization, are replaced by a smooth flowing first person narration combining dramatic recall with reflection and analysis. Most of all, the earlier major themes of a boy's adventures and of a vanishing farm life are now condensed and incorporated into larger, more compelling themes. They are still present in their own right but now also contribute to controlling powerful themes in the work as a whole.

Garland's career had been in decline since his peak period of the mid-1890's. *A Son of the Middle Border* re-established him as a major literary figure. It brought about his election to the American Academy in 1918 and was a primary factor in his being awarded a Pulitzer Prize in 1922.[15] Encouraged by the success of *A Son,* Garland wrote three more family autobiographical volumes, none of which reached the level of the first work. In 1930 he published *Roadside Meetings,* the first of four volumes of literary reminiscences. So after thirty years of a mixed literary career, including much autobiographical writing, Garland in 1917 discovered his final literary voice and gave himself almost entirely to autobiography until his death in 1940.

The closing scene of *A Son of the Middle Border* is a Thanksgiving dinner held by the Garland family at West Salem, Wisconsin, in 1893. The dinner takes place in a house which Garland had recently bought in order to settle his aged and weary parents who had left the Coolly country near West Salem over twenty-five years earlier to pioneer farther west. Garland, who has had a successful career as a writer in the East, sits at the head of the table and carves the turkey. "For the first time in my life I took position as head of the family and the significance of this fact did not escape the company. The pen had proved itself to be mightier than the plow. Going east had proved more profitable than going west!" (p. 464). Garland's reflections on this occasion summarize three of the principal themes of *A Son of the Middle Border,* themes which he states explicitly at this point but which appear dramatically and symbolically throughout the work.

A Son of the Middle Border is about the relationship of a young man to his parents, with that relationship significant not only for his personal development but for his self-discovery as a writer and for his understanding of his epoch. The conflict in the narrative is that of Garland's love for his mother and his rebellion against his father. As Garland grows to young manhood, his father represents to him pioneering and the hard work of the farm ("west" and the "plow") while his mother represents the established life of a settled area and an appreciation of Garland's expanding intellect and ambitions ("east" and the "pen"). *A Son of the Middle Border* dramatizes Garland's polarization of his experience into opposites symbolized by his parents. The thematic strength and suggestiveness of the work derive not only from Garland's symbolic use of a pervasive family conflict but from the "plot" which grows out of the conflict. Seeking to escape from his father's dominion and from

86

his father's ideals of the West and the plow, Garland "deserts" his mother, leaving her to his father and to the difficult life of a western pioneer wife while he pursues a career as a student and writer in the East. Gradually he is overcome by guilt until his life in the East is controlled by his drive to "rescue" his mother—to rescue her from further hardship and, in a sense, from his father. Garland's changing relationship with his parents, from rebellion and desertion to guilt and rescue, is the narrative and emotional center of the book.

The two other primary themes of the work stem from this center. The first deals with Garland's discovery of himself as an artist. He finds that the West is his basic subject, despite his desertion of it, and that his depiction of the West is inseparable from his rebellion against it and his guilt toward it. The second theme deals with Garland's discovery of himself as a westerner. As the son of a pioneer, he occasionally shares in the westering spirit. But as the member of a particular pioneer family, he associates his family's failure in the West with the end of the pioneering era. Garland therefore expands his personal autobiography into an account of an epoch. He does this not by writing about the epoch but by infusing an interpretation of his age into the story of his life.

Let me turn more fully to the first of these major themes, Garland's relationship with his parents. Garland's early memories of his mother and father introduce in the context of a boy's impressions the motif of a sympathetic, warm mother and a strong-willed, disciplinarian father. To the young boy the father is a heroic and adventurous figure who has fought the Confederates and who has lumberjacked in the Far North. But he is also a man with "terrifying" eyes and a willful nature. When Garland was still a child, the family visited the McClintocks, Garland's mother's family. On the way they reached the top of a hill which "gave a grand view of wooded hills to the northeast, but father did not wait for us to enjoy that. He started the team on the perilous downward road without regard to our wishes, and so we bumped and clattered to the bottom, all joy of the scenery swallowed up in fear of being thrown from the wagon" (p. 15). This little adventure is an allegory of the experiences of the Garland family over the next twenty-five years as Garland's father drives the family "downward" from the security and beauty of their Coolly farm to the perils and hardships of pioneering in Minnesota, Iowa, and Dakota.

Richard Garland's war experiences were the major source of Garland's characterization of him. A man used to discipline, order, and service, he imposed these on his family. But Garland's mother, Isobel, resembled her family, the romantic, poetic, brooding McClintocks, and Garland early in life identified his own temperament with hers and the McClintocks. When his father determined to leave their safe and placid valley for the hazards of new land farther west, Garland instinctively sided with his mother's reluctance and hesitation, even though he was also excited by the idea of pioneering. At a family gathering, he asks her to sing songs whose themes are the benefits of the settled life as opposed to the adventures of pioneering. Earlier in the evening she had sung a ballad of pioneering, "O'er the Hills in Legions Boys," singing it "submissively, not exultantly," for to her as to all pioneer women the song had meant "deprivation, suffering, loneliness, heart-ache" (p. 63). She had sung the ballad at Richard Garland's request, for "even in this choice of songs he generally had his way" (p. 63). But the youthful Garland asks her to sing "Pile the Wood on Higher," which she does "with pleasure, for this was a song of home, of the unbroken fire-side circle" (p. 64).

It is Richard Garland who uproots the Garland family, first from Green's Coolly in 1868, then the following year from their new farm in eastern Minnesota to Mitchell County, Iowa, and finally in 1881 to pioneer once more in South Dakota. Garland's response to these moves changes from a boy's excitement at adventure mingled with sorrow at losing friends to an increasing rejection of pioneering because of the suffering and hardship it brings his mother. Garland's rebellion against his father has another major cause in addition to Garland's association of his father with his mother's hardship. It is his father who is the taskmaster on the farm, who enlists the young Garland at the age of seven into a life of "service" to farm duties. At ten Garland is harnessed to the plow, and each year thereafter brings greater participation in the drudgery of farm labor as each farm increases in size and as his father asks more and more of him.

In 1876 the Garland family moved temporarily to Osage, Iowa, where Garland's father had been engaged as a wheat buyer for the Grange. Both Garland and his mother were overjoyed at their release from the bleakness and hardship of farm life. Within a year, however, the family returned to the farm, although young Garland was to spend half of each year in Osage attending the Cedar Valley Seminary. Initially Garland's principal reaction to his family's return to the farm was to rebel against his own required return each spring after the glories of town and seminary life. But increasingly he was also troubled by feelings of guilt as he left his mother behind on the farm each fall. Despite his realization of his mother's unending toil and failing health, his drives to rebel and to escape remain the dominant forces in his life during his seminary years. He discovers the power of his own will in a trivial conflict with his father over the purchase of a new hat, and discovers, too, that his talents as an orator are a way of making his personality felt by others. Gradually, then, Garland fused his desire to escape the domination of his father and his desire to escape the limitations of farm life into a powerful impulse toward rejection of his father's leadership of the family. This fusion was caused not only by his father's role as farm commander-in-chief but also by his lack of sympathy for Garland's interests in education in contrast to his mother's encouragement.

The opportunity for Garland's overt rejection of his father came with Richard Garland's decision to pioneer once again, this time in the newly opened lands of Dakota. Anxious to be his "own master," Garland struck out for himself, achieving freedom but at the same time leaving his mother to an even greater drudgery and bleakness. Although Garland remained in the West for several more years, and indeed at one time was himself infected by the Dakota land fever, he longed for further education and for a career in the East. Once in Boston, in 1884, he increasingly justified his "desertion" of his mother and assuaged his guilt by thinking of his drive toward success as a means toward aiding her. His visits to his parents' bleak Dakota farm in 1887 and 1888, and his mother's stroke in 1888 (which he blamed in part on the "madness" of his father), intensified this guilt-rescue motif into the dominant theme of Garland's representation of his Boston years.

Garland's attitude toward his family from 1887 to 1893 involved considerably more, however, than a desire to "rescue" his mother. Perhaps his developing friendship with the older W. D. Howells, whom he had met in 1887 and who responded to him with encouragement and understanding, relieved some of his hostility toward his father, who had offered neither of these qualities. In any case, Garland's attitude toward his family during these years was less emphatically a rejection of his father and more a desire to assume leadership of the family so that he might aid it as a whole. So he gradually began to perform some of the duties of family head, moving toward the time when he could control the fortunes of the family sufficiently to effect the "rescue" of his mother. He took charge of his younger brother and sister, and attempted to aid their careers and in particular to save his sister from a prairie womanhood. He lent his father money. And finally, in 1892, he threatened to remove his mother to West Salem by herself if his father did not move the entire family there.

Thus Garland's "victory" in 1893, at the Thanksgiving dinner, was complete. He had begun to relieve his guilt, first by arranging trips to California and the Chicago World's Fair for his parents, and then by settling them in their own comfortable home. His triumph over his father is symbolized by the irony of Garland paying for his father's last and farthest journey west (to California) with the proceeds of a lecture tour, and by Garland's assumption of the duty of carver at the Thanksgiving feast. But most of all his victory is contained in the return of his mother to a world which to Garland is a remembered world of maternal love and boyish response to that love, emotions later repressed by a family atmosphere which discouraged display of feeling. No wonder that Garland wrote that the preparation of the West Salem house for his mother was "as if for the entrance of a bride" (p. 463). His was indeed a family "love triangle," one which he closed at the triumphant moment of most love stories.

Much of the force and richness of *A Son of the Middle Border* stems from Garland's ability to combine the intensely personal theme of his family conflict with the objective reality of the setting in which it occurs, to combine the personal with a larger cultural theme which emerges out of setting and thereby to invest the cultural with some of the intensity of the personal. Garland's rebellion-rescue theme, in other words, is intimately linked with the East-West, pen-plow opposites contained in his final comments on his "victory." To take up the first of these, when Garland's father uprooted the family for further pioneering, the West in Garland's mind—the West as both direction and place—became associated with pain for his mother and with labor for himself. At first, despite his instinctive sympathy with his mother's antagonism to pioneering, he too had responded imaginatively to the promise of wealth and adventure in the image of the "sunset regions" in his father's song "O'er the Hills in Legions Boys." But in reality the sunset regions provided the unending labor of an Iowa farm and the desolate bleakness of a Dakota prairie. During Garland's boyhood the East was a parallel image of mythical possibility. It was a fabled world of immense cities in which were centered all culture and art. In Garland's boyish mind, "Writers were singular, exalted beings found only in the East—in splendid cities. They were not folks, they were demi-gods, men and women living aloof and looking down benignantly on toiling common creatures like us" (pp. 154–155). Gradually these images hardened in Garland's mind. The West is a land of false romance, its sunset regions demonstrably unreal on an Iowa farm. The East maintains its image of richness and stability, of tradition and culture. When Garland and his younger brother visited the East in the summer of 1882, they found their preconceptions confirmed by the splendors of Boston, New York, and Philadelphia and by the placid, wooded farms of New England. The West, of course, is the image of his father in its labor and uprootedness, the East of his mother, particularly in Garland's belief in the stability and peacefulness of its country life.

So to Garland in his young manhood the West is a false romance, the East a true one. The West is where he has labored fearfully, where his father has worked for thirty years to no avail, and where his mother has been all but destroyed. The East is where after some initial hardship he has made his talents felt and has gained a hold as an author and lecturer. It was thus almost inevitable that Garland would interpret his victory over his father and aid of his mother as a halt to their westward movement (his father's direction) and as a return to the East (his own direction). Garland made this reversal both explicit and dramatic by his depiction of West Salem at the time of his parents' return there. As Howells noted in his review of *A Son,* Garland portrayed West Salem as a New England village—calm, settled, peaceful.[16]

Garland developed the theme of the opposition between town and country life as parallel to that between the East and West. As a boy Garland had found romance and adventure on the farm itself, in observing the exciting events of threshing season or in wandering in the woods. During these early years his only sense of a deeper life outside the farm came from his vague aesthetic and emotional response to circuses and religious revivals. Gradually he discovered the world of books and bookish activities (such as debates and oratory) and expanded his interests from dime novels at ten to Hawthorne at seventeen. The physical drudgery of farm life now became an interruption to his developing intellectual and social capacities. The year's cycle of farm labor from spring to fall and of education at the Cedar Valley Seminary in the winter was essentially an emotional cycle of despair at finding himself once more behind the plow and delight at release into the social and intellectual activities of the town. The life of the mind to Garland thus became not only a goal in itself but a means of escaping farm and father, and Boston became not only a symbol of Eastern culture but an analogue to Garland's winter days at the seminary when he was at last free from fall plowing and husking. He is "profoundly happy" during these early years in Boston despite his poverty and loneliness, for they were not only "growing days" of study but were days of freedom as well (p. 331). Much of the cogency of the later sections of *A Son* derives from Garland's depiction of his career in the East as an escape and as a victory, a depiction which contributes to the details of his literary and political affairs an emotional relevance to his earlier portrayal of the hardship and confinement of farm life. It is out of this relevance that Garland can develop the final irony that he has found the excitement and wealth of the "sunset regions" not behind a plow in Iowa but as a writer in the East.

But to say that Garland "hated" the West is to indulge in the same simplification that Shreve does at the end of *Absalom, Absalom!* when he asks Quentin why he hates the South. Garland does not hate the West; he rather both loves and hates it. Howells, in his review of *A Son*, caught this quality in Garland and in the work. He noted that Garland's depiction of both the beauty of nature and the sordidness of the farm merged into a portrait of "the West which he has so passionately hated and finally so passionately loves." [17] Garland is like many Southern and Irish writers—Wolfe or Joyce or O'Casey—who have rebelled against their native lands but who find that their lands are inescapably part of their imaginations in a complex union of man and place which appears to flourish best in acts of rejection and rebellion. Two threads in this union are distinguishable in Garland—that of his relationship to the West as the son of a pioneer, and that of his relationship to it as a writer. In both instances, Garland is like Quentin in that the process of understanding his land is one of reliving his rejection of it and of rediscovering his love for it.

Garland evokes the pioneer spirit in *A Son* both in his father and in the McClintocks, particularly in his uncle David McClintock. The McClintocks are characterized as a Viking family, youthful, buoyant, confident. They are hunters and athletes as well as farmers, musicians and poets as well as pioneers. Throughout the work the McClintocks symbolize the pioneer spirit. They do so in a neutral emotional context in the sense that they are free from Garland's reaction against his father in his role of pioneer. At first, Garland believed the McClintocks heroic as he responded to their songs and energy. But when he encountered them in Iowa and California, he discovered in them the decline of the pioneer spirit. The McClintocks beat themselves against the land, and as they grow older and more tired, they become disillusioned with pioneering and see it—as Garland comes to see it—as a romantic lure. In *A Son of the Middle Border* Garland identifies his own youth with the full tide of the pioneer spirit and his maturity and adulthood with the disillusionment and decline of that spirit. He creates this sense of decline not only through his discovery that the "epic charm" of the McClintocks' westering is in truth only a futile uprooting, but through the details of his changing and expanding knowledge of farm life. So, for example, the idyllic purity he attributes in youth to the pioneer ideal is jaundiced by the coming of machine farming and by his recognition of the sexuality of farm and rural life. One of Garland's accomplishments, in other words, is his ability to allegorize the westward movement of America in his own life and in the lives of his family and of the McClintocks. He captures the buoyancy and excitement of a youthful America in his family's youth, the disillusion with pioneering in their maturity, and thus informs the otherwise abstract theme of the decline of the pioneering spirit with the concreteness and the emotional reality of his personal narrative. One feels the strength of this device particularly in such scenes as that in California (the final sunset region) when the old and bitterly weary David determines never again to play his violin, the violin which earlier had represented the joyous strength of the McClintocks. So when Garland's own family turns East in 1893 to settle in West Salem, it is to Garland an end to pioneering in America—and, by a remarkable coincidence, it is also the date of Frederick Jackson Turner's initial announcement of the same concept.[18]

Although Garland traces in *A Son of the Middle Border* his gradual disillusionment with the pioneer ideal, he cannot cut himself off from that ideal—just as Sean O'Casey was forever the Irishman. Garland had shared in the pioneer spirit as a boy, had given a "Going West" oration at his graduation exercises, and had succumbed to the spirit a last time as a Dakota land claimant. There is poignancy in Garland's account of the decline of the pioneering spirit and of his realization of its harmfulness, for he is portraying the decline and loss of an ideal he once believed in and acted upon. He depicts the loss of a core of idealism and therefore the loss of part of his life. He is a son of the middle border, in other words, and cannot escape the heritage of illusion and disillusion, the ambivalence of acceptance of the westering vision (the McClintocks) and rejection of it (farm and father) which is the fate of those on the line of pioneer advance. Although Garland resents bitterly the false lure of the sunset regions, he does so not only with an overlay of national nostalgia already current by 1917 but with a personal and family nostalgia for his lost youth and for the loss of ideals bred into his very nature.

A primary quality of Garland's relationship with his Western World is therefore that of loss. He has lost the innocence and freshness of his response to his world; indeed, that world itself, with its unfenced prairie and vigorous pioneers, is no more. Both his vision and the actuality are gone. But Garland developed side by side with this theme of loss a theme of gain. *A Son of the Middle Border* contains a theme found in much autobiography, one which Roy Pascal, in his *Design and Truth in Autobiography,* summarizes as "the story of a calling, . . . of the realisation of an urgent personal potentiality." In literary autobiography, Pascal notes, this "calling" takes the form of the writer telling us of "the evolution of his mode of vision in terms of his successive engagement with the world." [19] Garland's discovery of his calling as a writer occupies most of the last third of *A Son*. Once in Boston, he begins to discover the meaning of the world he had rebelled against and escaped from. He soon finds that this world of his mother and father, of the farm and of westering, is the one great emotional reality of his life and is in a sense his only literary material. He finds, in short, that his rejection of his world is his discovery of it, and that this discovery is his sole source of power as a writer.

Garland's earliest portraits of the West are conventional exercises in nostalgia and in the picturesque, as in his 1888 "Boy-Life" series. But there soon entered his work the effects of his visits to the West in 1887 and 1888 when he saw the bleakness and hardship of farm and village life from the perspective of his years in Boston. From this time his understanding of the world he had escaped became the center of his life as he portrayed in fiction the barrenness of that life and as he devoted himself to political and social reform movements which would aid the western farmer.

Garland's achievement of an aesthetic relationship with the world he rebelled against is inseparable from the central personal themes of *A Son of the Middle Border*. His success in finding himself as a writer allowed him to "rescue" his mother and to relieve his sense of guilt. His trips to the West in 1887 and 1888, in which all "the hard and bitter realities" of farm life came back to him "in a flood," are journeys in which his guilt feelings toward his mother are activated in proportion to his response to "the gracelessness of these homes, and the sordid quality of the mechanical daily routine of these lives" (p. 365). Garland's discovery of the aesthetic usefulness of the emotions of "intolerable poignancy" and of "half-hidden despair" contrib-

utes to a series of ironies in *A Son of the Middle Border.*
He had rejected his world only to find that his creative life
lies in that act, and he had used the negative act of rejection as a basis for the positive act of rescue. The close of
the book thus entails a double "victory." He has been victorious both in saving his mother and in discovering himself
as an artist, with the two triumphs emerging out of his
rejection of the West.

The best demonstration that Garland's aesthetic awakening lay in the discovery of his emotional relationship to his
parents and to the West can be found in the stories of
Main-Travelled Roads (1891). The two long stories—almost
novelettes—of the collection are "A Branch Road" and "Up
the Coolly." Both of these works center on a desertion-guilt-
rescue theme set in bleak farm communities. In "A Branch
Road" a young man leaves his sweetheart to the hardships
of prairie life because of jealousy. When he returns years
later, he finds her broken by the life of a farm wife. Wracked
by guilt, he attempts to make amends, but is clearly too
late. "Up the Coolly" is autobiographical in detail as well
as theme. Howard McLane (the same family name later
used by Garland in his "The Story of Grant McLane") is
a successful New York actor who returns home to his Wisconsin Coolly to find that farm life has embittered and
hardened his brother and dazed and weakened his mother.
Also tortured by guilt, Howard purchases the old family
farm for the family as a step toward atonement. These
stories, which are among Garland's best, reveal the relationship between this autobiographical theme and Garland's
most powerful creative response to the life of his area.

A Son of the Middle Border contains much of the traditional subject matter of autobiography, and since the life
depicted is principally that of a farm boy, and since the
style and form are not difficult, the casual reader is apt to
think that the work is obvious and direct. But in reality

it is a book of considerable complexity, its intertwined themes becoming constantly more suggestive as the youth grows and as his mind and his world change both in reality and in his understanding of them. Part of the depth of the work lies in the fact that its themes represent some of the basic paradoxes in the relationship of most artists to their families and to their areas. Garland is the son of a pioneer who has rejected his father and his father's goals and who has deserted his mother, yet who has translated rejection and desertion into self-discovery and success. He is a Westerner who has deserted his land yet who has discovered that he cannot and does not wish to desert it. He is the plowboy longing for books and schooling who learns that education leads him back to the subject matter of the plow. So the themes of the work turn on themselves, and one realizes at last that the "victory" dinner celebrates Garland's victory only in the senses of some increase in comfort for his mother and of his own minor success as an author—that the notes of melancholy and somberness which appear throughout the book are products of Garland's recognition that self-discovery is not happiness, though it may serve as the basis for art.

The "truth" of *A Son of the Middle Border* is not literal truth in two senses. First, the work contains many errors of fact, principally misdating.[20] More vitally, it is an account of Garland's life which stresses his relationship with his parents. The book is event shaped by recall and theme, the first defective, the second selective, and is thus a distortion of reality in the Aristotelian sense of the distortion of literal truth in order to achieve a larger truth. I emphasize these obvious characteristics of *A Son of the Middle Border* as art in order to introduce the idea that the work has another, though less immediately discernible, characteristic of art, a structure or form.

There are two major structural patterns in *A Son of the Middle Border*. The first derives from the physical movements of Garland and his family. The thirty-five chapters of the book divide into three parts: nineteen on Garland's youth in Wisconsin, Minnesota, and Iowa (1860–81); six on his wanderings after his father's move to Dakota (1881–84); and ten on his years in the East as student, teacher, and writer (1884–93). The first part stresses the growing rebellion of the young Garland against farm life. During these years Garland has only vague ideas about his goals. Rebellion is both his means and his end. The second part dramatizes a period of indecision on Garland's part as he moves between two worlds. He spends a summer in the East and finds his dreams of it confirmed, yet he joins the Dakota land rush, caught up by the land fever he had repudiated in his father. The last part deals with Garland's success in the East and with his victory in rescuing his mother. *A Son of the Middle Border* is thus not a book about Garland's prairie years with his later experiences an awkward appendix, as some critics have maintained. Without the short middle section on indecisiveness and the longer closing section on struggle and victory, the work would be incomplete both thematically and aesthetically. It would be an account of rebellion alone and would not have the symmetry and order lent by its sections on hesitation and on the finding of oneself and one's goals.

Garland's presentation of events in the last two sections of the book is determined by the primary theme of each in relation to the overall thematic movement from rebellion to hesitation to success. In the second part, for example, he narrated the few months spent in New England with considerable detail in order to emphasize that this area has an attraction and significance equal to Dakota, despite the much longer period he spent there. In the last part, his accounts of his activities in the East as a writer and reformer are frequently interrupted by reports of his trips west or of his thoughts of the West, thus keeping alive the goal of his activities in the East. The three parts, in short, are firmly conceived and dramatized as major divisions in Garland's career. Each has its own conflict and tone which contribute to the themes and movement of the work as a whole.

The second major structural pattern in *A Son of the Middle Border* is a circular one. Early in the book Garland devoted an entire chapter to an account of a farewell Thanksgiving dinner in 1867, shortly before the Garland family left Wisconsin for Minnesota. It was at this dinner that the opposing songs about pioneering had been sung and Garland had displayed his sympathy for his mother by asking her to sing "Pile the Wood on Higher." Garland's elaborate report of the Thanksgiving dinner at West Salem in 1893 is his conscious attempt to stress the circular pattern of his family's life. He and his mother, though defeated at the first dinner, are now triumphant, and the family has returned to the area of his birth. So Garland's decision to end his autobiography at thirty-three (he was fifty-seven in 1917) was not fortuitous. His decision was based on the thematic importance of his family's return to West Salem and the opportunity offered by the second Thanksgiving dinner to stress this importance by the device of structural circularity.

Garland not only imparted to *A Son* a fictional structure —that is, a form controlled by theme—but also relied on a number of fictional techniques of narrative and characterization. He was encouraged to use these techniques by his success in earlier stories and sketches in which an autobiographical theme was expressed through scene and symbol. The opening of *A Son,* which is based on Garland's story "The Return of a Private," illustrates the way in which he used some of these fictional devices. The story begins with several discharged Union soldiers on their way from Louisiana to their homes in Wisconsin. Its longest section is devoted to a dramatic presentation of the return of one private (Garland's father) to his wife, children, and farm. The theme of the story, that the hardship of the private's life will continue despite his thankfulness at rejoining his family, is rendered through dialogue and narrative. In his 1914 *Collier's* serialization of *A Son* Garland used this central portion of "The Return of a Private" in his first chapter, after a long introductory account of his grandparents and their origin. *A Son,* however, opens with the moment of the father's return and then shifts to an account of the grandparents. And even this account is now made dramatic by presenting it in conjunction with the family's visit to the McClintock farm. Garland, in short, drew upon earlier fiction and upon his knowledge of fictional devices for dramatic intensity and directness. Indeed, in this sense, *A Son of the Middle Border* is Garland's best work of extended fiction. With the possible exception of *Rose of Dutcher's Coolly,* his novels are weak in plot and character. They are weak, in other words, in fictional creativity, despite the excellence of particular scenes or settings. But *A Son* had the advantage of an intensely personal "plot" and dramatis personae. Here all of Garland's professional skill as a writer of fiction could be brought to bear upon a theme and plot which had always moved him and which required no inventiveness outside of his personal experience.

A Son of the Middle Border is not fictionalized biography, despite its fictional techniques, for throughout the book Garland imposes on past scene his own "present" voice as nostalgic reminiscencer or as analytic commentator. In his portrayal of his father's return from the war, for example, Garland describes Richard Garland's attempt to make friends with the young Hamlin, who had forgotten him.

"Come here, my little man," my father said.—*"My Little man!"* Across the space of half-a-century I can still hear the sad reproach in his voice. "Won't you come and see your poor old father when he comes home from the war?"

"My little man!" How significant that phrase seems to me now! The war had in very truth come between this patriot and his sons. I had forgotten him—the baby had never known him (p. 3).

The initial paragraph reveals the first of Garland's autobiographical voices, that of the nostalgic reliver of the earlier moment. His attempt is to add emotional depth to the moment by explicitly emphasizing the emotional reality of the act of recall. Garland used this device sparingly, no doubt recognizing the dangers of its overuse. The second paragraph contains Garland's other major autobiographical voice, that which analyzes the significance of the scene. *A Son of the Middle Border* is thus far from being an "objective" account of the past, for Garland openly colors the past with his mature feelings and ideas. As indeed he should, for as Roy Pascal notes, autobiography is essentially "an interplay, a collusion, between past and present," [21] an interplay in which the past is not only relived but reinterpreted. Part of the success of the book lies in Garland's ability to blend judiciously and smoothly dramatic scene and overt commentary. In the second half of the book there is more commentary and less of Garland's nostalgic voice. The events of Garland's later life called forth less reminiscent emotion and more analysis both because they are "adult events" and because they are for the most part "intellectual events" involving Garland's activities as a writer and reformer.

A final element of Garland's artistic strength in *A Son of the Middle Border* is his ability with concrete detail. As with most writers, he used detail in two ways: to evoke particular feelings at particular moments, and—through repetition and emphasis—to create symbols. The first use appears in such scenes as his recollection of school lunch hours in the winter, which were often spent "gnawing, dog-like, at the mollified outside of a doughnut while still its frosty heart made my teeth ache" (p. 115). These evocations of moment through the concrete are particularly vivid and frequent in Garland's narration of his prairie years. The other kind of detail, that broadening out into the symbolic, is the source of one of the major strengths of the book. Here one can distinguish between "motifs" of detail which have the suggestiveness of symbols but which are not elaborately developed, and more prominent symbols which serve as important thematic and structural threads.

The motif kind of symbolism includes plowing, mosquitoes, and manure (Garland's three principal aversions in farm life), which are often described or recalled in connection with the farm. It includes, too, Uncle David's violin as a symbol of the beauty and force of the westering impulse, and Edwin Booth (the great actor) as a symbol of the cultural life of Boston. Garland's ability to suggest the emotional and psychological reality of these and other such recurring details is responsible for much of the energy and coherence of the book.

Garland also used several more obvious and elaborate symbolic groupings. One of these draws on the imagery of the military to characterize Garland's father and the Garland family, an imagery which begins with the return of the soldier from the war and ends only with his "retreat" from Dakota to West Salem. Throughout *A Son of the Middle Border* the father is the "Commander-in-Chief" while Garland and the rest of the family are "soldiers." Garland's mother wears the "uniform" of a farm wife, the children perform "duties," and the westward moves of the family are "marches." The function of this metaphor of the family as a military unit is both to emphasize the power and dominance of Garland's father and to stress Garland's "desertion" of his mother. Another elaborate symbolic pattern in the book is that which arises from the songs which represent the opposing attitudes of Garland's mother and father toward pioneering.[22] "O'er the Hills in Legions Boys," in particular, supplies the oft-repeated image of the "sunset regions," with its connotations of wealth and adventure in the West. At first the image has its attraction for Garland as well as for his father. But as the book progresses, Garland begins to use the image with bitter irony and mockery whenever he describes his family's fortunes in Iowa and Dakota and the fortunes of the McClintocks in Iowa and California. It is appropriate, then, that the songs are again sung at the final Thanksgiving dinner, and that shortly before this event Garland combined the two major symbolic currents of the military and the "sunset" when he wrote of his father that "the flag of his sunset march was drooping on its staff" (p. 415).

Roy Pascal states that truth in autobiography "will not be an objective truth, but the truth in the confines of a limited purpose, a purpose that grows out of the author's life and imposes itself on him as his specific quality, and thus determines his choice of events and the manner of his treatment and expression." [23] Garland's ability is to create this "specific quality" of his life. He does not "tell us all," either of his career or of his deepest feelings. Rather, he creates a limited, but in itself complete, "story" of his life. He also interprets through his own life a phase of American life, that of the end of our westward expansion. *A Son of the Middle Border* tells not only of a son but of a middle borderer. It presents history as an aspect of family history and thus invests the first with emotional depth and the second with significance. It is the work of a minor writer who had the good fortune to undertake his one major theme when his skill and insight were equal to the theme and the task.

NOTES

* A portion of this essay has appeared, in somewhat different form, in the *South Atlantic Quarterly*. I wish to thank the editor of this journal for permission to reprint.

1. The fullest discussion of *A Son of the Middle Border* is by Jean Holloway, *Hamlin Garland: A Biography* (Austin, Texas, 1960), pp. 221–238. Garland himself wrote of the book (often repetitiously) in the following autobiographies: *A Daughter of the Middle Border* (1921), *Back-Trailers from the Middle Border* (1928), *Roadside Meetings* (1930), *Companions on the Trail* (1931), and *My Friendly Contemporaries* (1932). My account of the genesis of *A Son of the Middle Border* is based on these published recollections and on Garland's unpublished diaries (at the Huntington Library) and the extant manuscripts of the various versions of *A Son* (at the University of Southern California Library). Lloyd Arvidson lists the editions of *A Son* in "A Bibliography of the Published Writings of Hamlin Garland" (unpublished M.A. thesis, University of Southern California, 1952) and its extant manuscripts in *Hamlin Garland: Centennial Tributes and a Checklist of the Hamlin Garland Papers in the University of Southern California Library* (Los Angeles: University of Southern California Library Bulletin No. 9, 1962).

2. "Boy-Life on the Prairie," *American*, VII (January, 1888), 299–303; (March, 1888), 570–577; (April, 1888), 684–690; VIII (June, 1888), 148–155; (July, 1888), 296–302; (October, 1888), 712–717. I discuss this series in my *Hamlin Garland's Early Work and Career* (Berkeley, 1960), pp. 54–56 and *passim*.

3. These sketches are: "Holding Down a Claim in a Blizzard," *Harper's Weekly*, XXXII (January 28, 1888), 66–67; "A Pioneer Christmas," *Ladies' Home Journal*, XI (December, 1893), 11; "Boy Life in the West—Winter," *Midland Monthly*, I (February, 1894), 113–122; and "My Grandmother of Pioneer Days," *Ladies' Home Journal*, XII (April, 1895), 10.

4. The work is extant in two shorthand volumes, one at the Huntington Library, the other at the University of Southern California Library.

5. Garland's diary entry for December 25, 1898.

6. B. R. McElderry, Jr., has edited *Boy Life on the Prairie* (Lincoln, Nebraska, 1961), with an excellent introduction.

7. *Ibid.*, p. v.

8. These are "The Wife of a Pioneer," *Ladies' Home Journal*, XX (September, 1903), 8, 42; "Building a Fireplace in Time for Christmas," *Country Life in America*, VIII (October, 1905), 645–647; and "My First Christmas Tree," *Ladies' Home Journal*, XXVIII (December, 1911), 13. During 1914–1917 Garland published articles dealing with his relationship with Stephen Crane, James A. Herne, and W. D. Howells, portions of which he used in the later sections of *A Son of the Middle Border*.

9. Garland's diary entry for March 6, 1912.

10. Garland was also led to this change by the criticism of his friend Edward Wheeler, a poet and editor. See Garland's diary entry for January 7, 1914: "I stayed at home to work on 'The Sons of the Middle Border,' which after many revisions is nearly ready for the editor. It is now in the third person and not openly autobiographic. This change I made at the suggestion of Edward Wheeler."

11. *Collier's*, LIII (March 28, 1914), 5–7, 22–23; (April 18, 1914), 11–12, 21–22, 24–25; (May 9, 1914), 15–16, 26, 28–30; (June 27, 1914), 13–14, 31–33; (August 8, 1914), 20–21, 31–32.

12. *A Son of the Middle Border* (New York, 1917), p. 137. Citations appear hereafter in the text.

13. Garland's diary entry for August 2, 1914.

14. *Collier's*, LVI (March 31, 1917), 9–10, 25–26, 28–30; (April 21, 1917), 8–9, 27, 30; (May 26, 1917), 13–14, 49.

15. The prize was awarded ostensibly for *A Daughter of the Middle Border* (1921), but was principally for *A Son*.

16. W. D. Howells, "A Son of the Middle Border: An Appreciation," *New York Times Review of Books*, August 26, 1917, p. 309.

17. *Ibid.*, p. 315.

18. Turner, who was born in 1861 near Portage, Wisconsin, read his "The Significance of the Frontier in American History" at the Chicago World's Columbian Exposition in the summer of 1893.

19. Roy Pascal, *Design and Truth in Autobiography* (London, 1960), pp. 112, 135. Pascal's excellent work, and Wayne Shumaker's *English Autobiography, Its Emergence, Materials, and Form* (Berkeley, 1954), have contributed much to my understanding of autobiography as a form.

20. The most important of these errors is Garland's dating of his second trip to the West as 1889 when it actually occurred in 1888. See my *Hamlin Garland's Early Work*, p. 180, n. 36.

21. Pascal, *Design and Truth*, p. 11.

22. The role of these and other songs in *A Son of the Middle Border* has been well described by Ray B. Browne, "'Popular' and Folk Songs: Unifying Force in Garland's Autobiographical Works," *Southern Folklore Quarterly*, XXV (September, 1961), 153–166.

23. Pascal, *Design and Truth*, p. 83.

James Woodress

❧

Popular Taste in 1899: Booth Tarkington's First Novel

One of the engrossing mysteries of literary study is the popular book. Authors, publishers, and the critics never know if a particular work will strike the public fancy, and the scholar contemplating the subject of the popular book with hindsight can ask questions far more easily than he can answer them. Is it possible, for example, to analyze the component parts of a best seller to find the source of its popularity? Can one relate a best seller to its time and place? Are there certain subjects that are staple ingredients of the popular book? Is there any single common denominator of the best seller from age to age? Are the run-away

JAMES WOODRESS is Professor of English at the University of California, Davis.

best sellers merely more successful versions of the moderately popular book? I should like to examine these queries in the light of 1899 through the specific analysis of one popular book, Booth Tarkington's first novel, *The Gentleman from Indiana.*

Let us assume that the first requirement of the best-seller is the author's ability to tell a story well. Cooper in his day could spin a good yarn; so could Winston Churchill in 1900 and Margaret Mitchell a century after Cooper. Beyond that basic requirement, however, there seem to be some perennial topics that give their authors a headstart toward popularity. Historical fiction always has been salable from Sir Walter Scott to James B. Costain, and when it can be combined with sex and religion, as in *Ben Hur* and *Quo Vadis,* the formula seems certain to achieve popularity. Religion by itself always has been a potential best-selling subject and has produced such popular successes as *In His Steps* and the novels of Lloyd Douglas. Saccharine sentiment, popular in the mid-nineteenth century and written by those "damned scribbling women" that Hawthorne complained of, no doubt contributed to the success of best-selling romances like *St. Elmo* or *The Lamplighter.*

In addition to these perennial ingredients of the bestseller, there also seem to be topical interests that change from age to age and provide momentary stimulus to popular book sales. The importance of the slavery question certainly insured *Uncle Tom's Cabin* a wide distribution, and the contemporary interest in the race question must have played a large part in the recent success of *To Kill a Mockingbird.* Steinbeck's *The Grapes of Wrath* owed part of its success to the problems of the drought and depression in the thirties, just as Paul Leicester Ford's *The Honorable Peter Stirling* reached the best-seller lists because readers identified Grover Cleveland with the protagonist of the novel.

Beyond these examples and generalizations the investigation of the popular book becomes treacherous. The sensational best-sellers like *Ben Hur* or *In His Steps* seem easier to explain than the more modest successes. Lew Wallace and Edward Sheldon probably would have been successful in any age, for one has only to note the box office hits that have followed twentieth century filmings of *Ben Hur* or other Biblical dramas to see the perennial fascination of religion and history. Yet an examination of the moderate best-seller perhaps offers a better insight into the milieu of its period. Such a book was Tarkington's first novel, a work that is linked closely to the state of literary taste at the turn of the century. *The Gentleman from Indiana* probably could not have been a best-seller in 1860 or 1960.

Written by an unknown author, Tarkington's novel was a popular book which is not historical fiction, does not contain any titillating bacchanalia, does not exploit the subject of religion, and makes no use of any large event of topical interest. Its success most likely was due to a variety of factors reflecting public interests in 1899 plus, of course, the *sine qua non* of popular fiction, narrative ability. An analysis of the multiple factors that went into the success of the book provides a useful insight into the state of literary taste of that period. From the very beginning of his career Tarkington had the ability to interest a large audience, and his first novel is a mirror of contemporary interests.

Tarkington, who was thirty years old in 1899 when *The Gentleman from Indiana* was published, had been trying to write since leaving Princeton in 1894. His early efforts were costume romance, including *Monsieur Beaucaire,* which began a popular career after *The Gentleman* appeared, but his apprentice years were totally unsuccessful. When he turned to contemporary Indiana for his material, he produced a manuscript that S. S. McClure asked to read. McClure turned the novel over to Hamlin Garland for a critical opinion and accepted it for publication both in his magazine and in book form on the basis of Garland's enthusiastic response. Garland was so excited over the manuscript that he wrote Tarkington a letter "that changed everything for me" with its "four dumbfounding words: 'You are a novelist.' " [1]

The Gentleman from Indiana reached the bookstores in the fall of 1899 and in a few months appeared on the bestseller lists. It sold one hundred thousand copies within two years and was still selling eighteen thousand copies per year two decades later. The book was in print when Tarkington died in 1946 and only went out of print in the decade following his death. Plenty of copies still are available in secondhand bookstores. Compared with *Ben Hur* or *Uncle Tom's Cabin,* these sales are modest; but the book's appeal was immediate and lasting and made Tarkington a national figure overnight.

The novel that S. S. McClure received in the mail late in 1898 is a weird mixture of fictional elements. The disparate parts are woven together with considerable talent, but the entire concoction is a rather astonishing hodgepodge to analyze. It contains attacks on rural life and nostalgia for the small town, newspaper crusading against corrupt politics and a foray into honest politicking. It has a tender love story and a David-Jonathan relationship. It treats of mob violence of the Ku Klux Klan variety, and it contains a fair amount of comedy. Even feminism comes into the story in a significant manner.

The novel opens with the arrival of John Harkless, a world-weary young man of twenty-nine, in Plattville, Indiana, in the 1890's. He has just bought a rundown weekly newspaper which he proceeds to put on its feet and at the same time make into a crusading organ of civic virtue. He runs a crooked politician out of town and sends to prison ringleaders of the White-Caps, a rough crew of hoodlums who live at Six-Cross-Roads close to Plattville. He becomes a local hero, *sans peur et sans reproche,* whose disdain for his own safety requires that his fellow townsmen surreptitiously take turns in guarding him. He meets the perfect heroine in Helen Sherwood, a city girl who comes to visit her former school chum, Judge Briscoe's daughter. Romance begins—only to be interrupted after a lover's tiff by mob violence.

John walks off into the night, is beset by the white-hooded hoodlums, left for dead in a boxcar that turns up in the nearby city of Rouen (Terre Haute). While the hero is being patched up by specialists and is convalescent in the hospital, the petite Helen rolls up her sleeves and takes over management of the newspaper under an assumed name. She turns out to be a talented editor, makes the weekly paper into a daily, increases the circulation remarkably, and masterminds the rout of the corrupt politician who tries a comeback while Harkless is incapacitated. After weeks in the hospital and several months of recuperation in the home of a long-lost college classmate, Harkless returns to Plattville to find that he has been nominated for Congress and that the dynamic young editor who took over in his absence is none other than the beautiful Helen. The novel ends, of course, with wedding bells in the offing and the townsfolk beaming approval.

Reduced to a bald outline such as this, Tarkington's first novel sounds pretty deadly. The sentimental claptrap, the concealed identities, the *Weltschmerz,* the melodrama, the banalities, and the clichés—all of these elements make it heavy going today for anyone over eighteen. As with other best-sellers of bygone eras, the novel will remain, no doubt, hammock reading for adolescents. Yet Tarkington had real skill as a storyteller, and while his book is no longer a novel for adults, most of the writing is more than competent and some of it evocative. Tarkington had served his literary apprenticeship well, and several of the characterizations, incidents, descriptions anticipate the better moments of his later and more durable novels. The fact that this melange of fictional elements can hold together at all is an indication that Garland was right when he greeted Tarkington at the beginning of his career with the words: "You are a novelist."

Garland's enthusiasm for *The Gentleman from Indiana,* however, was based on more than Tarkington's narrative ability. Tarkington, in fact, was under no illusion that he had written a very good novel, and throughout his later career he always ranked this work low among his literary productions. But Garland apparently read the manuscript once and fired off his flattering letter. That Garland was never much of a critic is insufficient to explain his high opinion of the novel, because McClure and his partner, F. N. Doubleday, both shrewd takers of the literary pulse, concurred heartily in this view. Garland perhaps did not know himself why Tarkington's novel pleased him so much, but in retrospect one notes that Garland in 1898 was soon to become a writer of westerns for the *Saturday Evening Post.* His realistic *Main-Travelled Roads* (1891), *Prairie Folks* (1893), and *Wayside Courtships* (1897) were already behind him, having been written before 1892, and his best novel, *Rose of Dutcher's Coolly,* had been published three years before. Because Garland was in 1898 about to drop his realism for more popular fiction, *The Gentleman from Indiana,* a romantic story with realistic trappings laid in the contemporary Midwest, was made to order for his taste at that time. Garland's taste, moreover, mirrored the taste of many readers.

The opening of *The Gentleman* sounds much like the beginning of one of Garland's somber stories in *Main-Travelled Roads.* It begins with a jaundiced description of Midwest farm landscape:

There is a fertile stretch of flat lands in Indiana where un-agrarian Eastern travellers, glancing from car-windows, shudder and return their eyes to interior upholstery, preferring even the swaying caparisons of a Pullman to the monotony without. The landscape lies interminably level: bleak in winter, a desolate plain of mud and snow; hot and dusty in summer, in its flat lonesomeness, miles on miles with not one cool hill slope away from the sun. The persistent tourist who seeks for signs of man in this sad expanse perceives a reckless amount of rail fence; at intervals a large barn; here and there, man himself.

This introduction seems eminently compatible with the descriptions of worn-out farm wives and overworked farm boys, the poverty, drudgery, and numbing physical toil of Garland's Iowa farmers. Yet Tarkington went on to write what is essentially a romantic tale of young love.

The somber opening of *The Gentleman from Indiana* falls within a tradition already well established in America. The most critically esteemed writers, if not the most popular, were the realists: Fuller, Garland, Frederic, James, Crane, and others, whose spokesman was Howells. While these authors usually did not achieve the best-seller lists, they were attracting a growing audience. Garland's stories of Iowa farmers were more of a critical success than a popular success, but occasionally a realistic novel about small-town life achieved wide distribution. Perhaps the first of this type was Edward Eggleston's *The Hoosier Schoolmaster* (1871) with its genial but authentic genre scenes of life in Southern Indiana. More important was E. W. Howe's *The Story of a Country Town* (1884), a bleak and sobering account of unhappy people buried in a prairie town in north-western Missouri. Howe's novel was a best-seller despite the amateurish nature of its writing. Thus the criticism of small-town life in American fiction already was well established by 1899, and no doubt accounts in part for the success of Tarkington's novel.

One does not need to look far to find a source in American life for the belletristic criticism of rural America. Ignatius Donnelly's Populist Party platform of 1892 succinctly codified western discontent, and the farm problems of the late 1880's were certain to be mirrored in the fiction of the period. Tarkington's novel is a faint reflection of this western turmoil that reached its apex in the Presidential candidacy of William Jennings Bryan in 1896. This tradition in American literature continued beyond the 1890's in the "revolt from the village" literature of the twentieth century. One sees this clearly in an early Willa Cather story like "The Sculptor's Funeral," Edgar Lee Master's *Spoon River Anthology* (1915), Sherwood Anderson's *Winesburg, Ohio* (1919), and Sinclair Lewis's *Main Street* (1921).

When Tarkington's novel began its serialization, there were outraged editorials in the rural Indiana press over the unflattering picture of the Indiana small town. But the indignation did not last long, for the subsequent installments do not continue the initial tone of disparagement. There is some generalized satire of small-town mores and people, but before Tarkington had written another one hundred pages he was sounding just the opposite note. When one reads the entire book today, he is fairly astonished by the one-hundred-and-eighty-degree turn between chapters one and six.

By the time Tarkington had reached chapter six he was sugar-coating his picture of small-town life for another class of reader: those with the Rousseau hang-over. American cities, then as now, are filled with people who are one or two generations, or even only a few years, removed from the soil. These people like to think that virtue stems from the simple rural life, and they feed the myth with books that idealize small-town or country life. Just the year before Tarkington's novel appeared this type of reader had made a best-seller out of Edward Westcott's *David Harum*. They were charmed by the crusty old widower, banker, and crack-er-barrel philosopher, who thought "a reasonable amount of fleas is good for a dog" because they "keep him from broodin' on being a dog." Their children were equally charmed by Will Rogers, who made a movie out of *David Harum* a generation later.

Tarkington's novel also anticipated by one year another novel of this type, Irving Bacheller's *Eben Holden,* also a best seller. In this novel the title character is a homespun hired man and kindly protector of orphans. He lives the good bucolic life, practices good works, and dispenses practical wisdom. The type is familiar to a generation of American housewives who washed their dishes to the accompaniment of daytime soap opera. The more complex city life becomes, the more frustrating the traffic and noise, the more readers will enjoy fiction glorifying rusticity. Tarkington's novel worked this mother lode thoroughly.

In chapter six of *The Gentleman from Indiana* the circus comes to town, and John Harkless and Helen Sherwood attend. By this time Tarkington's descriptions have become pure nostalgic boyhood memories of the summers he spent visiting relatives in Marshall, Illinois, just across the state line from Indiana. Consider this passage:

> The length of Main Street and all the Square resounded with the rattle of vehicles of every kind. Since earliest dawn they had been pouring into the village, a long procession on every country road. There were great red and blue farm wagons, drawn by splendid Clydesdales; the elders of the family on the front seat and on boards laid from side to side in front, or on chairs placed close behind, while, in the deep beds back of these, children tumbled in the straw, or peeped over the sides, rosy-cheeked and laughing, eyes alight with blissful anticipations. There were more pretentious two-seated cut-unders and stout buckboards, loaded down with merry-makers, four on a seat meant for two; there were rattle-trap phaetons and comfortable carry-alls drawn by steady spans; and, now and then, mule-teams bringing happy negroes, ready to squander all on the first

Georgia watermelons and cider. Every vehicle contained heaping baskets of good things to eat (the previous night had been a woeful Bartholomew for Carlow [County] chickens) and underneath, where the dogs paced faithfully, swung buckets and fodder for the horses, while colts innumerable trotted close to the maternal flanks, viewing the world with their big, new eyes in frisky surprise.

This description could not have been more romantically idealized if it had come from Washington Irving's account of the Van Tassel farm as Ichabod Crane daydreams about Katrina's inheritance. Thus in tone and style there is something for everyone in this novel.

In content Tarkington's first novel combines the best of two fictional worlds. There is not enough realism to bother anyone who really prefers romance; yet there is enough to give a bow in the direction of realism. One begins the novel expecting Tarkington to be a follower of Howells, who had been preaching and promoting realism for twenty years, or Garland himself, who had written his own plea for realism in *Crumbling Idols* six years before. This sort of mixture, however, was a salable blend at the turn of the century, and Tarkington was not the only writer to profit by it. One might cite, for example, the case of Frank Norris, whose popular novel *The Octopus* does somewhat the same thing two years later. While Norris' *McTeague* and *Vandover and the Brute* are thoroughgoing pieces of naturalism, *The Octopus* blends romance and naturalism in a fashion that made it palatable to a much larger audience than the other two works. The railroad holds the San Joaquin Valley wheat growers in its tentacles and destroys them, but on another part of the stage romance flourishes. Norris, like Tarkington, supplied something for everyone in his novel.

Although McClure and Doubleday were charmed and Garland recommended the novel for publication, Howells withheld his approval of Tarkington's book. Howells visited Indianapolis on a lecture tour a few months after the novel appeared and was entertained by Tarkington and his sister. He acknowledged having read *The Gentleman from Indiana* but bestowed no praise. It was not until Tarkington wrote *The Turmoil* (1914) that he managed to suppress the romance and sentiment and produce a novel in the tradition of Howellesian realism. Then Howells wrote in his "Editor's Easy Chair" column: "So fine and strong a talent as Mr. Booth Tarkington's has its sins of romanticism in the past to answer for; but whoever reads his very powerful fiction lately current in these pages must own that he is atoning for far worse transgressions than can be laid to his charge." [2]

McClure's enthusiasm for *The Gentleman from Indiana* was shrewdly based on several prominent aspects of the book, the first of which is local color. Ever since the Civil War local color had been a standard ingredient of magazine fiction. The local color movement had produced Bret Harte, Sarah Orne Jewett, Joel Chandler Harris, George Washington Cable, and a host of others, all of whom had been very popular. Tarkington's novel, as I have noted, is tinctured with both realistic and idealized use of Indiana landscape and character. He satirizes, for example, Miss Tibbs, the local poetess of Plattville, and the idlers in the courthouse square; yet a few chapters later his heroine says to the hero: "Just one big jolly family. I didn't know people could be like this until I came to Plattville." To which the hero replies: "I believe they are the best people I know . . . kind to me . . . kind to each other . . . kind, good people." Ed Howe and Thomas Nelson Page rolled into one package! Yet Tarkington knew his small-town locale, and his book contains much authentic local color.

In addition to the local color, McClure certainly noted with favor Tarkington's exposure of vice and crooked politics in his novel. Just as the realistic and derogatory picture of the small town already had made a tradition in American literature, so had the literature of exposure. A quarter of a century before, Mark Twain and Charles Dudley Warner had pulled back the curtain a little way to reveal corruption in Washington in *The Gilded Age* (1873). Two years later DeForest in *Honest John Vane* created a dishonest Congressman who accepted a bribe in return for his vote on crucial legislation. The tradition was carried on by Henry Adams with an impressive portrait of a corrupt senator in *Democracy* (1880), and Ford's *The Honorable Peter Stirling* skillfully unmasked rottenness in state government in the last decade of the nineteenth century. The fictional expose continued without interruption into the twentieth century with the work of Upton Sinclair, Brand Whitlock, David Graham Phillips, and others. But even as Tarkington was attacking crooked politics in Indiana, McClure was about to discover the muckraking movement. Ida Tarbell was soon to be commissioned to make her remarkable study of the Standard Oil Company, and within a couple of years McClure was to assemble on the staff of his magazine the most brilliant trio of muckraking journalists ever brought together: Miss Tarbell, Ray Stannard Baker, and Lincoln Steffens.

Tarkington, in creating his crusading newspaper editor, made fictional use of the same kind of material that Steffens records in his study of governmental corruption in *The Shame of the Cities* (1904). John Harkless runs the crooked Congressman Roy McCune out of politics by obtaining evidence of a bribe McCune had accepted while in public office. Tarkington also made use of another kind of topical material in his introduction of the White-Caps (a kind of Ku Klu Klan), whose running battle with Harkless provides the central episode of the novel. Indiana, it may be remembered, had special trouble with the Ku Klux Klan as late as the 1920's, and at the turn of the century the problem of mob lawlessness or white-capping, as it was then called, was particularly acute. The reader of Tarkington's novel not only enjoyed local color, a love story, but he also could feel that he was reading something significant in the use of problem material.

A final element of the novel that McClure certainly thought salable in 1898 was the feminism. When John Harkless lies injured in the hospital, his male associates try desperately to keep the paper going. In a rather amusing scene they sit around the office trying to write enough copy to fill the next issue. They fail miserably. Then appears the peerless heroine Helen, who up to this time has been presented as the dainty, fragile, socially accomplished daughter of wealthy city parents. She moves in with no previous experience and reorganizes the office. The paper prospers under her direction in a manner to delight the hearts of all followers of Susan B. Anthony or Elizabeth Cady Stanton. Yet the feminism is not carried too far, for Helen at the end of the novel shows no disturbing signs of reluctance to relinquish her editorship and of not wanting to disappear into the nursery.

To sum up, what McClure, Doubleday, and Garland saw in *The Gentleman from Indiana* was a pretty well written novel that contained something for everybody. It was a romance that opened realistically. It was a love story told with enough realistic detail to please romantics who thought they ought to like realism. It had melodrama, it had comedy. It had mawkish sentiment and mild satire. It had a whiff of muckraking at a time when corrupt politicians and corrupt corporations were being called to account. It exploited the growing move toward equal rights for women, and gave nostalgic city folks a glimpse of their lost rural innocence. That the novel became a best seller seems due to its use of all these elements that struck notes of popular interest in 1899.

But Tarkington was not writing cynically to make use of popular material. Never in his career did he write solely to meet the demands of the literary market place. What he was able to do, however, mirrored the public taste. He had the happy knack of pleasing while being natural. This was the same sort of talent, perhaps, that made Longfellow the popular success he was a century ago. And with Longfellow, Tarkington seems destined to occupy a permanent place in American literature as a writer for youth. At the same time, as is the case with Longfellow, Tarkington's work reflects accurately the culture of his time.

NOTES

1. James Woodress, *Booth Tarkington: Gentleman from Indiana* (Philadelphia, 1955), p. 74.
2. *Harper's Monthly,* CXXX (May, 1915), 958–961.

C. Hugh Holman

❧ ☙

Europe as Catalyst
for Thomas Wolfe

It is customary to see in an American writer who spent a substantial amount of his artistically formative period in Europe the impact on him of his membership in two national cultures forming either a cosmopolitanism or an expatriated culture. Thus in the nineteenth century many writers seeing Europe in contrast to America found in it an aesthetic and moral challenge and emerged from their experience of the two cultures broadened, deepened, and enriched. This was particularly true of American writers in Italy.[1] In more recent times, most American writers seem to have sought in Europe a milieu more congenial to their aspirations and their inner selves than America and have

C. HUGH HOLMAN is Kenan Professor of English at the University of North Carolina.

embraced Europe as a truer spiritual—and often physical—
home than they could find in the Western Hemisphere.
This was true of England in the case of Henry James and
T. S. Eliot and of France in the case of the group we commonly call the "Lost Generation."

Neither of these responses describes with any complete-
ness the role that Europe played in the career of Thomas
Wolfe, although most of the writers who have attempted
to deal in any interpretive way with Wolfe's European experiences have treated him as being basically one of the
expatriates. George M. Reeves, Jr., in *Thomas Wolfe et
l'Europe,* a detailed examination of Wolfe in Europe, says:
"Wolfe appartient au groupe d'écrivains qu'on a appelé
La Génération Perdue. . . . Sa vie suit donc le cycle com-
mun à tout un groupe d'écrivains américains de l'entre-deux
guerres: révolte contre les Etas-Unis, fuite en Europe, et
retour en Amérique." [2] And Europe certainly played as
great a role in Wolfe's artistic development as it played in
the careers of the "Paris Expatriates," whose "recording
secretary" and best historian, Malcolm Cowley, included
Wolfe as a member of the group and saw his differences as
being primarily that he did not serve in World War I as
most of the expatriates did and that he preferred Germany
to France. Cowley even sees Wolfe's hunger for a lost and
unattainable home as typical.[3]

This is a classification with which Wolfe would have
been unsympathetic. In a speech at Purdue University in
1938, he said:

> I mention all this . . . because of its reference also to a
> charge that has sometimes been made by some of my friends.
> One of them, for example, not more than three or four years
> my senior, is very fixed in his assertion of what he calls "the
> lost generation"—a generation of which he has been quite
> vociferously a member, and in which he has tried enthusiasti-
> cally to include me. "You belong to it, too," he used to say.

"You came along at the same time. You can't get a way from it. You're a part of it whether you want to be or not"—to which my vulgar response would be: "Don't you you-hoo me!"

If my friend *wants* to belong to the Lost Generation—and it really is astonishing with what fond eagerness those people hug the ghost of desolation to their breast—that's *his* affair. But he can't have me. If I have been elected, it has been against my will; and I hereby resign. I don't feel that I belong to a lost generation, and I have never felt so.[4]

Yet, unmistakably Europe played a significant and perhaps a central role in Wolfe's life and literary career. From his twenty-fourth year, in which he made the first of seven trips to Europe, until his death just before his thirty-eighth birthday, Wolfe spent over one quarter of his time across the Atlantic.[5] In the critical formative period between 1924 and 1931—a period during which he was finding that extended prose fiction was his métier and, after writing *Look Homeward, Angel,* was seeking a theme and a subject matter for the rest of his work—he made five trips to Europe, totaling thirty-four months and representing forty-five percent of his time. A mere listing of the places which he visited or in which he lived for brief periods is impressive. It includes England, France, Switzerland, Italy, Germany, Austria, Czechoslovakia, and Denmark; and it touches almost every famous city which a visitor would normally have seen.[6] The two countries in which he spent the longest periods of time were England and France, although the country to which he felt the warmest spiritual affinity was clearly Germany.

His career as a writer of prose fiction began and flourished during his European travels. His first extended prose narrative, the semi-fictional account of his first voyage abroad, "Passage to England," he began on shipboard in the form of notes which he continued to compile in England. The formal writing of this narrative, which, typically, never appeared in its original form but the subject matter of which was used in portions of several of his books, he began in Tours.[7] He says of Eugene Gant in language remarkably close to that which he used many times about himself that

> He had come to Tours, telling himself that now at last, at last, he was going "to settle down and write," that he was going to justify his voyage by the high purpose of creation . . . with desperate resolve he sat down grimly now to shape these great designs into the stern and toilsome masonry of words. . . . And yet, write he did. Useless, fragmentary, and inchoate as were these first abortive efforts, he began to write now like a mad-man—as only a madman could write. . . . And in those words was packed the whole image of his bitter homelessness, his intolerable desire, his maddened longing for return. In those wild and broken phrases was packed the whole bitter burden of his famished, driven, over-laden spirit—all the longing of the wan-derer, all the impossible and unutterable homesickness that the American, or any man on earth, can know. They were all there . . . and in them was the huge chronicle of the billion forms, the million names, the huge, single, and incomparable substance of America.[8]

On his second European trip, while in Paris he began writing the rough outline of the book which became *Look Homeward, Angel.* In London during that trip the actual final form of the book began to be shaped in the summer of 1926, and much of the first third of the first draft was completed before he returned to New York in December of that year. His third European trip was also given over to intense work on his novel. Thus this first hauntingly evocative record of the autobiographical protagonist Eugene Gant was conceived from the vantage point of England and France and composed out of Wolfe's deep loneliness and hunger for America. It came into being, as he said in *The Story of a Novel,* because he "had felt the bitter ache of homelessness, a desperate longing for America, an overwhelming desire to return." [9]

Shortly after the draft of *Look Homeward, Angel* was completed and submitted to the publishers, Wolfe made his fourth European trip. During this journey, he spent a great deal of time in Germany and Austria. He was in Munich during the *Oktoberfest,* a festival celebrating the October beer. During the festival he became embroiled in a fist fight which became a brawl and received injuries that placed him for a time in a hospital. While he was hospitalized, he took stock of himself in a foreign land and he came, he says, to a reconciliation with the nature of the world. This reconciliation is the subject matter for the concluding chapters of *The Web and the Rock,* where he and his battered body conclude that "They had discovered the earth together . . . they had discovered it alone, in secrecy, in exile, and in wandering. . . . He knew that we who are men are more than men, and less than spirit." [10] Before he returned home from this fourth trip, he had learned of the interest of Charles Scribner's Sons in publishing *Look Homeward, Angel;* and thus the following year was spent in America putting the book which he had written in Europe into publishable form. It appeared in October, 1929.

In May, 1930, Wolfe returned to Europe, this time on a Guggenheim Fellowship, to begin work on his second novel. He was there for ten months, during which he frantically sought a subject and a theme, an organizing principle for his new book. In *The Story of a Novel,* he says of this period:

> I think I may say that I discovered America during these years abroad out of my very need of her. The huge gain of this discovery seemed to come directly from my sense of loss. I had been to Europe five times now; each time I had come with delight, with maddening eagerness to return, and each time how, where, and in what way I did not know, I had felt the bitter ache of homelessness, a desperate longing for America, an overwhelming desire to return.
>
> During that summer in Paris, I think I felt this great home-

sickness more than ever before, and I really believe that from this emotion, this constant and almost intolerable effort of memory and desire, the material and the structure of the books I now began to write were derived. . . . It was as if I had discovered a whole new universe of chemical elements and had begun to see certain relations between some of them but had by no means begun to organize the whole series into a harmonious and coherent union. . . . There was nothing at first which could be called a novel. I wrote about night and darkness in America, and the faces of the sleepers in ten thousand little towns; and of the tides of sleep and how the rivers flowed forever in the darkness. I wrote about the hissing glut of tides upon ten thousand miles of coast; of how the moonlight blazed down on the wilderness and filled the cat's cold eye with blazing yellow. I wrote about death and sleep, and of that enfabled rock of life we call the city. I wrote about October, of great trains that thundered through the night, of ships and stations in the morning: of men in harbors and the traffic of the ships.[11]

Thus he was writing down in notebooks and in great ledgers fragments which later were to find their way into his books and which were records in almost poetic form of his love for and his hunger for his native land. It was here, for example, that he first wrote down what finally became the famous passage on October in *Of Time and the River.* In its notebook form, it begins, "And in America the chinquapins are falling. The corn sticks out in hard and yellow rows upon dried ears, fit for a winter's barn and the big yellow teeth of crunching horses; and the leaves are turning, turning, up in Maine," [12] an obvious foreshadowing of Chapter XXXIX in *Of Time and the River* where these lines are transmuted into this passage, where the sense of contrast, of October remembered in a strange land is present as a hardly distinguishable but still echoing resonance:

Now October has come again which in our land is different from October in the other lands. The ripe, the golden month has come again, and in Virginia the chinkapins are falling. Frost sharps the middle music of the seasons, and all things living on the earth turn home again. The country is so big you cannot say the country has the same October. In Maine, the frost comes sharp and quick as driven nails, just for a week or so the woods, all of the bright and bitter leaves, flare up.[13]

That year in Switzerland, in Montreux, he found what was to be the theme for much of his work, the theme, as he expressed it, "of wandering forever and the earth again," a very appropriate theme for one possessed as he was with a desperate need for home and an endless urge to wander.[14] He returned in 1931 to America, where he continued to struggle with desperate energy that he describes with a remarkable frankness in *The Story of a Novel* to merge these experiences into a book. At last over his protests the vast manuscript was sent to the printer in 1934, and the book appeared in 1935 as *Of Time and the River.*

He did not return to Europe until 1935, and then for only two brief periods; but these were periods that seemed to have been profoundly constructive in shaping his final view of the world. In 1935 he was in Paris, London, and Berlin from March until July 4 and discovered that for the Berliners he was an internationally important figure; and in Berlin he had the heady experience of having a great nation literally at his feet—and, of all nations, the one to which, aside from America, he felt the closest kinship. It was natural enough, therefore, that in the following summer he should go again to Berlin to attend the 1936 Olympic games. Then he was gradually forced to see, despite the parties and adulation, the dark death's-head beneath the mask of Nazism. Though he had only two years remaining in which to realize the vision which he caught on that occasion and which he expressed most plainly in his short novel "I Have a Thing to Tell You," [15] this brief journey brought him face to face with a rampant evil that was loose in his world and forced him into a major and soul-searching re-evaluation of his easy acceptance of life

and the life principle as unqualified good. As Bella Kussy
says,

> In Germany under the Nazis he has seen the ultimate political
> and social effects of that vitalism which has been the supreme
> impetus and characteristic of his own life and work. Still sus-
> ceptible to its fascination and power, still conscious of it as
> basic and essential and all-pervasive in his own life, he sees that
> he must either accept its social consequences or reject it com-
> pletely; and he has enough humanity and resolution in him to
> do the latter.[16]

Out of this rejection comes what Miss Kussy calls "Wolfe's
new democratic 'social consciousness.' " Unquestionably the
greater maturity, social awareness, and objectivity of *You
Can't Go Home Again* result in large part from this instruction in the human capacity for evil.

Wolfe's European experiences clearly did serve to broaden
him and to enrich him, to instruct him in the nature of
his world, and to give him detachment and distance from
which to view his subject matter. Europe in this sense was
in a major way a catalyst for an intensely American talent.
"Catalyst" seems to me the appropriate figure, for a catalyst
is an agent, which introduced into a situation where elements are capable of reacting but are not doing so, results
in an interaction of these elements without itself participat-
ing in the reaction or being changed by it. Between Wolfe
and America a reaction occurred that might be called "catalysis," which is defined in *Webster's Third International*
as "an action or reaction between two or more persons or
forces provoked or precipitated by a separate agent or
forces, especially by one that is essentially unaltered by the
reaction." Europe served as this separate agent for Wolfe.

His European experiences were by no means unique, nor
was his response to them. It was essentially the response
of the self-conscious provincial who elects analysis over
adulation and looks upon Europe from the vantage point

of an openly American bias. In several respects, Wolfe's reaction to Europe was similar to some of Mark Twain's reactions, notably in *The Innocents Abroad*.[17] It is necessary to recognize that, as it did for travelers like Mark Twain, Europe was for Wolfe another frontier of experience but still an essentially American frontier. It was in this respect that he differed most significantly from those members of the "Lost Generation" who turned their backs upon the America of the middle class, the *Saturday Evening Post,* the Saturday night movie, the small town, and the Sunday band concert, and sought in a religion of art practiced in an environment of beauty a substitute for a way of life which they did not admire and in which they could not comfortably live.[18] They clustered around salons and in the offices of little magazines and were a powerful force in the maturing of American literary art. It is difficult to overestimate their value in the development of a sense of form and a formalist critical doctrine in American writing. But Wolfe was never happy or comfortable with them. Wolfe always tended to mock the aesthetes. In his long satiric description of Professor Hatcher's celebrated drama course at Harvard, he had laughed at those who found pretentious art a religious exercise. He was especially contemptuous of their "arty talk," which, he said,

> gave to people without talent and without sincerity of soul or integrity of purpose, with nothing, in fact, except a feeble incapacity for the shock and agony of life, and a desire to escape into a glamorous and unreal world of make believe—a justification for their pitiable and base existence. It gave to people who had no power in themselves to create anything of merit or of beauty—people who were the true Philistines and enemies of art and of the artist's living spirit—the language to talk with glib knowingness of things they knew nothing of—to prate of "settings," "tempo," "pace," and "rhythm," of "boldly stylized conventions," and the wonderful way some actress "used her hands." And in the end, it led to nothing but falseness and

triviality, to the ghosts of passion, and the spectres of sincerity. . . .[19]

In Francis Starwick in *Of Time and the River,* he drew a thorough and devastating portrait of a Midwesterner who has come East and then to Europe and who embraces all the shibboleths of the young art group. One episode that is revelatory of Wolfe's strong preference for America has to do with Starwick's enthusiasm for French names: "But their genius for names is quite astonishing!—I mean, even in the names of their towns you get the whole thing," he says, and then mocks the *"horrible"* appropriateness of some of the names in Eugene's region: "Beaverdam and Balsam, and Chimney Rock and Craggy and Pisgah and The Rat . . . Old Fort, Hickory, and Bryson City . . . Clingman's Dome and Little Switzerland . . . Paint Rock and Saluda Mountain and the Frying Pan Gap." [20] Here the guise of fiction has, for the moment, been dropped; these are quite literal names from the North Carolina mountains.

Wolfe himself was never a part of an artistic group. He was always separate from his fellows, and he lived in a solitary world. He declared in an autobiographical fragment which exists in many versions, one of which Edward Aswell published as "God's Lonely Man":

> My life, more than that of anyone I know, has been spent in solitude and wandering. . . . From my fifteenth year—save for a single interval—I have lived about as solitary a life as a modern man can have. I mean by this that the number of hours, days, months, and years that I have spent alone has been immense and extraordinary.[21]

He was a lonely and solitary traveler both at home and in Europe. Furthermore, those with whom he came in contact who were even on the edges of the expatriate movements he was offended by, the most startling example being F. Scott Fitzgerald whom he seems to have disliked intensely.[22]

He went to Europe initially with all the romantic expectations of a small town or country boy who loved books. England was for him the enchanted isle, rich in story, rich in all the range of literary associations. He went to England as "Heaven." [23] In London he declared himself to be "now lost in the beauty and mystery and fascination of this ancient and magnificent city." [24] In Paris, on the first journey, he felt himself "entering a new world of art and letters." [25] He made the standard pilgrimages and visited the literary shrines, and was, in general, a wide-eyed and romantic tourist. He was much like George Webber, of whom he wrote: "He was single, twenty-four years old, American. And . . . like certain tens of thousands of [young Americans], he had gone forth to seek the continental Golden Fleece." [26] But he came to see his romantic quest as a little ridiculous and mocked himself in ballad parody:

> The night was long, the way was cold: the ministrel young was overbold: he carried in his great valise, two pairs of socks and one chemise, and in his hand, to stay the curse, the Oxford Book of English Verse. Under a sky of leaden grey, he went from Chartres unto Potay, and from that point he journeyed on, until he came to Orléans.[27]

England he continued to like throughout his life. France he cared for hardly at all. The French people he distrusted and disliked, and seemingly only among the peasant class could he find Frenchmen with whom he felt at home. He wrote: "The Frenchman is lacking in true wisdom: he is tragically poisoned in his art, his life, his education. . . ." [28] The Germans, on the other hand, were his father's people; and somehow Germany was for him the Father Land. It was for him, as he described it as being for George Webber,

> the other part of his heart's home, a haunted part of dark desire, a magic domain of fulfillment. It was the dark, lost Helen that had been forever burning in his blood—the dark,

lost Helen he had found . . . old German land with all the
measure of your truth, your glory, beauty, magic. . . .[29]

What has been pointed out by many people about Wolfe
in relation to New York is also true of his relation to Europe, that he was the perennial provincial, the country boy,
fascinated by the city, fascinated by the world; and it was
with this open-eyed and provincial astonishment that he
looked out upon the Europe which he toured. He once
wrote a friend:

> . . . what mistakes I failed to make in Paris, I managed to
> make in other parts of the continent before I was through. I
> seem to have been born a Freshman—and in many ways I'm
> afraid I'll continue to be one.[30]

Not only was he rapidly plunged into the depths of loneliness and masses of mistakes on these solitary pilgrimages,
he also was angered by attacks upon America of the sort
that was common among the expatriate groups; and he rose
vigorously to the defense of his native land in terms that
would have been appropriate in the Rotary Club of his
native Asheville. He said, for example, in one letter to his
Mother:

> American vulgarity and American Philistinism is a source of
> much satire and jest; also the American tourist who spends his
> money here.
> I suppose, like all nations, we have our vulgarities; but I
> have seen no group of people more vulgar in its manners, its
> speech, and the tone of its voices than the French middle class.
> And no matter how materially-minded our own people have
> been, or are now, there is a certain satisfaction in knowing
> that, at least, they wash themselves with some regularity.
> I shall never go about waving my country's flag—I believe
> I recognize a great many of our faults, but the faults I recog-
> nize are not the faults Europeans accuse us of. That is what
> sometimes annoys me. They may curse us all they please if

they only curse us for sins we have committed; but they are forever cursing us for things we are not guilty of.[31]

These European experiences would hardly have been the raw materials for a writer aiming at a well-made novel of the School of Flaubert or Henry James; and to appreciate fully what Europe contributed to Wolfe, it is necessary to recognize that his true subject and his consistent one, binding together into a unity the diffuse parts of his sprawling books, is his own deep immersion in experience and, in particular, the experience of being an American. He is not a novelist in the true sense of the word; he is a maker of epics; and, like Whitman, he recognized that the American epic was ultimately the song of the democratic man sung by himself. In his common experiences of the length and breadth, the light and darkness, the beauty and the ugliness of his land and his people, Wolfe found the subject for his work. In attempting to realize it, he created self-contained, dramatic, lyric, and rhapsodic passages which become, like the segments of "Leaves of Grass," short but total records of parts of his experience. What Europe gave him more than anything else was not its storied history or the beauty of its landscape or the grace of its culture or the ability to associate with great men but simply a sense of difference, an awareness that somehow these differences defined what it is to be American. He went to Europe not to escape but to seek the dream of a paradise. He found not paradise but loneliness. Out of that loneliness came his subject. Out of that subject there came a desperate awareness that the American artist must seek and find new traditions and new methods.

What emerges finally from his experience with Europe is not his expatriation or necessarily any internationalism in his cultural view but rather awareness of an artistic task that the American writer must undertake in difficulty and with fear but in which he must succeed if, as Wolfe sees it, he is to be both artist and American. Without Europe, his relationship to his own land and his own past might never have been clear to him. Hence Europe was a catalyst, not an actor in the reaction; and out of that catalysis came the declaration with which he closed *The Story of a Novel,* perhaps as profound a judgment about the complex fate of being an American as he was ever to make:

It is not merely that in the cultures of Europe and of the Orient the American artist can find no antecedent scheme, no structural plan, no body of tradition that can give his own work the validity and truth that it must have. It is not merely that he must make somehow a new tradition for himself, derived from his own life and from the enormous space and energy of American life, the structure of his own design; it is not merely that he is confronted by these problems; it is even more than this, that the labor of a complete and whole articulation, the discovery of an entire universe and of a complete language, is the task that lies before him.

. . . Out of the billion forms of America, out of the savage violence and the dense complexity of all its swarming life; from the unique and single substance of this land and life of ours, must we draw the power and energy of our own life, the articulation of our speech, the substance of our art.

For here it seems to me in hard and honest ways like these we may find the tongue, the language, and the conscience that as men and artists we have got to have. Here, too, perhaps, must we who have no more than what we have, who know no more than what we know, who are no more than what we are, find our America.[32]

Thus did the catalytic Europe bring the artist Wolfe to an awareness of his subject America. As Kathleen Hoagland said of Wolfe, "I know why he writes like he does. He's in love with America." [33] Europe made him achingly aware of that love.

NOTES

1. Nathalia Wright, *American Novelists in Italy, The Discoverers: Allston to James* (Philadelphia, 1966), and Van Wyck Brooks, *The Dream of Arcadia: American Writers and Artists in Italy, 1760–1915* (New York, 1958).

2. George M. Reeves, *Thomas Wolfe et l'Europe* (Paris, 1955), pp. 83, 142. Another monograph, Daniel L. Delakas, *Thomas Wolfe, la France, et les romanciers français* (Paris, 1950), also takes this view. Neither Reeves nor Delakas sees the issue as a simple one, and both put Wolfe's work apart from that of the expatriates. Reeves, for example, while he asserts that Wolfe's experience is like that of "La Génération Perdue," declares his work to lie "en dehors du principal courant littéraire de son époque" (p. 83).

3. Malcolm Cowley, *Exile's Return: A Literary Odyssey of the 1920's* (New York, 1951), pp. 9, 291–292.

4. *Thomas Wolfe's Purdue Speech: "Writing and Living,"* ed. William Braswell and Leslie A. Field (Purdue University, 1964), pp. 36–37.

5. These biographical data are assembled from *Thomas Wolfe's Letters to His Mother*, ed. John S. Terry (New York, 1943); *The Letters of Thomas Wolfe*, ed. Elizabeth Nowell (New York, 1956); Elizabeth Nowell, *Thomas Wolfe: A Biography* (New York, 1960); Richard S. Kennedy, *The Window of Memory* (Chapel Hill, 1962), and Delakas, *Thomas Wolfe, la France, et les romanciers français*, which has a very useful "Tableau Chronologique de la Vie de Wolfe" on pp. 143–147, which is very detailed on Wolfe's European travels.

6. An almost unbelievable listing of cities he visited is given in the "Tableau Chronologique" in Delakas. The postcards listed in *Wolfe's Letters to His Mother* also help us to see his coverage of Europe.

7. Kennedy, *The Window of Memory*, pp. 97–106, has a good account of this work.

8. Wolfe, *Of Time and the River* (New York, 1935), p. 858–859.

9. Wolfe, *The Story of a Novel* (New York, 1936), p. 31.

10. Wolfe, *The Web and the Rock* (New York, 1939), pp. 692–693.

11. *The Story of a Novel*, pp. 30–31, 35–36, 37–38.

12. Nowell, *Thomas Wolfe*, p. 168.

13. *Of Time and the River*, p. 329.

14. *The Letters of Thomas Wolfe*, to Maxwell E. Perkins, July 17, 1930, pp. 240–245. This is a very important letter, which deserves examination in its totality, and is too richly instructive to be reduced to the brief summary I have given of it.

15. In *The Short Novels of Thomas Wolfe*, ed. C. Hugh Holman (New York, 1961), pp. 233–278, in the form in which it was published in the *New Republic*, LXXXX (March 10, 17, 24, 1937), 132–136, 159–164, 202–207. A longer version appears in Wolfe's *You Can't Go Home Again* (New York, 1941), pp. 634–704.

16. Bella Kussy, "The Vitalist Trend and Thomas Wolfe," in *The World of Thomas Wolfe,* ed. C. Hugh Holman (New York, 1962), p. 110. The essay originally appeared in *Sewanee Review,* L (July-September, 1942), 306–324.

17. See Bruce R. McElderry, Jr., *Thomas Wolfe* (New York, 1964), pp. 64–66, where he comments on similarities between Wolfe and Mark Twain. See also McElderry's article, "The Durable Humor in *Look Homeward, Angel," Arizona Quarterly,* XI (1955), 123–128.

18. Cowley, *Exile's Return,* is excellent on the ideals of this group.

19. *Of Time and the River,* p. 135. The material on Hatcher's class—almost all of it satiric—occurs on pp. 130–135, 167–175, 282–304, 309–324.

20. *Ibid.,* pp. 698–699.

21. Wolfe, *The Hills Beyond* (New York, 1941), p. 186.

22. See, among many possible places, *The Letters of Thomas Wolfe,* pp. 262–266, particularly his description of Fitzgerald "in the Ritz Bar where he was entirely surrounded by Princeton boys, all nineteen years old, all drunk, and all half-raw" (p. 263).

23. *The Letters of Thomas Wolfe,* p. 67: "I'm going to Heaven in September [1924]. That is, to England."

24. *Ibid.,* p. 71.

25. *Ibid.,* p. 74.

26. *The Web and the Rock,* pp. 302–303.

27. *The Letters of Thomas Wolfe,* p. 92.

28. *Ibid.,* p. 93.

29. *You Can't Go Home Again,* pp. 703–704. I have attempted to describe in more detail Wolfe's reaction to Germany in my article Thomas Wolfe's Berlin," *Saturday Review,* L (March 11, 1967), 66, 69, 90.

30. *The Letters of Thomas Wolfe,* pp. 192–193.

31. *Wolfe's Letters to His Mother,* pp. 114–115.

32. *The Story of a Novel,* pp. 92–93.

33. In "Thomas Wolfe: Biography in Sound, An NBC Radio Broadcast," published in the *Carolina Quarterly* (Fall, 1956), 9.

ENGLISH
LITERATURE

Meredith Thompson

❧ ❧

Current and Recurrent Fallacies in Chaucer Criticism

The vast proliferation of published comment in the humanities now causes increasing professional and even public concern. A few years ago we discovered humanists to be less "productive" than scientists; something really had to be done; we withheld promotions, raised enormous research funds, made it ever so easy to go from pen to print, etc. The results have been gratifying and terrifying. The quantity itself is suspect: too frequently desperate professors have acquired the second-rate journalists' trick of blowing up minor points into full-length articles, glittering with specious jargon and distinctions that never needed to be made. All this is well-known and not easy to remedy.[1]

MEREDITH THOMPSON is Professor of English at the University of British Columbia.

But the trouble does not stop there. Especially with older greater authors like Chaucer, most of the chief technical and aesthetic problems have long since been pursued as far as available evidence soberly permits, and the continuing search is not likely to turn up any large new body of significant data. Yet delightful Chaucer increasingly attracts would-be exponents of his art. After these have mastered Chaucer studies to date—no small task if accomplished —what is left to be done? Not, save rarely and minutely, scholarship in the primary sense. Furnivall, Skeat, Manly, Robinson, etc., though they will go on being looted, can never be totally dispossessed. What is left, inexhaustibly it would seem, is interpretation or more properly re-interpretation. On the positive side this may represent the right and necessary bringing into play of any aspect whatever of modern knowledge, critical technique, etc. that sheds new light. But often, even in the work of undoubtedly learned critics, interpretation goes farther and farther beyond the text or ignores it completely. This is also well-known and perhaps irremediable. It is somewhat as Rossini is reported to have said to the young composer, "Your opus is both beautiful and new: but the beautiful in it is not new, nor the new beautiful."

What follows here will endeavour to save Chaucer from some of his friends and interpreters. He will of course survive all of them; but meanwhile it seems a pity that divers distortions should run so strongly and far, that valuable thought and print must be expended to combat them, and that university students too often waste their time dovetailing interpretations instead of reading Chaucer for themselves. But one cannot do all things in one chapter. Individual interpretations will not be discussed in detail, nor rival interpretations offered. Hopefully it will yet prove useful to identify certain fallacies—not only logical fallacies —which occur and recur in Chaucer criticism and in criticism generally, whether or not the examples given in each case seem appropriate.

For ease of reference, I have before me four very accessible anthologies of Chaucer criticism,[2] and I shall largely refer to essays therein. These may be said to represent almost every kind of Chaucer criticism in the twentieth century, including some of the most famous studies written. Then if I am ever unwittingly guilty of unfair quotation out of context, I hope the whole context will not be far to seek. Moreover, I cannot think of a single one of these essays that does not contain fresh insights, however much its main purport or passing details may seem to me questionable. Above all, I am delighted to find in J. S. P. Tatlock, not, as it happened, the original instigation, but certainly welcome support of one who sets out upon a task that can hardly prove popular. Says Tatlock,

> Even some fairly good critics after absorbing a minimum from a poem will enlarge upon it, with easy eloquence and only too obvious enjoyment, out of their own bowels, following the "practice of those two prudent insects, the bee and the spider"; stimulating perhaps, but infirm. Especially a critic must be wary about taking subtle though possible implications of word or act very seriously (as he might well with an actual person), unless confirmed by what is more overt (*W*334).

This could be said to define the fallacy of fallacies, from which most of the others stem: reading too much into the text. But it is no easy matter to determine what is too much. Tatlock seems to take refuge mainly in the author's intent; others like C. S. Lewis (*SII*16) in the literary tradition of Chaucer's time—both intent and tradition often highly debatable. As or more debatable results are apt to come from the view that literary works are *per se,* and may or should be re-interpreted according to the pre-occupations of each succeeding age and critic, regardless of the astonishing vicissitudes through which Chaucer's reputation has already passed. By critical fallacies, therefore, I mean critical excesses, frequently involving new and perhaps good points of departure which, all too often, are carried out to lengths of absurdity and made to exclude all other approaches. The "evidence" and pleading in such cases would not stand in any court of law if more real property were at stake than the meaning of works of art. In practise various fallacies of method leading to fallacies of interpretation are blended. Starting with the latter, I shall try to isolate some of these; yet in doing so, I will not presume to pass judgment on the whole work of the critics concerned, but only on those aspects which I honestly feel result in the unsatisfactory appraisal of Chaucer.

I shall begin with what might be called the *realistic fallacy* and defined as unwarranted implication of real-life contexts, forgetting that Chaucer's and most art is conventional and mimetic rather than photographic. For many readers, the best example of this fallacy in our volumes would be Kittredge's famous theory of the "Marriage Group" (*W*188f, *SI*130f), for me sufficiently demolished by H. B. Hinckley (*W*216f), though more could be added (as by C. H. Holman, *W*240). What interests me at the moment, however, is not the grouping nor interpretations as such of the tales concerned, but the apparent assumption that the tellers are real persons of whom Chaucer has shown a part and the critic, from his own knowledge of human psychology, may freely extend—in this case, to prove his theory. I quote a few bits with some added italics: "Now the substance of the Wife's false doctrines was not the only thing that must have roused the Clerk to *protesting answer* . . . The Wife's discourse . . . embodies a rude personal assault upon the Clerk, whose quiet mien and habitual reticence made him seem *a safe person to attack . . . He saw it; the company saw it.* He kept silent, *biding his time.*"

This (and there is much more) somehow sounds like the kind of psychologizing and pontificating of which nineteenth century criticism, especially of Shakespeare, is full. (Chaucer criticism has never had an E. E. Stoll.) None of the above quotation can be proven beyond debate, and the italicized phrases are not authorized by the text of Chaucer at all. Nevertheless it is, in many ways, an attractive theory, at least in the spirit of Chaucer, whom it might well have amused. But it remains a highly circumstantial *theory;* and to speak of "Chaucer's Marriage Group," as most people do, suggests that something of an argumentum ad hominem and the otherwise great name of G.L.K. are involved.

The realistic fallacy—satirized, I presume, when James Sledd speaks of "Griselda's children, whose sex life will be ruined by their childhood experiences" (*W*233, *SI*167)—is one of the oldest and still dangerous pitfalls in Chaucer criticism. The eternal discussion of each tale's appropriateness to its teller is full of it: so also comment like that of B. H. Bronson on Chaucer's real and literary personalities (*infra* and *W*271f). A special variety of the realistic fallacy might be designated the *historical fallacy,* as when Wayne Shumaker (*O*65f), unnecessarily enough, reads into the Wife of Bath's portrait extensive descriptions of the actual continental pilgrimages of Margery Kempe, a most incongruous companion for Dame Alys. To those who haven't read Margery, Shumaker's account is very interesting; the worst to be said is that it exaggerates the importance of Alys's having "passed many a strange strem" and supplies details *for Alys* which even Chaucer might not have known. The extensive historical researches of J. M. Manly—here anticipated in "A Knight Ther Was" (*W*46f)—have vastly enriched the background of Chaucer's works. Only the unwary, perhaps, need fear being trapped: since first reading Manly, I confess I am almost unable to think of Chaucer's Prioress without something of Elizabeth of Hainaut in her make-up. As for that very clever Leslie Hotson (*W*98f)—he traps the wary, too. Shades of Esdras Barnivelt, Apoth!

A somewhat opposite pitfall may be called the *anachronistic fallacy* and defined as unwarranted implication of noncontemporary (usually too modern) elements in interpretation. I consider fallacious only that which is unwarranted and excessive. Modern psychology, for example, has long since given new meaning to much literature which precedes it; but it becomes fallacious (or ridiculous) in extreme and forced application. The following comment on the *Book of the Duchess* is a fairly clear case of the latter: "By a wonderful leap of psychological insight, and in strict accord with truth rediscovered in our own century, his private grief has been renounced by the Dreamer, to reappear externalized and projected upon the figure of the grieving knight. The modern analyst, indeed, would instantly recognize the therapeutic function of this dream as an effort of the psyche to resolve an intolerable emotional situation (etc.) . . . the knight's long and rapturous eulogy of his lost lady would serve, in the Dreamer's unconscious, to discharge the latter's sense of guilt for the disloyalty of wishing the death of that Merciles Beaute" (Bronson, *W*281). This is the first time, so far as I know, that Chaucer (in or out of his works) has ever been suspected of homicidal tendencies. Moreover, I should probably be held guilty of what I have just called the realistic fallacy if I noted (in his defence) that when he wrote the *Book of the Duchess* (1369–70) he had apparently been married to Philippa for several years, probably happily enough. There is, of course, some truth in Bronson's psychologizing, and it is possibly only my opinion that he exaggerates the quite conventionally lovelorn state of the Dreamer in order to bolster his theory of the whole work as an amorous triptych. But this is not my chief complaint: whether discernible here or not, such psychological depths are as old as human nature; yet, in Chaucer's formal aristocratic world, life, love and even death were less matters of passions concretely than of patterns abstractly, both in conception and action, as Bronson earlier indicates. It is just this surface of enamel-work in patterns which gives medieval art much of its character and which the modern analyst is apt to ignore or thrust aside in order to discover (if it is a discovery) that beneath it, as beneath the surfaces of all periods, the same basic human passions lie. In more general terms, the anachronistic fallacy (like the intellectualizing fallacy, discussed later) usually results in oversophisticated interpretations which are bound in some measure to be specious, through application of critical techniques which do not suit medieval literature and which—though ultimately it probably doesn't matter—Chaucer might well not have understood.

Much more widespread aspects of oversophistication are related to the many varieties of what might be called the *schematic fallacy* and defined as the unwarranted implication of schemes—unities of design, purport, etc.—frequently conveyed to a waiting world by the numerous "reopenings," "rediscoveries," "revisitings," etc. of Chaucer's works. Since these previously undiscerned schemes are usually inferred to be deliberate on the author's part and, understandably perhaps, since other and dissonant internal evidence tends to be slighted, this process often enhances the poet's art to the point of apparent perfection even in his earliest immature efforts, so that Chaucer, like the British monarch, can do no wrong. Distinguishable, but closely related to the schematic fallacy, is therefore what might be called the *perfective fallacy.* Objection to the former is that thereby Chaucer's works are too often made out to be what they are not; and to the latter that his highly interesting and gradual artistic development is so frequently underestimated.

To this reader, the volumes before us contain a large number of highly interesting essays which nevertheless illustrate excessive schematization, usually offered as the only true interpretation, etc. This phenomenon is not easy to explain: it may be related to the ever-increasing scientific expertise of criticism, plus the confidence (often rather naive) that the mysteries of art have their codes which can (always?) be "broken" if only the right formula, clue, or tactic be found; or it may indicate more fundamental disparities between the scholarly, hence logical, mind and the creative imagination. Thus C. Muscatine writes of the *Knight's Tale,* "It has resisted satisfactory interpretation" —one is tempted to add "Bully for it!"—"where poems of much more complicated structure . . . and much more varied style . . . have yielded brilliant results to criticism" (*W*6of). This deficiency he endeavours to repair; and, though he may not be absolutely accurate in remarks on the limitations of his predecessors, "the traditional critics," he does once again make us aware of the beautiful symmetries of design for which the *Knight's Tale* has long been famous. Unfortunately (in my view), he does not stop there. The main symmetries, if charted, would produce triangular groupings of persons, etc. leaving Theseus at the top. Thus, so the argument runs, Theseus is the central character and hence the most important. Moreover, as king, he controls the action and is thus seen to be the instrument of cosmic necessity and order of which even the purely aesthetic symmetries of the poem are indicative. In his philosophic speeches and in his own person he demonstrates an ideal of the noble life, despite dangers to it, which is the unifying principle of the whole poem. For quite parallel reasons, one would have to consider the Prince of Verona as the chief character in *Romeo and Juliet,* a play unified by a message on behalf of civic harmony and the avoidance of feuds. To Muscatine's theory, William Frost (*SI*98f) adds some very good suggestions, but he has a rather unrestrained fondness for tabulation. Thus the *Knight's Tale* has 3 concentric circles of interest (amorous, ethical, theological), 3 atmospheres (classical, realistic, chivalric), 3 abiding attributes (noble, tragic, superhuman), 3 ways in which Palamon and Arcite differ, 3 aspects of destiny, 3 ceremonious events, 3 causes of the final solution, etc. Fortunately no very startling distortions are involved in this process of worrying the text; but it is a good example, in a small way, of what may be considered the schematic fallacy.

Less hampered by moderation than Muscatine and Frost is A. W. Hoffman in his interpretation of the *General Prologue* (*W*30f, *O*9f). Apparently disregarding the usual view of the opening description of spring (ll. 1–18) as a piece of literary convention, he finds it significantly symbolic, archetypal and doctrinal, serving as a key to the design and meaning of all that follows. Thus the principal symbols, the bird (*"smale foweles"?*) and the saint (Becket), represent a dualism of nature and supernature, whose two voices— " 'Go, go, go,' says the bird; 'Come,' says the saint."—ring through the poem. Hoffman argues strongly; and it is always possible that some readers will recognize the *General Prologue* in what he has to say about it. For example: "The phallicism of the opening lines presents the impregnating of a female March by a male April, and a marriage of water and earth. The marriage is repeated and varied immediately as a fructifying of 'holt and heeth' by Zephirus, a marriage of air and earth . . . these symbols as parts of a rite of spring have a long background of tradition . . . Does not the passage move from an activity naturally generated and impelled to a governed activity, from force to *telos?* Does not the passage move from Aphrodite" (suggested by April) "and *amor* in their secular operation to the sacred embrace of 'the hooly blisful martir' and of *amor dei?*" and later: " 'Go, go, go,' the bird's voice, is a major impulse in the portrait of the Squire and in the Squire's pilgrimage; the Knight's pilgrimage is more nearly a response to the voice of the saint." When the Squire "carf biforn his fader" it was "perhaps a suggestion of the present submitting to the serious and respected values served and communicated by the past, the natural and the imposed submitting of the son to his natural father, and beyond him to the supernatural goal, the shrine to which the father directs his pilgrimage." And finally, "the exterior unity . . . is made stronger and tighter . . . by . . . a theme of love, earthly and celestial . . . sounded in different keys all through the portraits." To prove this, amidst better evidence, are quoted lines containing, "he loved chivalrie," "lovede venerie," "love-knotte," "love-dayes," "A fat swan loved he," "wel loved he . . . a sop in wyn," "he loved gold in special"—most of which, to this reader, would not exactly substantiate a theme of love, earthly or celestial, any more than the summoner's "fyr-reed cherubynnes face" and trumpet-great voice are "reminders of noble and awesome aspects of divine justice." In fact, among the many essays in these volumes in which there is unwarranted schematic forcing and, usually, unwarranted elaboration, Hoffman's may serve as a rather advanced case.

At the same time, Hoffman may be said to illustrate what might be called the *ideological fallacy,* the unwarranted implication of ideas, if in fact the ideas can at most be assumed rather than proven, and especially if they are the basis of an unjustified scheme. Nevertheless, Hoffman impresses this reader that what he is concerned with is, naturally enough, the art of Chaucer and with ideas as means of artistic unity. Various other critics (in our volumes) seem to suggest that for them and therefore for Chaucer the ideas are the chief *raison d'être* of a work, whatever other virtues it may have. Interpretations of this order—except, of course, for Chaucer's prose pieces—willy-nilly illustrate a special kind of ideological fallacy which might be called the *didactic fallacy,* that is, unwarranted emphasis upon ideas so as to suggest that the poet's main purpose was to teach. In this connection, divergent views of medieval aesthetic seem to be held. That literature was much more regularly infused with ideas than in later periods is obvious—also that ideas, given the synthetic nature of medieval thought, very noticeably belonged to larger systems or schemes. But this surely does not mean that from one or a few ideological allusions in a work we may assume the whole thought context, as is now so commonly done. Nor should we forget that the Middle Ages apparently found ideas entertaining for their own sake, as part of the "doctrine and sentence" with which works were leavened and adorned, often somewhat mechanically or superficially by our standards. Regarding Chaucer's doctrinal additions to *Il Filostrato,* C. S. Lewis says, "If the author was so 'courteous beyond covenant' as to give you an extra bit of *doctryne* (or of story), who would be so churlish as to refuse it on the pedantic ground of irrelevance? . . . On the other hand, he would be a dull reader, and the victim rather than the pupil of history, who would take all the doctrinal passages in Chaucer seriously" (*SII*23).

To no specific author was Chaucer more indebted for *doctryne,* especially in the middle period of his writing, than Boethius. Since much of Boethius's popularity resulted from his having given attractive expression and "logical" support to widely-held views about Fortune, Fate and human values on the whole consistent with Christian teaching, it has become easy for critics to extend the range of Boethian influence in Chaucer, far beyond that proven by incontestable verbal reproduction or by the evidence of tenets peculiarly the Roman philosopher's. In my view, therefore, the works of Chaucer which, like *Troilus and Criseyde* and the *Knight's Tale,* draw much upon Boethius, are especially apt to receive interpretations embodying schematic, ideological and perhaps didactic fallacies. At

any rate, a considerable number of essays in our volumes
are wholly or partly Boethian interpretations, which usually
means Christian interpretations at the same time. Thus,
Dale Underwood, writing of the *Knight's Tale,* finds that
a "pattern of progressive order in the poem thus corre-
sponds to the pattern of progressive order in Boethius'
'Consolation' " (*O42*). He considers it a shortcoming in
Theseus that "he sees . . . only a portion of his text" (i.e.,
Boethius). Underwood concludes: "The poem is finally,
then, the poet's theatre, world, and tale, in which he images
the form and principle not only of Fortune and of man
but, encompassing and transcending these, the universe of
divine order" (*O43*). At the very least, I think, this is putting the cart before the horse, with the result, intended or
not, of overemphasizing ideological factors in the poem.
It is really the Victorian "moral fallacy" in another guise.

But this is a relatively mild example. In recent decades,
the urge to find extra-aesthetic meaning in literary works
has very frequently carried the schematic-ideological-didac-
tic fallacies to much greater lengths. The result is "a kind
of *discordia concors";* and what Dr. Johnson said of the
Metaphysical Poets might oft be better applied to criticism
and critics of this order: "The most heterogeneous ideas
are yoked by violence together . . . their learning instructs,
and their subtlety surprises; but the reader commonly
thinks his improvement dearly bought, and, though he
sometimes admires, is seldom pleased." One extreme may
be called the *allegorical fallacy* and defined as unwarranted
implication of underlying level(s) of meaning, usually schematic. This is no new thing: Lawrence long since ridiculed
the mythological criticism of his day by construing *Jack
and Jill* as a cosmic allegory of the sun-god. But there
probably never was a time when critics felt freer to con-
jecture ostensible parallels to the whole or any part of a
literary work, often with only the faintest and/or equivocal

prompting from the text—or with none—and to insist that such constitutes the "interpretation" thereof, "now for the first time discovered, etc." Prevailing sociological, political, religious, scientific, etc. notions of the author's or critic's times have been offered with full academic seriousness as the indispensable "keys" to understanding. The procedure may look scientific: behind it is often a strangely naive reliance on oversimplified or mechanical devices to unlock the mysteries of great art. And often, too, either the "interpretation" turns out to be extraliterary, i.e., to be something different from the work itself, or, at least, it tends to distort the very real relations between the work and its background, to confuse work and background, etc. By this time, moreover, it would generally be admitted that the purism of certain "new critics" did not quite provide an acceptable alternative.

The most exaggerated kind of allegorical fallacy in the history of Chaucer criticism is that involved in the use of the so-called "exegetical method" in the hands of D. W. Robertson, Jr., and his followers. In spite of the fact that Robertson has been most ably answered by senior Chaucerians and medievalists—e.g., by Dorothy Bethurum (*SII*226f),[3] this approach continues to attract younger scholars seeking novel projects, and, by this time, has been applied to a wide variety of early literature extending as far back as *Beowulf.* In a word, Robertson, more or less following Augustinian tradition, applies the allegorical methods of medieval scriptural interpretation to literature of all kinds, including works of Chaucer. His rationale of this procedure richly illustrates the fallacies of formal logic, viz., fallacies of generalization (and its opposite), of analogy, of *non sequitor,* etc., and is marked by a curious rigidity and simplesse. Having noted opinions of certain twelfth century writers—as Alanus de Insulis's that literature will have a *nucleus* of allegorical import beneath its *cortex* of surface meaning, and Hugh of St. Victor's that the *sentence* (i.e., Alanus's *nucleus*) represents at least three levels of meaning or reference: tropological, allegorical, and anagogical—he proceeds to apply this scheme as an interpretive measuring-stick to all medieval literature whatsoever, all Chaucer included. In so doing, he underplays many ideological and aesthetic complexities of the period and of its dynamic evolution through centuries after the twelfth toward greater secularism in outlook and greater realism in artistic expression, of which Chaucer and his time represent what is already an advanced and climactic stage. To Robertson and his disciples, interpretation consists mainly of finding for details of the text supposed parallels or at least analogies in other writings, so as to demonstrate its symbolic-allegorical nature, its expression of the tenets and traditions of medieval Catholicism, often by inference schematically. This process frequently reveals both considerable subtlety and considerable range of cross reference, and is basically apologetic. It characterizes a (disproportionate?) number of essays in those two of our volumes issued by the University of Notre Dame Press—even more in a subsequent volume of *Beowulf* essays from the same press. The interpretations given are often, to say the least, extreme. They may be said to illustrate a special blend of several aforementioned critical distractions, which may be called the *christian-clerical fallacy*, that is, the unwarranted assumption of medieval Catholic doctrines (frequently of monastic origin and outlook) as necessary keys to literary interpretation. This, probably, is what William Empson had in mind when he noted how much "neo-Christian cheating has made nonsense of the English literature of earlier periods." [4]

Unfortunately, startling examples are not at all difficult to find. Robertson is one of many who consider Boethius the source of Chaucer's conception of tragedy, which is at least plausible if not just provable. But Robertson goes much farther than this. In an essay (*SII*86f) purporting to prove *Troilus and Criseyde* "a typical Chaucerian tragedy," he soon supplements the relevant and familiar passages of the *Monk's Prologue* and *Tale,* the *Boece,* etc. with others from Isaiah, John of Salisbury, St. Augustine, Peter Lombard, etc., and so concludes that Troilus' "three stages of tragic development . . . correspond to the three stages in the tropological fall of Adam: the temptation of the senses, the corruption of the lower reason in pleasurable thought, and the final corruption of the higher reason," the last through "the substitution of Criseyde for divine grace." For when Troilus was first of all smitten by her beauty:

> *And sodeynly he was therwith astoned,*
> *And gan hir bet biholde in thrifty wise.*
> *"O mercy, god!" thoughte he, "wher hastow woned,*
> *That art so fair and goodly to divise?"* (I, 274–277).

only Robertson (or one of his "school") could comment, "The death of the spirit implied in Chaucer's lines was observed by a still older clerk (*Eccles.* 9:8–9): Turn thy face from a woman dressed up . . . For many have perished by the beauty of a woman, and hereby lust is enkindled as fire." (Similarly *Eccles.* 9:2 and *Prov.* 23:33–34 to which reference is also made.) Explanation of the lovers' behavior by the conventions of courtly love is completely excluded: "There is no historical evidence for this sort of thing . . . and there is good reason to doubt that the term 'courtly love' as it is usually understood has any validity at all" (*SII*106). Troilus' love is "idolatrous lust" merely of Criseyde's "figure" and "competence in bed"; "Criseyde . . . reveals the pride and self-love upon which her "love" for Troilus is based"; Pandarus is "a priest of Satan," etc. Other of this critic's interpretations are equally wild: In the *Nun's Priest's Tale,* "the dangers of the service of Venus in marriage are once more shown, and in this instance the idea is applied by implication to the relationship between a priest and his flock"; the hunting horn which the dreamer hears in *The Book of the Duchess* somehow sounds "the call of Christ and His Church for the human soul"; the theme of *The Parliament of Fowls* is the "neglected appeal of divine love." Reviewing works in which these gems occur, the *Times Literary Supplement* (6:11:64) noted: "This is a country into which most critics will shudder to follow Robertson. In terms of logic the name of the country is *reductio ad absurdum*."

Such reaction is typical of most authoritative criticism. The suspect nature of Robertsonian scholarship has been so frequently pointed out, one can only marvel at the persistence of this "school" and the audience which it seems to attract. Many of its "interpretations" of Chaucer's works are so very incongruous, one might wonder if Robertson will not soon declare it was all a comic hoax, that we may end by having a good laugh together. But this seems unlikely.

However great Robertson's sins against scholarship, his sins against art are greater. By this time, as was said, the "method" has been applied to a wide range of medieval literature, including Chaucer. And, in every piece of such criticism that I have read, the literary works discussed seem to be represented as having their various *raisons d'être* as religious tracts—in effect, just that. Now, important as ideas may be in medieval works, other critics today would argue that intrinsic literary values have little to do with ideas as such. So they say; but the concern of this paper is to identify some critical excesses, not to substitute one excess for another. Obviously the importance of the "message" differs from author to author and work to work: Chaucer is not Langland; but even in *Piers Plowman*, despite Robertson and his colleague B. F. Huppé, one symbol or a tangled gardenful does not necessarily make a *summa*.

Chaucer was evidently a good fourteenth century Christian, interested up to a point in certain doctrinal questions, concerned considerably over abuses in the church. But beyond that, as everyone except the Robertson "school" knows, he is the great secular, the humanist whose breadth of affirmation is of itself a renaissance and foreshadows a greater. Symbolism and allegory are elements especially in his earlier works, but it is the "cortex" which more and more mattered to him, the teller of tales. To represent *all* his works primarily as religious and moral exempla is to shift focus away from supreme narrative art and cause serious distortion. To represent *Troilus and Criseyde* as a proselytizing of the more morbid aspects of monkish asceticism, especially as regards human love—out of whatever motive or myopia—is shameful. So much better C. S. Lewis: "*Troilus* is what Chaucer meant it to be—a great poem in praise of love. Here also, despite the tragic and comic elements, Chaucer shows himself, as in the *Book of the Duchess, The Parlement,* and the *Canterbury Tales,* our supreme poet of happiness." [5] This too is based on assumption, which comes closer—if I may also assume—to what people have always felt about Chaucer. It may further imply what, again, the ideological critics miss or undervalue, that Chaucer wrote, as he is read, with delight—only secondarily to instruct, primarily to give pleasure—that also, when he chooses, he is the greatest humorist in the language, or certainly in verse narrative. Surely it is a dolorous thing to extract religious significance from the *Miller's Tale,* as does P. E. Beichner C.S.C. (*SI*117f), rather than enjoying, with E. M. W. Tillyard (*O*45f), the highest art of sheer fun.

All of the fallacies so far discussed may be called *fallacies of interpretation,* various excessive (and to that extent erroneous) views as to the significance of Chaucer's works. These views result from equally fallacious critical methods, as e.g., many interpretations reflecting unwarranted allegorizing are due to (misapplication of) the exegetical method. While one cannot completely separate *fallacies of interpretation* from *fallacies of method,* a few more mainly of the latter sort deserve mention.

Perhaps the most common of these, which is involved in most unsound criticism, may be called the *rationalistic fallacy* (or *assumptive fallacy*) and defined as the unwarranted reliance upon logical "proof" based on insufficient empirical evidence. The critic seizes on some passage(s) in the text and arrives at a first assumption, which may itself be unproved or unprovable, whence he proceeds to a second based on the first, a third based on these two, *ad inf.,* getting closer and closer to what he set out to prove and further and further from what Chaucer wrote. There are some shining examples among various essays already cited. Another good one is a "Robertsonian" interpretation of the Pardoner by R. P. Miller (*SI*221f). After a good deal of adroit rationalizing from theological citations, he concludes, "The eunuch is the *vetus homo,* who by wilfully cutting himself off from grace presumptuously sins against the Holy Spirit. Chaucer suggests this spiritual state by using the image of eunuchry, reinforcing his point by allusions to the concept of the *veteres homines* who, according to Paul, "have given themselves up to lasciviousness, etc." Armed with this and other assumptions, we pass into the *Tale,* where the tavern boy warns the riotoures of Death. "Thus taughte me my dame," says he. To Miller, he is the true *novus homo,* "whose 'dame' is the Church"; and, therefore, as "symbolic opposite" to him is the Old Man of the *Tale,* another *vetus homo,* " 'all forwrapped' save his face: for the *vetus homo* represents the state of spiritual death." Finally: "What should be clear, however, is the consistent philosophical pattern artistically presented through the manipulation of Scriptural images . . . It should also be more evident how the *Pardoner's Tale* fits generally into a scheme of opposition between Charity and Cupidity in the *Canterbury Tales* as a whole." Or, at least, one thing leads to another.

To anyone who will object that it is unfair not to show the arguments by which such statements are arrived at, I would reply that the volumes I am using are very accessible and that it is in some ways better to show such statements (and others quoted earlier) in naked isolation, since no amount of rationalizing, of assumptions based on assumptions, can ever make them more than merest hypothecations of what might possibly be the substance of Chaucer's works. That is just the point. At the outset of this paper Tatlock was quoted in most just protest against excessive reading between lines and unwarranted elaboration. Protest as strong should be made against the arbitrary and univocal qualities of much recent criticism. Many interesting suggestions become irritating to the informed reader simply because the critic (perhaps too eager to make a "discovery") declares them to be proved beyond all further debate and to eliminate all other interpretations of the work(s) concerned. Much of the rationalizing designed to substantiate these "certainties" is flimsy, and strays too far from what Chaucer wrote; but even if it is clever as can be, it becomes wearisome.

Many of the fallacies already discussed may be said to exemplify another fallacy which, like the abuses Tatlock describes, is not only very basic but involves both method and resulting interpretation. This may be called the *intellectualizing fallacy* and defined as the unwarranted imposition of the scholarly mind upon the art of literature. The scholarly mind tends to be logical, precise, definite, etc.: art is often the opposite. When a small scholarly mind appraises great art, the results are apt to be disastrous. Even Robertson admits, "Much criticism of medieval literature is vitiated by a certain pedantic seriousness on the part of the critics" (*SII*106). For example, the scholar may conceive the creation and interpretation of literature as something too orderly or analyzable. "The present writer," says W. C. Curry (*W*185), "once entertained the perilous theory that Chaucer may have fashioned Dame Alisoun in accordance with astrological principles . . . But upon more mature consideration I have concluded that such a theory in application is so mechanical and so simple in its execution that the resultant figure is likely to be little better than a highly colored dummy . . . I do not know how Chaucer has created such a character, but I suspect that the soul and personality of this woman was conceived in the poet's imagination as a complete whole." This, from the chief authority on Chaucer's astrology, has the scholarly caution and wisdom of good criticism. To me, it seems to say that, however much Chaucer was a man of learning and ideas, he was primarily a man of feeling and imagination, the counterpart in his day of the great novelist in ours.

But the *intellectualizing fallacy* is more than pettiness, pedantry, and overprecision. It is probably not to be avoided entirely even in the most brilliant criticism—or perhaps less so there—for whatever submits the living body of art to abstract analysis, to formulation in respect of principles, even aesthetic principles, or to any whatever explanation which loses sight of the degree of immediacy in its origins and impact, can at best be partial, at worst quite false. "We murder to dissect." This is probably a very simple application of semantic theory, if not of philosophical aesthetics. In the light of Plato's example of the painter (or poet) and the bed, much literary criticism is yet a further remove from the thing itself, and some aesthetics (paradoxically?) even beyond that. Nevertheless, it is frequently appropriate to discuss an early writer in language he would not understand: he may have builded more than he knew or, in any case, analytical technique and terminology have developed greatly since his time. However, when R. Baldwin (O26–7) says of the *General Prologue:* "In transfixing *travel* details to static *effictiones,* the character is broadened proleptically with peculiar pilgrim intimations"; and "This Tabard-highroad tension creates a double illusion. It would seem that a deliberate bilocational, bifocal, and bitemporal effect is achieved by Chaucer. As a result, the fiction, by extension, moves on many levels, not the least of which is the bodying forth of the *vita est peregrinatio* motif in the timelessness of salvation"; or when A. Mizener (W364) writes: "The character of Criseyde is primarily an instrument for, and a unit in, a tragic action; it is therefore statically conceived and is related to the action by congruence rather than by cause and effect. For both Troilus and Criseyde are the victims of an act determined not by Criseyde's character, but by the dramatic necessities of the action." They may, up to a point, be doing no more than elaborating the obvious, in the case of Baldwin, by rather highfalutin jargon; but also these critics may likewise, to some extent, be oversubtilizing Chaucer's art and making it seem too premeditated and deliberate. If they are, they represent an extremely common kind of distortion found in the criticism of all periods.

A strange conclusion seems inevitable: that the scholar is by no means necessarily the best interpreter of literature; and the critic, if he is to avoid numerous pitfalls, must be as much artist as scholar. Something of the sort was apparently in Noel Coward's mind when he wrote, "I find it very interesting . . . to read criticisms and analyses of my plays written by people . . . who appear to have an insatiable passion for labelling everything with a motive. They search busily behind the simplest of my phrases, like old ladies peering under the bed for burglars, and are not content until they have unearthed some definite, and usually quite inaccurate reason for my saying this or that. This strange

mania I can only suppose is the distinctive feature of a
critical mind as opposed to a creative one." [6] A similar contrast is in Yeats' *The Scholars,*

> *Bald heads forgetful of their sins,*
> *Old, learned, respectable bald heads*
> *Edit and annotate the lines*
> *That young men, tossing on their beds,*
> *Rhymed out in love's despair*
> *To flatter beauty's ignorant ear.*
>
> . . . .
>
> *Lord, what would they say*
> *Should their Catullus walk that way?*

or even Chaucer?

As noted above, one aspect of the *intellectualizing fallacy*
is the use of overtechnical language if it causes distortion,
a special instance, I presume, of Bacon's "Idols of the
Market-Place," the deceptive power of words themselves.
Another, a contrasting hazard in the use of critical language
(which we are least eager to censure), may be called the
stylistic fallacy and defined as the unwarranted elaboration
of critical style, so as to give, in some measure, a false impression of the work(s) under discussion.[7] Nineteenth century critics seem to have been especially prone to this kind
of distortion. Behind it, somewhere, is usually the notion
(which is at least half-true) that criticism is a fine art in
itself, and that in appraising his favourite authors the critic
should endeavour to produce a verbal parallel as beautiful
as they. The result is apt to be emotional criticism, florid
and, when meaningful, tending to overpraise and something less than absolute accuracy. If the object be a Shakespeare or a Chaucer, the disparity may not be as noticeable
as when enthusiasm has less justification. J. R. Lowell's in-
sistence that Gray's *Progress of Poesy* "overflies all other
English lyrics like an eagle" is probably a clear case; but
so also is his estimate of the Black Knight's Duchess: "one

of the most beautiful portraits of a woman that was ever drawn . . . with no romantic hectic or sentimental languish . . . such a figure as you would never look for in a ballroom, but might expect to meet in the dewy woods, just after sunrise, when you were hunting for late violets." Less so, but also somewhat excessive is Arnold's: "Of Chaucer's divine liquidness of diction, his divine fluidity of movement, it is difficult to speak temperately. They are irresistible, and justify all the rapture with which his successors speak of his 'gold dew-drops of speech' " (*O*6)—even if the 'gold dew-drops' is Lydgate's phrase. On occasion, words can also make off with more recent critics; but perhaps— though this is a pessimistic guess—words are now more apt to be accompanied in their flight by the ideas as well. A possible case is from Hoffman (as above): "Beyond their knowing, beyond their power or impotence, impotently both Pardoner and Summoner appeal for the natural love —melody of bird-song and meadows of flowers—and both pray for the celestial love, the ultimate pardon which in their desperate and imprisoned darkness is their only hope: 'Com hider, love, to me!' " (*W*42). Turning the pages of these four volumes, the reader may find other glowing passages for himself.

But all this is a matter of degree, and whether the degree be actually "unwarranted" some would debate no matter what examples of professional criticism were chosen. And yet the fallacies discussed above, and probably others, do flourish, at times irresponsibly and arrogantly, even among very learned and clever men. Chaucer will indeed survive them; but, meanwhile, many young students of Chaucer are being misled by logical claptrap, pseudoscientific terminology, irrelevant erudition and, I suppose, the imperious manner and the sponsorship even of good journals and presses. Chaucer is not Milton, Blake, Joyce, etc.: I should like to propose seriously that he does not always need such elaborate interpreting, nor has benefited from much of it. To quote the same *TLS* again: "Apart from everything else, we keep wondering why Chaucer, who for all his subtlety was notoriously fond of making his points plainly, should here have kept his text so clear of necessary indications." These words refer to the *Nun's Priest's Tale* (and Robertson's "interpretation" thereof), but might well apply to the most of Chaucer.

And so, Bruce Robert McElderry, Jr., I offer you this groatsworth which, considering both the subject and the occasion, should certainly be at least a bobsworth.

NOTES

1. A recent discussion is William Arrowsmith, "The Shame of the Graduate Schools." *Harper's Magazine* (March, 1966), pp. 51–59.
2. *Chaucer: Modern Essays in Criticism,* ed. Edward Wagenknecht (New York, 1959); *Discussions of the Canterbury Tales,* ed. Charles A. Owen, Jr. (Boston, 1961); *Chaucer Criticism: Volume I: The Canterbury Tales; Volume II: Troilus and Criseyde & the Minor Poems,* eds. Richard Shoeck and Jerome Taylor (Notre Dame, Ind., 1960, 1961). These are referred to in the text as *W, O, SI,* and *SII,* respectively. Titles and original sources of the essays are indicated in these volumes.
3. See *Critical Approaches to Medieval Literature, Selected English Institute Papers, 1958–1959,* ed. D. Bethurum (New York, 1960).
4. *Punch,* XXIII (April, 1965), p. 81.
5. *The Allegory of Love* (New York, 1958), p. 197.
6. *Play Parade* (Garden City, N.Y., 1933), pp. vii–viii.
7. This is the most usual case; strictly, the stylistic fallacy would involve any unsuitable language, high or low.

Irving Ribner

❧ ❧

The Morality of Farce:
The Taming of the Shrew

One of the traditional functions of comedy, as we all know
—and as was constantly repeated in Renaissance critical
treatises—was to serve as a moral commentary upon human
relations. Shakespeare's comedies achieve this end in the
highest degree, for there is no one of them which does not
in some way explore the meaning of human love, and of all
human relations there is none more vital or important than
this. While we have come to recognize the profundity of
this exploration in such plays as *The Merchant of Venice,
Measure for Measure,* or *The Winter's Tale,* we tend to
dismiss as inconsequential his concern with love and marriage in the earliest comedies, or to sum up what he has

IRVING RIBNER is H. Rodney Sharp Professor of English at the University
of Delaware.

to say as merely conventional repetition of commonplace Elizabethan attitudes. What Shakespeare for most readers seems to be saying about the love relations between men and women in such plays as *The Comedy of Errors* and *The Taming of the Shrew* has seemed incredibly naive, silly, and certainly of no relevance to our modern world.

I would suggest that Shakespeare's complexity in these plays has generally been underestimated, and that we cannot take the seemingly didactic speeches of characters as expressions of Shakespeare's moral attitudes. In these plays Shakespeare is already experimenting with a technique by which moral statements are examined and evaluated in terms of the larger dramatic context in which they occur.

Let me illustrate this with a well known scene in *The Comedy of Errors*. Modern readers have always been somewhat dismayed by the advice which Luciana offers her unwelcome lover, Antipholus of Syracuse, whom she takes to be her sister's husband:

> *If you did wed my sister for her wealth*
> *Then for her wealth's sake use her with more kindness.*
> *Or, if you like elsewhere, do it by stealth.*
> *Muffle your false love with some show of blindness:*
> *Let not my sister read it in your eye;*
> *Be not thy tongue thy own shame's orator:*
> *Look sweet, speak fair, become disloyalty;*
> *Apparel vice like virtue's harbinger;*
> *Bear a fair presence, though your heart be tainted;*
> *Teach sin the carriage of a holy saint;*
> *Be secret false* (III, ii, 5–14).

This advice, which seems to condone adultery so long as it is kept secret, is usually taken as the rather naive young Shakespeare's statement of a conventional Elizabethan view of the demands of honor, and we forgive him for the patent absurdity to modern ears of what he is saying.

But we must remember that we are in Ephesus, the city

of witchcraft and deception, and that Antipholus is already so bewildered by the strange things which have happened to him that he is no longer sure of who he really is. Luciana is counselling the substitution of appearance for reality, and she is urging it upon a man already so overcome by deception that he has lost awareness of his own identity. The context into which Luciana's moral advice is put renders the advice ludicrous and patently false, and this, I would suggest, was how Shakespeare conceived that his audience should receive it. He is not proposing an Elizabethan view of honor based upon outward appearance. He is exposing, by its poetic and dramatic context, the hollowness and worthlessness of any concept of honor or propriety not based upon reality.

Shakespeare has only begun to find this method of moral commentary in *The Comedy of Errors,* and his attempts are awkward and halting. But with his achievement here in mind, we can turn with greater understanding to *The Taming of the Shrew,* his first full scale treatment of domestic relations, and one in which we may find his technique considerably advanced. Although this play has always been among the most popular of Shakespeare's plays on the stage, it has also been one of those most slighted and denigrated by the critics. Many scholars still refuse to believe that Shakespeare was the author of the entire play, and some would still remove it from the canon entirely— partly, I suspect, because what he seems to be saying about marriage seems so silly. Most of these writers who do accept Shakespeare's authorship fail to see much relation among the play's plots, and they tend to regard the play as a dramatic failure. Quiller-Couch reflected what is still a dominant view when he wrote:

> To call *The Shrew* a masterpiece is not only to bend criticism
> into sycophancy and a fawning upon Shakespeare's name. It

167

does worse. Accepted, it sinks our standard of judgment, levels it, and by levelling forbids our understanding of how a great genius operates; how consummate it can be at its best, how frequently bad at its worst.[1]

There is only one point on which I would agree with Quiller-Couch. That is that by taking *The Shrew* seriously we may have some insight into how a great genius operates, for I believe that in this play Shakespeare considerably advanced the method—already begun in *The Comedy of Errors*—which he was to use with ever-increasing skill and precision in his later comedies.

We have in this play a skillful combination not of two, but of three stories, each representing an origin and a literary tradition utterly alien to those of the other two. The combination is ingenious, and we must now recognize it to have been Shakespeare's original achievement, for there is no longer reason to suppose that Shakespeare's play was based upon a lost earlier play of which the anonymous *Taming of a Shrew* provides a corrupt version. *The Taming of a Shrew* whose existence for so long was permitted to obscure the brilliance of Shakespeare's achievement, is now generally recognized as based upon Shakespeare's play rather than as anterior to it. It was the attempt of an unknown literary hack to imitate Shakespeare's work, filling in his effort with liberal borrowings from such unlikely places as Marlowe's *Tamburlaine* and Joshua Sylvester's translation of Du Bartas.[2] *The Taming of a Shrew* is only important as illustrating what a mess a dramatist of lesser genius than Shakespeare could make of equivalent material.

At the heart of Shakespeare's *Taming of the Shrew* is a coarse medieval antifeminist joke which has come down to us in several versions, the most interesting perhaps being the mid-sixteenth century ballad, *A Merry Jest of a Shrewd and Curst Wife Lapped in Morel's Skin for her good behaviour*. This ballad Richard Hosley would regard as the actual prime source of Shakespeare's play.[3] Implicit in this story of wife-beating and submission is the notion of woman as subordinate to her husband, as much his property as the old plowhorse, Morel, in whose raw skin the errant wife of the ballad is finally wrapped. It is a view of woman which the author of *A Shrew* unequivocally presents, and it is a view which Petruchio himself in Shakespeare's play clearly proclaims:

> *She is my goods, my chattels; she is my house,*
> *My household stuff, my field, my barn,*
> *My horse, my ass, my anything* (III, ii, 223–225).

Most critics of the play have taken these lines as an expression of Shakespeare's moral attitude, and there is usually the lame apology that he is merely expressing the common Elizabethan view for the delight of an audience to whom it was more congenial than it may be to most of us today. Geoffrey Bullough, for instance, tells us that Shakespeare's play is "as much a social comedy preaching the subjection of women as was *A Shrew,* but its effect is more witty and civilized."[4]

With the material of his crude ballad source Shakespeare combined the Bianca-Lucentio subplot which he took from George Gascoigne's *Supposes.* This choice was a stroke of true genius, its effect beyond the comprehension of the author of *A Shrew* who replaced Shakespeare's underplot with a gauche and utterly ineffective one involving the wooing of Kate's two sisters. This he may have regarded, in fact, as an embellishment, for it must be noted that a single more gentle sister for Kate is already present in the ballad source, *A Merry Jest.* The *A Shrew* author is amplifying Shakespeare's play, not providing a model for it, as some earlier commentators have supposed.

In adapting Gascoigne's early play, itself based upon a sophisticated Italian original and written for an Inns of

Court audience, Shakespeare emphasized even beyond anything in his source the tradition of elegant Petrarchan love-
making in which Gascoigne's story had its origins. Shakespeare removes the pregnancy of Gascoigne's heroine which
is an essential part of his plot, so as to suggest a more ele-
vated kind of love-making in which the lady's chastity must
always be preserved and which must culminate in marriage.
In Shakespeare's subplot the woman is not her husband's
chattel to be beaten into submission by him, but a goddess
upon a pedestal to be worshiped. Love is not entirely a
matter of legal possession secured by marriage contracts; it
is an all-embracing passion which makes the lover the slave
of his mistress and which consumes him utterly until he is
united with the object of his desires:

> *Tranio, I burn, I pine, I perish, Tranio*
> *If I achieve not this young modest girl* (I, i, 97–98).

This, of course, is at the opposite extreme from Petruchio.
The usual explanation is that the subplot was intended as
a contrast which by its very absurdity enforces the contrary
view of domestic felicity in the Petruchio-Kate relationship.
And this view is usually regarded as fully vindicated by the
supposed victory in the contest of wives with which the
play ends. Those who take this final scene in literal terms
as a vindication of Petruchio's view of marriage tend to
ignore the animal context in which the scene is cast. Petruchio bets upon his wife as he would upon a hawk or a
hound, and his victory is that of any good trainer of dogs.

Those who might be tempted to take the Bianca-Lucentio
relationship as representing a more refined view of marriage closer to Shakespeare's heart must be reminded that
this marriage is based entirely upon deception and that, in
spite of Lucentio's Petrarchan protestations, Shakespeare to
emphasize its essential crassness must reduce it before it can
be concluded to crude commercial terms not unlike those

in which Petruchio courts his Kate. The supposed Lucentio, who is really Tranio in disguise, bids like a merchant against Gremio for the prize (II, i, 345 ff). If Petruchio is cast as the animal trainer, these lovers are reduced at last to traders at a horse sale. Bianca is merely the "commodity" which Baptista awards to the highest bidder, pending a binding legal guarantee of his bid:

> *I must confess your offer is the best;*
> *And, let your father make her the assurance,*
> *She is your own; else you must pardon me* (II, i, 385–388).

To see in either of these love relations Shakespeare's view of marriage we must conclude that he saw the most vital of all human relations either as the act of buying an animal or as the act of beating one into submission.

But the real key to Shakespeare's moral commentary on marriage may perhaps be found in the third story with which Shakespeare combined these two. This is the old *Arabian Nights* tale of "the sleeper awakened," a folklore motif which has come down to us in many versions. What is significant about it is that it poses again the problem of the relation of appearance to reality, and this questioning of the very nature of reality in Shakespeare's play, as in *The Comedy of Errors* is a framework in which the other two plots are set. The relations of Katherine to Petruchio and of Bianca to Lucentio are both seen as a kind of play within a play—a fantastic performance staged before an old man rendered incapable of distinguishing the true from the false. The Christopher Sly induction is absolutely essential to *The Taming of the Shrew* because it furnishes the frame of reference in which the other two plots are to be seen, and in this perspective the wooing of Kate is as absurd as the wooing of Bianca. We do not have, as some suppose, a presentation of two views of marriage, the one finally to be judged more valid than the other; we have the holding up to ridicule of two views of marriage, and as the Petruchio-Kate relation receives the greater dramatic emphasis, it is the one found most wanting.

At the same time that the Christopher Sly induction introduces its confusion between appearance and reality it relates this theme to the problem of courtship and marriage, for the most prominent thing about which Sly is confused is the identity of woman and the true nature of the seemingly dutiful and loving wife. Throughout the performance before them Sly in reality will be sitting next to Bartholomew the page who will seem to him to be the model of the loving wife ready to serve her supposed husband with

> *What is't your honour will command,*
> *Wherein your lady and your humble wife*
> *May show her duty and make known her love?* (111–113).

As the play within this play opens Bartholomew appears to Sly to be all that Katherine will become as the result of her taming:

> *My husband and my lord, my lord and husband,*
> *I am your wife in all obedience* (Ind., ii, 104–105).

And the theater audience's sense of Sly's delusion will prepare it to see Petruchio's supposed victory as the same kind of delusion. When the Bianca-Lucentio subplot is introduced, again the theme of false identity appears. This entire subplot will depend upon confusion of persons. Lucentio will assume the disguise of his servant, wooing under false pretense, and when he has won his lady the final scene will reveal her not as the meek young girl he had fallen in love with, but rather as a wife as willful and as disobedient as her sister Katherine had seemed at the play's beginning. The subplot consists, of course, of a whole set of "supposes" and these are linked thematically to the induction as they are to the main plot, for Christopher Sly is as uncertain of reality and of his own identity as are the characters he is watching. Only the theater audience knows the truth, and this awareness causes it to see the self-delusion of Shakespeare's characters.

The taming of Katherine in Shakespeare's source consisted essentially of the beating of a wife into submission. In Shakespeare's play this physical element is greatly toned down, although elements of it survive. What we have instead is, in fact, the teaching of Katherine to question reality and to accept falsehood as truth, just as it is accepted by Christopher Sly. A few illustrations may suffice.

Petruchio's initial approach to Baptista is one of pretending to believe what the audience knows is false. He describes Katherine as we have already been made to see in a previous scene that she is not:

> . . . *hearing of her beauty and her wit,*
> *Her affability and bashful modesty,*
> *Her wondrous qualities and mild behaviour* (II, i, 48–50).

And as an opening gift he presents Baptista with a teacher to instruct Katherine, who we know is not "Licio, born in Mantua" as Petruchio calls him, but simply the disguised Hortensio.

This deliberate pretense that falsehood is truth is maintained in his first encounter with Katherine herself:

> . . . *I find you passing gentle.*
> *'Twas told me you were rough and coy and sullen,*
> *And now I find report a very liar;*
> *For thou art pleasant, gamesome, passing courteous* (II, i, 241–
> 244).

The treatment of Katherine in Petruchio's house is largely a matter of his denying what she knows to be true until she herself is confused about reality, and this process

173

of confusion is only completed upon the road to Padua
when she is ready to agree that the sun is the moon and
that a withered old man is a fair young girl, just as Christopher Sly believes that the page beside him is a loving wife.

The process of taming thus becomes a denial of truth and
a destruction of that power of reason which separates man
and woman from the lower animals. That its final effect is
to reduce the tamed wife to the level of an animal is made
clear by the very soliloquy in which Petruchio compares
his "politic reign" as husband to the taming of a hawk by
its master:

> *My falcon now is sharp and passing empty;*
> *And till she stoop she must not be full-gorged,*
> *For then she never looks upon her lure.*
> *Another way I have to many my haggard,*
> *To make her come and know her keepers' call,*
> *That is, to watch her, as we watch those kites*
> *That bate and beat and will not be obedient* (IV, i, 172–178).

The animal terms of Petruchio's courtship have, in fact,
been made clear from the beginning. At the end of their
first encounter, he pretends to examine Kate in the terms
with which a would-be purchaser would survey a horse:

> *Why does the world report that Kate doth limp?*
> *O sland'rous world! Kate like the hazel twig*
> *Is straight and slender, and as brown in hue*
> *As hazelnuts, and sweeter than the kernels.*
> *O, let me see thee walk: thou doest not halt* (II, i, 251–256).

Limping is a defect one looks for in horses, not in wives.
To be "brown in hue" can be meritorious only in horses,
for Elizabethan women were prized for the whiteness of
their skins, darkness in complexion being, in fact, regarded
as a sign of a lecherous disposition. When Petruchio asks
that his prospective bride be paraded before him like a

horse in a ring, we are being well prepared for the crude animalism of the wife-context of the play's final scene.

In *The Taming of a Shrew* the Christopher Sly framework is maintained throughout the play, and the final scene is a return to reality in which we find Sly again a beggar out on the street. He then announces to the tapster that he has learned how to tame a shrew and will go home to practice his lesson upon his own wife. This is a fitting conclusion for the medieval antifeminist joke which is the substance of this play. Why this final episode is not in Shakespeare's play has been the subject of much debate. I do not think it necessary to suppose, as some have done, that our text represents a shortened version or is in some way corrupt. Richard Hosley has shown by an examination of all Elizabethan induction plays that Shakespeare's failure to complete his was no way unusual. The answer may be that for Shakespeare to have ended his play as *A Shrew* ends might have destroyed the effect of his work which he had been building toward from the very beginning.

The complications of Shakespeare's play actually are over at the end of the first scene of the fifth act. The second scene is a kind of epilogue which serves a function similar in the total structure to what might have been served by the concluding element of the Christopher Sly story which Shakespeare omitted. It is the same kind of final summing up of the play's moral content. It is Shakespeare's substitute for a return to reality—a return to a reality which is not reality at all. The characters of the play have now seemingly abandoned their disguises, and in the contest of wives which is the chief substance of the scene we are to see what has been the result of all the action of the play—the revelation of what a true, dutiful and loving wife should be.

And what do we find? Bianca and the widow are themselves revealed as shrews and Kate is revealed as the trained hawk or dog of her master. Is this reality? By his constant stressing of false appearance Shakespeare has led us to the point where this final revelation seems as much a fancy and an idle dream as Sly's stay in the lord's palace. We continue to see in this final scene a vision of domestic felicity such as might be seen by a beggar disguised as a lord, incapable of distinguishing man from woman and uncertain even of his own identity. Rather than the crude return to reality at the end of *The Taming of a Shrew* Shakespeare gives us a seeming return to reality which is merely the embracing by Petruchio, Lucentio and the rest of an absolute delusion. We continue to the very end of the play to see a conventional Elizabethan statement about marriage through the eyes of a Christopher Sly.

It is thus not necessary for us to forgive Shakespeare for presenting an outmoded view of marriage and to say that the play is redeemed in spite of this by its exuberance, farce, or comic characterization. The play actually ridicules two views of man's relation to woman, and in this ridicule there is important moral commentary. It is this moral commentary, in fact, which holds together the separate parts of the play and makes of it the delightful experience which it is.[5]

NOTES

1. Ed. *The Taming of the Shrew* (Cambridge, 1928), p. xxiv.
2. See Peter Alexander, "A Case of Three Sisters," *TLS,* July 8, 1965, p. 588.
3. "Sources and Analogues of *The Taming of the Shrew*," *HLQ,* XXVII (1964), 289–308.
4. *Narrative and Dramatic Sources of Shakespeare* (London, 1960), I, 64.
5. All Shakespeare references have been to the New Kittredge Edition (Waltham, Mass., 1966).

French Fogle

⊸❧ ⊱❧

The Action of
Samson Agonistes

Over the past thirty years *Samson Agonistes* has had no lack
of commentators who sought meaning and dramatic unity
in the action of the tragedy.[1] It has been viewed as Milton's
autobiography, as political commentary on the Restoration,
and as Milton's most detailed portrayal of the human condition in a universe controlled by providence. Many of
these studies have yielded valuable insights into the artistic
and philosophic workings of Milton's mind and into the
nature of Samson's spiritual state and development. But
continuing efforts to discover "the meaning" of *Samson*
provide evidence of dissatisfaction with solutions already
presented. Probably no great literary work can be made to

FRENCH FOGLE is Professor of English at Claremont Graduate School.

yield its full meaning to the pressure of a single critical approach. It is surprising, however, to find that in all this critical endeavor so little attention has been paid to the formulations of seventeenth-century theology as a means of understanding what happens to Samson in the play. Milton, though casting his work in classical form and adapting his treatment of theme to the spirit of Greek tragedy, was writing, as he says in *The Reason of Church Government,* with the advantage "over and above of being a Christian." It would seem inevitable that in dealing with the story of a great man fallen from high position into sin and misery and his eventual spiritual recovery Milton should utilize the currently available Protestant formulations of the process of regeneration, a process which Milton himself defined and described in some detail in the *Christian Doctrine* and which was an absorbing preoccupation of most of the divines of the period. It can throw much light on the steps by which Samson was transformed from abject slave, in mind and body, to heroic champion and martyr.

The series of provocative and intensive studies of *Samson Agonistes* by William Riley Parker in the 1930's and 1940's defined a theme and a pattern of action for the drama which have been dominant in most major treatments of the play since that time. According to Parker the theme of the play is the hero's regeneration and reward, and the pattern of action is the record of Samson's progress upward from an initial state of self-pity and near despair through a series of trials and illuminations to a level of moral renewal at which he became once more God's champion, the instrument of divine revenge on the Philistines. Parker used the word "regeneration" in its general meaning of being born again in a spiritual sense, of achieving a new and higher spiritual nature. "Obviously," he continued, "Samson's regeneration is not, in the strict sense, Christian, for the Holy Spirit and the purifying power of Christ are

missing. But repentance and faith, the 'co-efficients of regeneration, on the human side,' are present; and the idea
of regeneration itself is essentially Christian rather than
Hebrew. It is to be found in the Old Testament, but 'out-
wardness is prominent' there." [2]

Parker saw Samson's regeneration as requiring at least
four stages: he must achieve patience; he must achieve
faith; he must conquer the weakness which led to his fall;
and he must recognize and obey the call to further service.[3]
In the encounters, first with the Chorus, and then with
Manoa, he was seen as achieving patience; in the episode
with Dalila he demonstrated his mastery of the weakness
which had been his ruin; and in his response to the Officer's
second summons to perform at the festival of Dagon he
showed evidence of recognizing and obeying a call to further service. The course of Samson's regaining of faith was
much more difficult to delineate, involving first an acknowledgment of personal responsibility for his failure, and second a portrayal of his resistance to both Dalila and Harapha, which gave him the strength to admit his guilt. Having
surmounted these trials, Samson emerged as heroic champion and martyr.

The list of critics who have played variations on the
theme of regeneration in interpreting *Samson* is imposing.
Merritt Y. Hughes subscribes both to the view that it is a
drama of regeneration in which the key is the hero's faith
in himself and God, and to the breakdown of the action
into the four steps of regeneration.[4] M. M. Mahood sees
the tragedy as a drama of regeneration, although the pattern of action follows the descending-ascending curve represented by the three stages of (1) thirst for glory; (2) renunciation of glory; and (3) bestowal of glory unsought.[5]
To Miss Ellis-Fermor the play is a drama of inward struggle
giving us a "steady psychological progression from despair
through heroic conflict upwards to exultation and the final

assumption into beatitude. . . ." [6] M. E. Grenander, elaborating the "middle" which Dr. Johnson so sadly missed, divides the God-Samson relationship into five stages: first, Samson's initial state of enjoying divine favor; second, his loss of that favor by his revelation of his secret to Dalila; third, his demonstration of worthiness of renewed favor (a) in the Manoa incident, where he evinces a desire to expiate his crime, and (b) in the Dalila incident, where he remains firm against her blandishments; fourth, in the challenge to Harapha, where he "hopes once again to act as God's agent"; and fifth, his complete restoration, as God chooses him to visit destruction on the Philistines at the theater.[7] Elizabeth Mary Pope, followed by Michael Krouse, regards the major action of the play as centering in three trials, standing in "triple equation" to those undergone by Christ in *Paradise Regained,* trials by which Samson's faith is tested: trial by physical necessity through Manoa, trial by fraud through Dalila, and trial by violence and fear in the person of Harapha. The events following the retreat of Harapha then seem to be simply those to be expected on Samson's restoration to full faith in God.[8]

To Don Cameron Allen the play is the record of Samson's recovery from a condition of near despair, witnessed in the exchanges between Samson and the Chorus after the departure of Manoa, through a regenerative process sparked mainly by the taunts of Dalila and Harapha.[9] When Samson vanquishes Harapha in what Allen calls (p. 93) the most important scene of all because it is the hinge of the tragedy, God has in effect vanquished Dagon and Samson's course is now easy, "for the way upward, the patient surrender to faith, once the obstacles in the hard lower levels are cleared, is as easy as the effortless descent to despair." Samson's subsequent triumph at the theater is, to quote Allen again, "not so great as [his] conquest of doubt and despair" (p. 94). Without rejecting other more "secular" psychological analyses, Allen shifts the emphasis to the problem of Christian despair and "the regeneration of a desperate man" which "includes in its circular scope all of the theological dicta on the genesis and cure of despair" (p. 83).

In his meticulous and sensitive study of Samson's moral growth, Arnold Stein prefers to call the process "moral re-integration" rather than "regeneration." [10] Each stage of the action is minutely examined for its nuances and promises; each line of verse is hammered out to implications of almost "ayery thinnesse." Although Samson may experience psychological ups and downs in the course of the drama, Stein holds that his moral reintegration is steadily and surely advanced through the intense pressure exerted by Samson on some fundamental questions, such as those of guilt and self-respect, political justice and divine justice, and the full facing of the self in these terms. With each encounter he acquires a new and higher degree of heroic knowledge, until, at his departure from the stage, "he looks at things human, and himself in their midst, with a clarity that penetrates and understands to the last detail, but seems to see as from a great distance. He speaks as from a distance, beyond involvement, with a cold intensity of feeling that seems beyond feeling, with an energy of mind and expression raised to a great height, yet mastered, incisive, authoritative, final, with nothing left over, no shadows, no tension." [11] Stein's study marks some kind of culmination in the attempt to understand Samson's career in this-worldly terms, to see the action as a course in the self-education of the hero, to place him on a par with the secular protagonists of Greek tragedy. Minimal stress is placed on the divine role in the process of regeneration, which to the seventeenth century, including Milton, was the only way in which the alienated soul could be restored to divine favor through the illumination of the understanding and the renovation of the will. Unless we interpret the action of *Samson* in the terms which Milton and his time accepted as marking the regeneration of fallen man, we may, it is true, devise a pattern which will lead us convincingly from the opening scenes to the final catastrophe, but it may or may not be the action Milton intended to portray. Closer attention to seventeenth-century formulations of the regeneration which Samson undergoes may promote fuller understanding of the process.

One would not willingly sacrifice any of these studies of *Samson,* even though some of them may appear to be over-ingenious and though at times the drama seems forced to yield what the critic has thought must be there. Yet each of them has increased our knowledge of the play, even if only by forcing us to renewed attention to it. The most cursory examination of the play will reveal that the Samson of the opening lines is not the same Samson who dies in glory among the choice nobility of Philistia. Something has happened to him to lift him from private ruin to public triumph, and one may call this regeneration and then proceed to define it in one's own terms. But when the regenerative process is seen as a steady psychological progress upward to higher and higher levels of heroic knowledge and insight, when it becomes almost exclusively a matter of growing inner illumination and fuller self-awareness, the text of the play itself begins to crumble under the weight of interpretation.

As an instance, the Dalila episode has been interpreted as marking a major advance in Samson's moral recovery from the despair resulting from the encounter with Manoa. His resistance to the temptation to which he had once fallen prey and his admission of guilt to the very one who had been the instrument of his fall are noted as clear evidence of his added strength and grace. But, as many have pointed out,[12] he had proclaimed his own responsibility as early as line 46, when he cautioned himself against doubting divine prediction and said, "Whom have I to complain of but my-self?" and a few lines later had admonished himself: "I must not quarrel with the will/ Of highest dispensation" (60–61). He had also confessed his guilt to both the Chorus and Manoa. Perhaps it took special courage to admit to Dalila's face his culpability and his priority in sin, but such awareness was no new thing in Samson's own con-sciousness. As for his resistance, variously interpreted as his substituting obedience for disobedience or sealing his repentance with action, could one expect anything less from the victim in the midst of his suffering faced so soon again with the external cause of his misery? It doesn't always in-dicate growth in moral stature when one refuses to touch the hot stove a second time. Is it not almost inconceivable that he should succumb again, no matter how artfully the pressures were applied? Further, one might wonder whether the savagery of his repulse of Dalila did not evidence his continued weakness, or at least his moral insecurity, rather than any major acquisition of strength. And what was Sam-son's own comment on the episode? "God sent her to de-base me,/ And aggravate my folly" (999–1000). It may be true, of course, that Samson, immersed in the situation, cannot know as fully what he has gained from the encounter as can the critic blessed with both hindsight and foresight, but it is equally apparent that some of the critical elabora-tions on the incident have gone far beyond the reasonable limits of the text. Why should Samson say that God sent her to debase him unless he felt debased, and why to ag-gravate his folly unless he felt his folly actually aggravated? —not perhaps in the *fact* of his having resisted Dalila's blandishments but by the frenetic manner in which he had done so. At least one can say that his attitude, so far as we can read it from the text, bears few of the marks of one who had just gained a significant moral victory. When I hear, then, that in this scene Samson "is walking towards purification and the right understanding of the love of God," [13] or that here "he shows himself worthy to be chosen by God once again," [14] I can only wonder whether a pattern of regeneration, preconceived, has not been pressed upon the poem rather than received from it.

The meeting with Harapha has also been seen by most critics as fraught with spiritual significance for Samson. To one, it is the moment when Samson finds his faith completely, it is the final spiritual victory, and "his soul is ripened to dwell with God." [15] To another, it is the most important scene of all, "the final event of the tragedy in miniature," for "By the victory over Harapha, who symbolizes all that is valiant in Philistia, God, working through Samson, has put Dagon down." [16] To almost all, it marks the renewal of Samson's will, his awakening from the lethargy so pronounced in earlier scenes, and it gives him the impulsion to go on and complete his destined task.

Important things do happen in this scene, but one's credulity is strained when one is asked to believe that Samson's actions represent a ripening of soul or a final event in the tragedy in miniature. As with the Chorus, Manoa, and Dalila before, Samson does confess the justice of his punishment and he does assert his confidence that God will triumph over Dagon. But this is no great advance in his spiritual effort. The two new notes that appear in the scene are his hope of pardon for past offenses (very important, though he had had the grace earlier to ask for pardon, l. 521) and his willingness to use his strength in some manner, however misdirected, in the God-Dagon contest. Hope of pardon, as contrasted with mere request for pardon, is essential to his regaining a sense of dignity and worthiness that will finally banish the earlier mood of despair. But the grotesque, almost comic aspects of the scene make one wonder whether this activation of the will has been devoted to good ends. "The challenge of muscles," as

Arnold Stein calls it,[17] is easy and refreshing for Samson because it arouses his old pride in his physical strength, the pride he had felt when, as he had said, "like a petty God/ I walk'd about admir'd of all and dreaded/ On hostile ground, none daring my affront" (529–531). It is difficult to see how one "inspired" could mistake this circus proposal (a blind man armed only with an oaken staff against a fully accoutered giant) for a chance to deliver Israel or Samson from the Philistian yoke. Even should Samson succeed in shattering the carcass of this "Tongue-doughty Giant," presumably he would still be a captive grinding in chains and Israel no better off than at present. The fact is that Samson here is on the point of confusing his willfulness with God's will, as he earlier had when he *thought* his marriage to Dalila was lawful simply because he "knew from intimate impulse" that his earlier marriage to the woman of Timna "was of God" (222–223, 231). How simple it would all be if he could find his role (and his pleasure) in just destroying one Harapha after another. The relish with which he looks forward to Harapha's "clatter'd Iron" (1124) and "shatter'd sides" (1241) does not seem the mark of the tempered, triumphant, and inspired champion of God that some critics have seen in Samson at this stage. His will to action is an important step forward, to be sure, but that will, while remaining alert and dynamic, must become more receptive to divine direction than it is in this scene. The tension in the drama, far from being relaxed by the near-emergence of the hero into beatitude, is here greatly heightened as we see Samson, now with the illuminated mind and renovated will of the regenerate man, on the verge of wasting his hard-fought spiritual gains by allowing his old warrior's blood-lust to displace the divine mission of freeing Israel in his endeavors. It may have been one of the more inscrutable of God's mercies that on this occasion he frustrated Samson's fervid desire for action in order that his will might be made more receptive and his mind more sensitive to the divine mission when the opportunity came.

From this review of two main episodes in Samson's career I hope it is evident that I am not resisting the idea of *some* kind of change and development in the character of Samson. To do so would be to deny any dramatic interest to the play, and I think it has that in abundance. My main objection is that the idea of regeneration *as it has been applied to the drama* has resulted in either an oversimplification or an oversubtilization of the action, and it remains unsatisfying because one feels an uneasy disparity between the critical conclusions and the play one reads.

The regenerative process as an informing principle of *Samson Agonistes* seems to have been utilized (a) as a means of maintaining the essentially Greek spirit of the drama against the charge, notably by Sir Richard Jebb, that it is more Hebraic than Greek, and (b) as an answer to Dr. Johnson's notorious charge, in *Rambler* 139, that the play has no middle, that "nothing passes between the first act and the last, that either hastens or delays the death of Samson." These critical maneuvers (both defensive, it is interesting to note), designed to supply a hero who was Greek as well as Christian and to fill the vacuum which Dr. Johnson abhorred, may well have produced a protagonist who is something less than Christian (and I do not mean just because he was pre-Christian) and a middle so distended that even Dr. Johnson might have been persuaded to qualify his remark.

Without denying the value of many of the critical studies referred to here, we might find it instructive to look at Milton's own definition of regeneration and consider its meaning in the light of other seventeenth-century explications of how it worked. In the *Christian Doctrine* (I, xviii; Columbia Edition, XV, 367) Milton says, "Regeneration is that change operated by the Word and the Spirit, whereby the old man being destroyed, the inward man is regenerated by God after his own image, in all the faculties of his mind, insomuch that he becomes as it were a new creature, and the whole man is sanctified both in body and soul, for the service of God, and the performance of good works." Admittedly, this is *Christian* doctrine that Milton is defining, but its relevance to the times before Christ is made explicit. Regeneration, he says, is by the Father, not by the Son, "for no one generates, except the Father." And later, discussing Saving Faith, which is one of the effects of regeneration, he stipulates that "the ultimate object of faith is not Christ the Mediator, but God the Father. . . . For the same reason it ought not to appear wonderful if many, both Jews and others, who lived before Christ, and many also who have lived since his time, but to whom he has never been revealed, should be saved by faith in God alone; still however through the sole merits of Christ, inasmuch as he was given and slain from the beginning of the world, even for those to whom he was not known, provided they believed in God the Father. Hence honorable testimony is borne to the faith of the illustrious patriarchs who lived under the law, Able [sic!], Enoch, Noah, &c. though it is expressly stated that they believed only in God" (I, xx; CE, XV, 403–405). We are justified in assuming, therefore, that to Milton the operation of the Word and Spirit in Samson's regeneration had the same form and function as a Christian operation.

Two points of this definition invite special attention. The first is that the regeneration takes place "in all the faculties of his mind," that is to say, as Milton specifies, "in understanding and will," and he goes on to point out that "this renewal of the will can mean nothing but a restoration to its former liberty" (*ibid.*, p. 371). We should underscore here *the will* as one of the faculties regenerated, and *freedom* as one of its qualities, for, says Milton *(ibid., p. 373),* "if the will of the regenerate be not made free, then we are not renewed, but compelled to embrace salvation in an unregenerate state." Whatever the mysteries involved in the problem of free will and essential grace, Milton at least clung doggedly to the position that good works could emanate only from a will acting independently, not compelled by any extraneous power, including grace. The grace might have to be bestowed before the will could be really free, but in any case true regeneration was impossible without that essential freedom.

The second point to be stressed is the purpose of the regeneration—"for the service of God, and the performance of good works." *Action* is thus seen as the end for which the understanding is illuminated and the will renewed. Without the product, the process is meaningless and abortive, and without either of the ingredients the product is impossible. This intimate, indissoluble relationship among these three elements of man's inner and outer life were basic to Milton's conception of morality. Remove any one of them and there is no effective regeneration. So much would seem to be fundamental with respect to the life of the individual human being, devoted to the service of God.

The complications become almost staggering, however, when God's Understanding, God's Will, and God's Works are brought into close relationship with those of the individual. Man's understanding must be illuminated *by* something from outside, that is, the light or mind of God, and not just something that *appears to be* the mind of God, or the morally good. The will is renewed only by being made freely responsive to the will of God, not by the mere act of willing, no matter how strongly. And the works are good only as God pronounces them good, not as they are mere actions proceeding from the will. In attempting to adjust these three elements of man's regeneration to the divine faculties, self-deception is a constant threat, since the human understanding has its own pretensions and the will its own private desires and human works their own specious glory. At any point in the equation the self may try to appear as a factor equal to God.

Milton's whole life was in one sense an attempt to establish and maintain this triple harmony with the divine life, but of all the steps in that mysterious process of regeneration, none was more fascinating, none more difficult for Milton than that of achieving a harmonious relationship between his will and the divine will. The whole history cannot be reviewed here, of course, but two periods stand out in his experience when the problem of the will seems to have been critical. One was at the time of his twenty-third birthday, after the failure of his series of religious poems so enthusiastically launched with the Nativity Ode just two years before, when he sat almost passively, wanting the grace to use his talents and awaiting the will of Heaven. The strong will to serve, evident in Elegy VI to Diodati, had been frustrated by the admitted failure of "The Passion," and it was clear that pious intentions and the exertion of the human will alone were not enough. Another occasion came just three years after his total blindness, when he conceived of his best service to God as consisting in the patient bearing of his mild yoke. It was one of the alternatives available to Samson after the Harapha encounter. But mere submission and resignation were no solution for either protagonist. Each had a talent which could not be hidden. What was required was a moment of dynamic receptivity, when the illuminated mind and the renovated will in perfect balance with the divine mind and will could use those talents in the true service of God. When Milton, faced with the alternative of patience instead of heroic action, felt his own rousing motions, his will was receptive and responsive with its full powers to what was felt to be God's will. *Paradise Lost* and *Paradise Regained* stand essentially as profound treatments of the will in its various states and relationships and functions—free and enslaved, obedient and rebellious, passive and active. And it is Milton's concern with this problem of the will in the whole process of regeneration which provides much of the drama of *Samson Agonistes* and supplies a clue to a fuller understanding of its action. A few points will have to suffice here.

Samson's initial state is as near despair and loss of faith as Don Cameron Allen has portrayed it, subject to what Milton calls the four several degrees of death, the first of which produces guiltiness, which "is accompanied or followed by terrors of conscience. . . . It is attended likewise with the sensible forfeiture of the divine protection and favor; whence results a diminution of the majesty of the human countenance, and a conscious degradation of mind. . . . Hence the whole man becomes polluted . . . whence arises shame. . . ." (*CD*, I, xii; CE, XV, 203–205). He is also suffering from the second degree of death, called spiritual death, "by which is meant the loss of divine grace, and that of innate righteousness," which "took place not only on the very day, but at the very moment of the fall" (Samson's as well as Adam's). It "consists, first, in the loss, or at least in the obscuration to a great extent of that right reason which enabled man to discern the chief good, and in which consisted as it were the life of the understanding. . . . It consists, secondly, in that deprivation of righteousness and liberty to do good, and in that slavish subjection to sin and the devil, which constitutes, as it were, the death of the will" (*ibid.;* CE, XV, 205–207). He is then the victim of both partial spiritual blindness, and paralysis of the will. Nevertheless, says Milton, even in the state of spiritual death some remnants of the divine image remain in man and the liberty of the will is not entirely destroyed; otherwise it would be difficult to vindicate the justice of God (*ibid.;* CE, XV, 209–213).

And so Samson in his state of partial spiritual blindness is not unaware that God's will *had been*, at least, that he should perform great exploits. In his present misery he descends to self-pity and comes close to blasphemy in questioning the justice of Providence for permitting this abysmal descent from the high station, "separate to God" (31), which had been foretold; but he recovers, enough at least to remind himself that "highest dispensation" (61) is not at fault but his own "impotence of mind" (52). There is some moral health in this acknowledgment, but his impotence is in his will as well as in his mind. If it *had been* God's will that he should perform heroic deeds, it could only continue to be so; this he could not see at the moment—hence, the "death" of his will to act. But he had also allowed his own will to be paralyzed by the enormity of his present suffering. When the Chorus enter they observe him "As one past hope, abandon'd,/ And by himself given over" (120–121), that is, without will and therefore without hope. In the ensuing exchange Samson questions the unequal yoking of his mean wisdom with immeasurable strength, but in his first confession to the Chorus of his guilt, it is his will which he indirectly condemns. He had married the woman of Timna against the wishes of his parents, but he knew "from intimate impulse" (223) that what he did was the will of God to begin his work of Israel's deliverance. She being unfaithful, it was then easy for Samson to interpret his own particular impulse toward Dalila as also being of God. In his pride he had identified his willfulness with the divine will. Or, as Arnold Stein puts it, "the precious, individual favor of the 'intimate impulse' [had been] rationalized in a logical analogy to indulge a 'motion' from self." [18] He has the moral strength and vision at least to admit that he himself was the prime cause of his fall, but the recognition of the defective will within him makes him fear to exercise that faculty.

The almost complete denial of the will is evident in the following scene with Manoa. Again he confesses his responsibility, not only for his private disgrace but also for the public shame to God and honor to Dagon, and with the full facing of his guilt he is content to turn the whole contest over to God and Dagon. His own will to action is close to extinction, so close that he cannot approve even his own father's offer of minor domestic solace. It has sometimes been taken as a sign of his moral growth that he refuses Manoa's offer, but his reasons for refusing—simply to "pay on my punishment" (489) and expiate if possible his crime—do not bear the marks of real renovation, and he is properly admonished by Manoa against such indulgence in suffering. He is close to total apathy. This is correctly regarded as the low point in Samson's career and it is the point at which his will is weakest. A certain degree of moral understanding is not absent, nor is repentance, which is an effect, in regenerate man, prior to faith, as Milton says (*CD*, I, xix; CE, XV, 387). But will is absent. Complete withdrawal from all action is the only thing Samson can will— and that is death, of course. He has gone through certain progressive steps in repentance—"namely, conviction of sin, contrition, confession, departure from evil, conversion to good" (*CD*, I, xix; CE, XV, 385)—but all of these, as Milton points out, "belong likewise in their respective degrees to the repentance of the unregenerate." So that these steps toward repentance do not necessarily mark the regenerate man. To repentance must be added the second effect of regeneration, which is saving faith, and this has its real source in the will: "the source from which faith originally springs, and whence it proceeds onward in its progress to good, is a genuine, though possibly in the first instance imperfect, knowledge of God, so that, properly speaking, the seat of faith is not in the understanding, but in the will" (*CD*, I, xx; CE, XV, 407). Until, then, that will is activated and faith achieved, there is the danger that the whole regenerative process may be frustrated—or may not begin at all, since the kind of mortification experienced by Samson to this point, according to Milton, "cannot be a constituent part of regeneration, inasmuch as it partly precedes it (that is to say, as corruption precedes generation) and partly follows it; in which latter capacity it belongs rather to repentance" (*CD*, I, xviii; CE, XV, 373).

It is one of the ironies of the Dalila episode that she who had been the instrument of Samson's loss of strength became a means, not of his recovery of strength, but of his recovery of a will to use that strength. His rejection of her proposal was only a negative act of will, but it *was* an exercise of will, and the chief value of the experience to Samson was not so much in moral enlightenment as in the revelation that he still had the power to act, even if it were only in the rejection of evil offered. This power is given further development in the encounter with Harapha, now in a positive fashion. Here was tangible evil, to be fought by methods with which he was familiar and with powers he knew himself still to possess, and his awakening will makes him eager to join battle. It is a nice question as to whether his returning trust in the living God stirred up this urge to action in him, or whether the confidence in his own power to act led to his affirmation of faith. The change evident in him is probably the result of the interaction of both operations. But it is clear that the stimulus offered by Harapha aroused in Samson a confidence in his own powers which enabled him to see himself, however uncertainly, as possibly God's champion and gave him a will to carry out his divinely appointed destiny as deliverer. It is probably not of primary importance that Harapha was an unworthy object of such powers. It has already been suggested that Harapha was not the key to Israel's deliverance and that Samson's repeated challenges bear strong marks of human pride. But there is in Samson, unmistakably, a *renewed will* that has regained much of its former freedom and one that is at least seeking the divine will. Sanctification has not been completely attained, however, for even after the victory over Harapha, Samson still looks on death as a possible, and not altogether undesirable, end of his present suffering. Having achieved repentance, saving faith, and a renewed will, he could still fail to reach the grand objective through his preoccupation with self and a confusion of his desires with God's intent.

And now we come to the critical point of the action. Possessed of a fresh awareness of God's continuing purposes and of a renewed will, free to act, Samson now needs only the occasion for its exercise. The Chorus suggest the alternatives open to Samson in a moving celebration of the glorious careers of those deliverers whom God invests with heroic magnitude of mind and celestial vigor to execute His errands on the wicked, followed by a suggestion that patience is more often the exercise of saints. Either way may be acceptable. This is the choice that Samson must make, and it is a choice that he is for the first time free to make.

At his first summons by the Officer to appear before the lords of Philistia, Samson chooses the way of patience—or rather, of inaction. He devises both religious and personal reasons why he "will not come," and the Officer retires for further instructions. The question of moral responsibility in the case of compulsion is discussed by the Chorus and Samson, who finally begins to realize that God's purposes are not to be confined by place or circumstance, or thwarted by human conventions and laws. He sees finally that God may use His servants for his ends even "in Temples at Idolatrous Rites." It is at this point that Samson feels the "rousing motions" which make him reverse his earlier decision. These motions have generally been regarded as the final illumination to Samson's understanding (they have been called "better thoughts" and "the inner voice"),[19] but they surely have primary meaning in terms of Samson's *response* to his enlightened mind. The very words themselves are active—"rousing," "motions." They represent an impulsion to act, a free response by his receptive but nonetheless dynamic will. It was the moment when the divine and the human will became one, and it was through the action alone, as the culminating step in the process of regeneration, that the patient saint became the heroic martyr who won for himself, as well as for us, calm of mind, all passion spent.

N O T E S

1. To simplify documentation I list here the studies to which main reference is made in the following essay: W. R. Parker, *Milton's Debt to Greek Tragedy in* Samson Agonistes (Baltimore, 1937), and "The Greek Spirit in Milton's *Samson Agonistes*," *ESEA*, XX (1935), 21–44; A. S. P. Woodhouse, "Tragic Effect in *Samson Agonistes*," *UTQ*, XXVIII (1959), and "*Samson Agonistes* and Milton's Experience," *Transactions of the Royal Society of Canada*, Ser. 3, XLIII (1949), Sect. II, 157–175; Don Cameron Allen, "The Idea as Pattern: Despair and *Samson Agonistes*," Chap. iv in *The Harmonious Vision* (Baltimore, 1954); James Holly Hanford, "*Samson Agonistes* and Milton in Old Age," in *Studies in Shakespeare, Milton and Donne* (New York, 1925), pp. 167–189; Arnold Stein, *Heroic Knowledge: An Interpretation of* Paradise Regained *and* Samson Agonistes (Minneapolis, 1957); M. M. Mahood, *Poetry and Humanism* (London, 1950); Una Ellis-Fermor, *The Frontiers of Drama* (New York, 1946); Elizabeth M. Pope, Paradise Regained: *The Tradition and the Poem* (Baltimore, 1947); F. Michael Krouse, *Milton's Samson and the Christian Tradition* (Princeton, 1949); Merritt Y. Hughes, Introduction to *Samson Agonistes*, in *John Milton: Complete Poems and Major Prose* (New York, 1957); M. E. Grenander, "*Samson's* Middle: Aristotle and Dr. Johnson," *UTQ*, XXIV (1954–55), 377–389; G. A. Wilkes, "The Interpretation of *Samson Agonistes*," *HLQ*, XXVI, 4 (August, 1963), 363–379.

2. *Milton's Debt*, p. 242.

3. *Ibid.*, p. 238.

4. Intro. to *SA*, in *John Milton*, p. 537.

5. *Poetry and Humanism*, pp. 237–238.

6. *Frontiers,* p. 32.

7. *"Samson's* Middle," p. 381.

8. Pope, *Paradise Regained,* Chap. v; Krouse, *Milton's Samson,* pp. 125–126.

9. *Vision,* pp. 87–88.

10. *Heroic Knowledge,* p. 141.

11. *Ibid.,* p. 190.

12. G. A. Wilkes is one who has taken exception to the regeneration theory, maintaining that the essential theme of the drama is "how the fallen Samson is to serve God's 'uncontroulable intent'," and that what makes the action cohere "is the sense of providence undeflected by anything in its path, making use of Samson's betrayal, his blindness, and his chains in its 'uncontroulable intent'." See "The Interpretation of *Samson Agonistes,"* pp. 370–371, 379.

13. Allen, *Vision,* p. 91.

14. Grenander, *"Samson's* Middle," p. 381.

15. Parker, *Debt,* p. 46.

16. Allen, *Vision,* p. 93.

17. *Heroic Knowledge,* p. 180.

18. *Ibid.,* p. 146.

19. See Woodhouse, "Tragic Effect," p. 212.

Murray W. Bundy

✥

Milton's Exalted Man

The theme of Milton's first epic had been "man's first disobedience," the consequences for mankind, and the promise of redemption through the Son of God, second Adam. In the sequel, *Paradise Regained,* this final victory is achieved "By one man's firm obedience fully tri'd/ Through all temptation" (I, 4–5), not, as one would expect, with the climax in the Passion, but in the encounter with Satan in the desert. As late as 1879 so little had been done to determine the meaning of the poem that it was described as "little more than a paraphrase of the temptations as found in the synoptical gospels," [1] and early in this century there were few to question that view. Fifty years ago A. H.

MURRAY W. BUNDY is Professor Emeritus of English at Washington State University.

Gilbert initiated the serious attempt to define Milton's aim by setting the temptations against the background of New Testament commentary culminating in the Reformation.[2] More recently Elizabeth M. Pope provided a useful survey of this entire tradition, enabling readers to view the poem in the light of a patristic trilogy of vices such as gluttony, avarice, and vainglory or of a Protestant analysis of distrust, idolatry, and presumption.[3]

This view is, one observes, primarily concerned with vices rather than with the virtues exhibited in resistance to them. The poet, however, was intent upon the illustration, under the conditions of the humiliation, of that Godlike behavior which justified his exaltation, both in the proclamation in *Paradise Lost*, "By Merit more than Birthright Son of God" (*PL*, III, 309), and at the end of *Paradise Regained:* "Hail, Son of the Most High, heir of both worlds." This involved, not alone "firm obedience," but a complex pattern of related virtues, explicitly named and comprehended under the title "consummate virtue."

This approach to an artistic whole of more than two thousand lines enables one to relate to the materials derived from *Luke* (and *Matthew*) many extensive passages which exemplify virtues not involved in the synoptic accounts and amplify those which are: the proclamation of God to Gabriel (I, 130–167); the initial soliloquy in the desert (I, 196–293); the debates preceding the visions on the mount (II, 406; III, 250); the conditions of the offer of the kingdoms as divorced from the temptation itself (IV, 154–194); and the tempest and dreams of the last night (IV, 394–483). It will also explain the disproportionate length of the second temptation.[4] Here Milton found the materials beginning with the banquet and extending to the vision of Athens for the elaboration of virtues peculiarly appropriate to "the Exalted Man."

A shift in emphasis from vices to virtues helps to set the poem in proper perspective as a fulfillment of plans enunciated as early as 1642. At that time Milton was seeking "what king or knight, before the conquest, might be chosen in whom to lay the pattern of a Christian hero," [5] and he suggested the suitability of the short epic in the style of Job. When, in his search for a protagonist, he asked whether the dramatic or epic form might be "more doctrinal and exemplary to a nation," he was concerned with means, not ends. The Cambridge Manuscript is the record of the fruitless search for the ideal hero, first in English history before the conquest, then in Scottish, and, finally, in the Bible. With the results of that search we are familiar: the dramatic plans for a poem on the Fall and eventually the epic. We are prone to forget that Milton had been balked in his search for a hero. *Paradise Regained* was to become not only a sequel to the longer epic but a realization of a goal, presenting as hero the new Adam, achieving by obedience and other virtues the good lost by the first protagonist. The poet was thus able to embody that full pattern of a Christian hero and to exercise poetic abilities comparable, he had written, to the office of the pulpit, "to inbreed and cherish in a great people the seeds of virtue and public civility."

Milton was a Renaissance didactic poet in the tradition of Spenser, and, like him, he sought to have "ensampled a good governour and a virtuous man," [6] and to bring in his hero "through the cave of Mammon, and the bowr of earthly blisse, that he might see and know, and yet abstain." [7] Like Spenser, he stressed the Christian virtues, and he presented vices as they involved the principles of choice. Adam, the defective hero, had made the wrong choices. Christ, in a poem which would justify the proclamation of him as Son of God, undergoes temptations, not that they may be properly designated, but that they may be seen as essential in the proving of "the Exalted Man." This was a *good* temptation, "that whereby God tempts even the righteous for the purpose of proving them, not as though he were ignorant of the disposition of their hearts, but for the purpose of exercising or manifesting their faith or patience. . . ." [8] The poem illustrates the central ethical doctrine of *Areopagitica:*

> He that can apprehend and consider vice with all her baits and seeming pleasures, and yet abstain, and yet distinguish, and yet prefer that which is truly better, he is the true wayfaring Christian.[9]

The hero of *Paradise Regained* is, to use Jeremy Taylor's title, the "Great Exemplar." In this last volume, in which *Samson Agonistes* is the companion-piece, we are asked to think of *Christus Agonistes,* in which the desert is to be Christ's "Victorious Field/ Against the Spiritual Foe" (I, 9–10) and the deeds are to be "above Heroic," God describes the contest to Gabriel as the first phase of a triumphant struggle:

> But first I mean
> To exercise him in the Wilderness.
> There he shall first lay down the rudiments
> Of his great warfare (I, 155–158).

The angelic chorus anticipates

> Victory and Triumph to the Son of God
> Now entring his great duel, not of arms,
> But to vanquish by wisdom hellish wiles.
> The Father knows the Son; therefore secure
> Ventures his filial Vertue, though untri'd,
> Against whate're may tempt, whate're seduce,
> Allure, or terrifie, or undermine (I, 173–179).

Milton might have presented this conflict in Gethsemane or on Calvary. Perhaps he had been deterred by memories of the uncompleted Passion poem, or perhaps the emphasis on Pauline doctrines had become less congenial.[10] Whatever the reason, the choice of the wilderness as the scene brought the advantage of making the evidence of "consummate virtue" follow immediately the proclamation, "This is my beloved son," at the baptism. In comparison with *Paradise Lost* the sequel gives to the theme of redemption a new dimension. The justification of the ways of God to men in the first epic, even after the dialogue of Father and Son in Book III and the philosophy of history in Book XII, is incomplete; and the paradox of a fortunate fall [11] hardly satisfies the demands of a rigorously logical theodicy. It is true that the endowment of man with free will as the condition of moral choices and the grace involved in man's redemption had been adequately set forth; but, until there is a fuller development of the nature of the Incarnate Son as he encounters the world, the flesh, and the devil, there is something arbitrary about the fiat in Heaven. For Milton it was not enough that the Son be presented as vicarious sacrifice for alienated humanity. Before the Passion he must show himself "worthy of his Birth Divine," and, in doing so, demonstrate the capacity of human nature, which in his humiliation he had assumed, to achieve atonement, not as a passive acceptance of Grace, but as the activity of regenerated man, the encounter with sin of the true warfaring Christian.[12]

This view is anticipated at one point in *Paradise Lost,* in a passage in which the past tense is anticipatory and therefore prophetic of the earthly ministry. The Father, accepting the Son as mediator of his grace, proclaims that, in fulfilling the office of Redeemer, the Son

> *hast been found*
> *By Merit more then Birthright Son of God,*
> *Found worthiest to be so by being Good,*
> *Farr more than Great or High; because in thee*

> *Love hath abounded more then Glory abounds,*
> *Therefore thy Humiliation shalt exalt*
> *With thee thy Manhood also to this throne;*
> *Here shalt thou sit Incarnate* (III, 308–315).

The language is paradoxical: the Son by his Merit, by being good under the conditions of his humiliation, will be exalted to the throne where he will "sit Incarnate."

There is a comparable view in *Paradise Regained*, the Father's speech to Gabriel:

> *this man born and now up-grown,*
> *To shew him worthy of his birth divine*
> *And high prediction, henceforth I expose*
> *To Satan* (I, 140–143).

At length, in the completed plan of Redemption, the Son will drive him back to Hell:

> *His weakness shall o'recome Satanic strength*
> *And all the world, and mass of sinful flesh;*
> *That all the Angels and Aetherial Powers,*
> *They now, and men hereafter, may discern,*
> *From what consummate vertue I have chose*
> *This perfect Man, by merit call'd my Son* (I, 161–166).

The purpose of this battle in the desert, the laying down of "the rudiments of his great warfare" before the Son is sent forth to conquer Sin and Death, is ostensibly a preliminary exercise. It is, however, primarily a justification of two proclamations, to the Angels who heard the first, and to men at the baptism who heard the second. They may discern the righteousness of the Exaltation in Heaven, against which Satan had rebelled, and that second Exaltation resulting from the humiliation, the consummate virtue of "this perfect Man, by merit call'd my Son."

For this *agon* in the desert, in which virtues encounter vices, the poet had provided a prose synopsis in *Christian*

Doctrine, Book II, entitled "The Worship of God, consisting chiefly in good works." At this point it becomes necessary, even at the risk of slight repetition later, to view portions of the first ten chapters in perspective, to indicate the main divisions, to name the virtues grouped under various headings, and to mention the vices or "opposites" by which these virtues are tested. A few virtues irrelevant to the poem will be ignored.

Of three main divisions of Book II the first deals with the general virtues of the Understanding and Will. Those of the Understanding are *Wisdom* and *Prudence* (II, ii; CE, XVII, 27). Opposed to *Wisdom* are "a false conceit of wisdom" and "human or carnal wisdom." *Prudence,* "an indispensable seasoning of every virtue," is that "by which we discern what is proper to be done under the various circumstances of time and place" (II, ii; CE, XVII, 37). The general virtues of the Will are *Sincerity* or *Integrity,* and *Constancy.* These general virtues are pervasive in *Paradise Regained.* One of them, wisdom, is the subject of intensive testing.

We turn to special virtues pertaining to the worship of God, divided into Internal or External Worship. The former, consisting "mainly in the acknowledgment of one true God, and in the cultivation of devout affections toward him," involves *"Love, Trust, Hope . . . Fear . . . Patience,* and *Obedience"* (II, iii; CE, XVII, 51). The opposites of Trust are distrust of God, an overweening presumption, carnal reliance, and a trust in idols. To the *Fear of God* are opposed carnal security and "a fear of anything except God." Patience, "whereby we acquiesce in the promises of God," has as an opposite "impatience under the divine decrees." Finally, *Obedience* is "that virtue whereby we propose to ourselves the will of God . . . and serve him alone."

Turning from Internal to External Worship, we find as

the first of two topics *Invocation or Adoration of God* (II, iv; CE, XVII, 81), a seemingly unlikely topic for development in the poem. The opposites, however, point to its pertinence: idolatry, the tempting of God (under which Milton quotes *Matt.* 4:7), and the practice of magical arts. Under External Worship, the second subject, *Sanctification of the Divine Name,* provides occasion for a chapter entitled "Zeal" (II, vi), important for the understanding of Christ's reaction to blasphemy.

The third part of Book II, concerned with our duties toward our neighbors, seems irrelevant; but the discussion provides much of the material for the treatment of the second temptation. Milton begins, as before, with general virtues (II, viii; CE, XVII, 197). These, *Love* and *Righteousness,* are exercised partly toward ourselves. Love for neighbors depends upon self-love, and righteousness demands the rendering to oneself of what is due. "The love of man toward himself consists in loving himself next to God . . ."; and "Righteousness toward ourselves consists in a proper method of self-government" (II, viii; CE, XVII, 201, 203). This egoistic center is essential to the understanding of the temptations included in the expansion of the visions on the mount. This is vital Miltonic doctrine. In 1641 he had written: "But there is yet a more ingenuous and noble degree of honest shame, or, call it, if you will, an esteem, whereby men bear an inward reverence toward their own persons." [13] After having defined this self-esteem in *Christian Doctrine* he added a sentence without which a part of *Paradise Regained* cannot be understood:

> From this, as from a fountain, the special virtues in general derive their origin; inasmuch as under the head of righteousness toward ourselves are included, first, the entire regulation of the internal affections; secondly, the discriminating pursuit of external good, and the resistance to, or patient endurance of, external evil (II, viii; CE, XVII, 203).

This division is followed in the enumeration of the special virtues. First, the internal affections to be regulated are mentioned in pairs: love—hatred, joy—sorrow, hope—fear, and anger. Second, in the discriminating pursuit of external good, there are "special virtues which regulate our desire of external advantages" (II, ix; CE, XVII, 213). Among these is *Temperance,* comprehending sobriety, chastity, and decency. It is strange that as an aspect of the last Milton names contentment, "that virtue whereby a man is inwardly satisfied with the lot assigned him by divine providence." Opposites are "anxieties respecting the necessities of life," covetousness, and "murmuring against the wisdom of God in making provision for the wants of this life."

At this point, in the midst of a paragraph, are found "the virtues more peculiarly appropriate to a high station": Lowliness of mind, with opposites of arrogance and vainglory, and Magnanimity, with opposites of an ambitious spirit and pride. It is significant for the bearing of this upon the poem that there is allusion here to the example "of Christ in rejecting the empire of the world" (II, ix; CE, XVII, 235–243).

The third division of special virtues derived from self-esteem, concerned with "the resistance to, or the endurance of evil," names Fortitude, with opposites of timidity and rashness, and Patience, with opposites, among others, of impatience and a "stoical apathy" (II, x; CE, XVII, 247–253).

This is the prose pattern of the Christian hero from which Milton shaped *Paradise Regained.* The Son of God, second Adam, exemplifying, in his encounter, firm obedience and related virtues described in *Christian Doctrine*— Wisdom, Trust, Zeal, Lowliness of mind, Magnanimity, Patience, to mention some of them—lays down in the wilderness "the rudiments of his great warfare."

The first temptation involves both love and trust, virtues

of internal worship. *"The love of God* is that by which we prefer him above all other objects of affection, and desire his glory"; and trust, considered as an effect of love, is "that whereby we wholly repose on him" (II, iii; CE, XVII, 51, 53). In reply to Satan's contrast of the testimony of John at the baptism with the situation in the desert, the Son simply affirms trust: "Who brought me hither/ Will bring me hence . . ." (I, 335–336). The temptation to turn stones into bread invites a miracle which would imply doubt, distrust of the proclamation at the Jordan, and, as irrelevant, provision of food for others in an uninhabited desert. The reply is a noteworthy expansion of *Luke:*

> *is it not written*
> *(For I discern thee other than thou seem'st)*
> *Man lives not by Bread only, but each Word*
> *Proceeding from the mouth of God, who fed*
> *Our Fathers here with Manna?* (I, 347–351).

The completion of *Deut.* 8:3 and the identification of "this barren waste" with the scene of the fasts, also of forty days, of Moses and Elijah, invite comparison of the trust and obedience of these three with the distrust and disobedience of the children of Israel, who, after having been fed with manna, were rebuked by Moses. God could have performed a miracle in the desert again, but for the Son to have done so would have been a questioning of his reliance upon the Father: "I can of myself do nothing." "Why dost thou then suggest to me distrust,/ Knowing who I am . . ." (I, 355–356).

The remainder of Book I, after this expansion of the first temptation, continues the illustration of virtues belonging to the worship of God by introducing the theme of wisdom, a general virtue of the Understanding. The adversary pleads his obedience to God in having tested both Job and Ahab and now in testing the Son of God, his love having led him to contemplate the excellence of the Savior, and his "love of neighbor" having impelled him to aid mankind "by presages and signs/ And answers, oracles, portents and dreams" (I, 394–395). Satan affects love both of God and neighbor, a travesty of the Miltonic pattern.

A wise Savior instantly detects the lies and sophistry in this, the first of the long debates. Satan, he replies, had been permitted to test patient Job, a "good" temptation not to be confused with the "bad" temptation of Ahab, in which he was "a liar in four hundred mouths." This distinction introduces a sharp contrast between Job's perfect trust and its opposite, "a trust in idols," described in *Christian Doctrine* both as idolatry and the practice of magical arts. In Milton's view of history under the old covenant this reliance upon oracles, which is distrust of God, was idolatry:

> *For God hath justly giv'n the Nations up*
> *To thy Delusions; justly, since they fell*
> *Idolatrous* (I, 442–444).

"Henceforth Oracles are ceast" (I, 456), and one of the themes of the "Nativity Ode" assumes its full significance as the Son proclaims: "God hath now sent his living Oracle/ Into the World, to teach his final will . . ." (I, 460–461).

The second temptation, with related materials, extending from II, 302 to IV, 364, nearly half of the poem, is a development of the themes of self-love and self-esteem.[14] Here the poet exemplifies at length those three aspects of the latter already mentioned: the regulation of the affections, the discriminating pursuit of external good, and the resistance to, or patient endurance of, evil.[15] At the center of the poem and its apex, Milton weaves about the scriptural visions of the mount a proffered banquet, long debates, and the vision of Athens as developments of the main theme, the consummate virtue of "this perfect Man, by merit call'd my Son." In the exhibition of virtues derived from a proper self-esteem, the Son of God fulfills the paradoxical prediction that the humiliation will exalt his manhood to the throne, that the victory under the conditions of the incarnation will be a second justification of God's ways to men, proving through temptation that by "being good" he merited that exaltation. Here will be found the chief virtues defined in the prose: wisdom and prudence, sincerity and constancy, zeal, temperance, moderation, lowliness of mind, and magnanimity, fortitude and patience.

Temperance is first tested when Satan proffers a banquet as rightly due to the Son of God, the homage of nature to the Exalted Man. The virtue is explicitly denoted:

> *To whom thus Jesus* temperately [16] *reply'd:*
> *Said'st thou not that to all things I had right?*
> *And who withholds my pow'r that right to use?*
> *Shall I receive by gift what of my own,*
> *When and where likes me best, I can command?* (II, 378–382).

In this avoidance of "the acceptance of riches, advantages, or honors" he also illustrates magnanimity, having been "actuated by a regard to [his] own dignity, rightly understood."

At this point one would have anticipated the testing of chastity as an aspect of temperance; but, as many have observed, the poet has already eliminated it: Belial's proposal, "Put women in his eye," had been met by Satan's scornful rejection. In the dismissal, however, it should be observed that the stress is upon the virtues. Sensuality would have been beneath the notice of one both wise and magnanimous: "wiser far/ Than *Solomon,* of more exalted mind" (II, 205–206).

The action proceeds to the trial of contentment, "that virtue whereby a man is inwardly satisfied with the lot assigned him. . . . Poverty is not to be accounted a disgrace. . . . We are forbidden to glory in riches, or to put our confidence in them" (II, ix; CE, XVII, 223–227). The opposites or vices are anxieties concerning the necessaries of life, covetousness, and "a murmuring against the wisdom of God in making provision for the wants of this life." All of this is implied in Satan's assault upon contentment:

> *Great acts require great means of enterprise,*
> *Thou art unknown, unfriended, low of birth,*
> *A Carpenter thy Father known, thy self*
> *Bred up in poverty and streights at home;*
> . . . .
> *Get Riches first, get Wealth, and Treasure heap* (II, 412–427).

The reply brings together the virtues explicitly named in the prose as issuing from self-esteem:

> *Yet he who reigns within himself, and rules*
> *Passions, Desires, and Fears, is more a King;*
> *Which every wise and vertuous man attains* (II, 466–468).

Here the three nouns designate the three realms in which self-government can be disturbed: the affections, the pursuit of external good, and the endurance of external evil. Milton is obviously following his prose pattern.

Like Spenser, having brought his hero through the cave of Mammon and the Bower of Bliss (but in the reverse order), he makes this speech on the true King the transition to Book III, which will be concerned with virtues "more peculiarly appropriate to a high station." Now, at the very end of Book II, in anticipation of the treatment of these virtues, we hear a paradox which will pervade the remainder of the poem:

> *Besides to give a Kingdom hath been thought*
> *Greater and nobler done, and to lay down*
> *Far more magnanimous, then to assume* (II, 481–483).

"Lowliness of mind," Milton had written, "consists in thinking humbly of ourselves, and in abstaining from self-commendation, except where occasion requires it" (II, ix; CE, XVII, 235). To this were opposed arrogance, a desire of vainglory, and boasting. "Magnanimity is shown, when in . . . the acceptance or refusal of riches, advantages, or honors, we are actuated by a regard to our own dignity, rightly understood" (II, ix; CE, XVII, 241).[17] To this were opposed an ambitious spirit and pride.

In the debate at the beginning of Book III Satan uses arrogance and vainglory as means of assailing lowliness of mind, and ambition and pride in tempting magnanimity. He appeals to arrogance first through flattery:

> *Thy actions to thy words accord, thy words*
> *To thy large heart give utterance due, thy heart*
> *Contains of good, wise, just, the perfect shape* (III, 9–11).

Attacking humility and abstinence from self-commendation, he subtly suggests:

> *wherefore deprive*
> *All Earth her wonder at thy acts, thy self*
> *The fame and glory, glory the reward*
> *That sole excites to high attempts the flame*
> *Of most erected Spirits?* (III, 23–27).

To all of this "our Savior calmly replied," and vainglory is dismissed as "the blaze of fame," dependent only on popular favor. Once more we hear the familiar theme, "Fame is no plant that grows on mortal soil." Glory is not to be sought by conquest and the applause of conquerors, who "swell with pride and must be titl'd Gods."

> *It may by means far different be attain'd*
> *Without ambition, war, or violence;*
> *By deeds of peace, by wisdom eminent,*
> *By patience, temperance* (III, 89–92).

This magnanimous protagonist, "actuated by a regard to [his] own dignity," concludes: "I seek not mine, but his/

Who sent me, and thereby witness whence I am" (III, 106–107).

This rejection of glory leads Satan to shift his attack: the Father, whom the Son had just invoked, not "content in Heav'n by all his angels glorified," requires glory from men. In rejecting glory, Satan insinuates, the Son least resembles the Father. This is blasphemy, and it elicits the zeal of the Son, described as "an ardent desire of hallowing the name of God . . . ," adequately introduced here: "To whom our Saviour fervently reply'd" (III, 121). The adverb again furnishes the cue.

We are told that Satan "yet of another Plea besought him soon" (III, 149). To explain his tactics we must continue with the chapter on "Zeal"; one of the opposites of zeal was a "too fiery zeal." Satan attempts to divert a righteous zeal into a vicious extreme: since "to a Kingdom thou art born," and the time is ripe,

> *If Kingdom move thee not, let move thee Zeal,*
> *And Duty; Zeal and Duty are not slow;*
>
> . . . .
>
> *Zeal of thy Father's house, Duty to free*
> *Thy Country from her Heathen servitude* (III, 171–176).

The virtue requisite at this moment is patience: "All things are best fullfil'd in their due time,/ And time there is for all things" (III, 182–183). Combined with this are trust and obedience under the conditions of the humiliation:

> *What if he hath decreed that I shall first*
> *Be try'd in humble state, and things adverse,*
> *By tribulations, injuries, insults,*
> *Contempts, and scorns, and snares, and violence,*
> *Suffering, abstaining, quietly expecting*
> *Without distrust or doubt, that he may know*
> *What I can suffer, how obey? who best*
> *Can suffer, best can do; best reign, who first*
> *Well hath obey'd; just tryal e're I merit*
> *My exaltation* (III, 188–197).

The experience on the mount repeats the themes of the debates in visual terms. The *agon* has been presented in the medium of rhetoric, which, in comparison with poetry, Milton had written, is "more subtle and fine," and he turns now to materials closer to poetry, "more simple, sensuous, and passionate." To understand Satan's appeal in terms of sensory impressions, it is necessary to be aware of a psychology of temptation familiar to Milton and already used in *Paradise Lost*. The Devil can insinuate evil imaginations through his knowledge of the thoughts and especially the images already present in the mind of his intended victim. These he can transform into provocative dreams and visions. He had been successful in fashioning Eve's dream and making it an essential prelude to the Fall.[18] He also knew what Jesus had been contemplating in the soliloquy in the desert:

> *To rescue* Israel *from the* Roman *yoke,*
> *Then to subdue and quell o're all the earth*
> *Brute violence and proud Tyrannick pow'r,*
> *Till truth were freed, and equity restor'd:*
> *Yet held it more humane, more heavenly first*
> *By winning words to conquer willing hearts,*
> *And make perswasion do the work of fear* (I, 217–223).

The three visions on the mount are attempts to pervert these three aims. The rescue of Israel from the Roman yoke, through taking sides in the Roman-Parthian conflict, would tempt to carnal reliance. The subduing of violence and tyrannic power, by the supplanting of Tiberius, would lead to pride and ambition. The making of persuasion do the work of fear would through the vision of Athens lead to human or carnal wisdom. Temptation, Milton knew, often lies in the perversion of legitimate goals. In all of this not only lowliness of mind and magnanimity will again be assailed, but also temperance, contentment, obedience, and that "better fortitude of patience."

The first temptation, to help the Parthians against the Romans, suggesting ambition and violence, the Savior calls "much ostentation vain of fleshly arm" (III, 387), and, tempted both to "carnal reliance" and "imprudent zeal," in fulfilling prophecy, he asserts both complete trust in God and patience: "My time . . . is not yet come" (III, 396–397). The second temptation, to unseat Tiberius, with further appeals to imprudent zeal, pride, and ambition, is met by an "unmov'd" Son of God:

> *Nor doth this grandeur and majestic show*
> *Of luxury, though call'd magnificence,*
> *More than of arms before, allure mine eye,*
> *Much less my mind* (IV, 110–113).

This expansion of synoptic materials, involving carnal reliance, imprudent zeal, vainglory, ambition, and pride, necessarily less explicit in naming the vices than the preceding debates, serves again to illustrate trust, obedience, and related virtues, but in particular that patience to wait for the time of fulfillment: "when my season comes to sit / On *David's* throne" (IV, 146–147).

At this point Milton took a surprising liberty which has elicited little comment: only after the offer of the kingdoms has been rejected does an impudent tempter name the condition, "if thou wilt fall down, / And worship me as thy superior Lord" (IV, 166–167). Why this isolation of the condition from the gift? The answer may lie in the poet's addition to *Luke,* "as thy superior Lord," providing a second occasion for an emphasis on trust and one of its opposites, idolatry, the worship of anything save God. A second explanation lies in the occasion for another display of zeal in the presence of blasphemy. Satan had dared "to the Son of God to propound / To worship thee accurs'd" (IV, 178–179). It is *with disdain* (always indicating in Milton strong aversion) that the Savior pronounces him more accurst "For this attempt bolder than that on *Eve,*/ And more blasphemous" (IV, 180–181). In the garden he had tempted Eve from true worship to the adoration of a tree, both idolatry and blasphemy. In the desert he is bolder, as the blasphemy lies in the offer, "To me my own, on such abhorred pact,/ That I fall down and worship thee as God." Zeal achieves its climax: "Get thee behind me," and the Adversary stands unmasked, "That Evil One, Satan forever damn'd." [19] The poem as a tragedy of the antagonist is nearing its catastrophe.

Thus the offer of the kingdoms is separated from that of Athens: "Be famous then by wisdom." This last vision is, if we accept Satan's statement, a trial whether in higher sort than angels or men Christ may be called the Son of God, and it is a step toward the testing of the third day of his nature as higher than that of perfect man. It is not primarily a temptation to seek wisdom, but to pervert the aim of the Son "to make perswasion do the work of fear." As such it is the culmination of Milton's presentation of wisdom as a divine attribute. "Wisdom," he had written, "is that whereby we earnestly seek after the will of God . . . ," and to this he had opposed "human or carnal wisdom." As a general virtue of the understanding it is therefore a counterpart of Obedience, "whereby we propose to ourselves the will of God as the paramount rule of our conduct . . ." (II, iii; CE, XVII, 69). These two complementary themes, knowing and doing the will of God, run through the poem like *motifs* in a symphony. At the outset Satan had viewed his adversary as one who in youth had displayed "all vertue, grace, and wisdom" (I, 68). After the proclamation in heaven, the angels had sung of him as "Now entring his great duel, not of arms,/ But to vanquish by wisdom hellish wiles" (I, 174–175). Now wisdom is to be lifted to a transcendent plane as an aspect of consummate virtue of one who is more than mere man. Can it, under the conditions of the Incarnation, rely in part or rely at all upon its human or carnal counterpart?

In *Paradise Lost* Eve succumbed to Satan's sophistry in praise of this lower wisdom. In the dream she had been invited to taste of the tree of knowledge and "be henceforth among the Gods/ Thyself a Goddess" (V, 77–78), and after her fall she adores this tree "of operation blest/ To Sapience" (IX, 796–797). Adam partook with her, fondly overcome by female charm, and having preferred her to Heavenly wisdom:

> *All higher knowledge in her presence falls*
> *Degraded, Wisdom in discourse with her*
> *Looses discount 'nanc'd and like folly shews* (VIII, 551–553).

After Adam's participation, he praises Eve as "exact of taste,/ And elegant, of Sapience no small part" (IX, 1017–1018).

The shorter epic records a comparable testing of wisdom (and obedience) by the subtle presentation to the Son of the virtues of that tree of Sapience before which Eve had bowed in adoration, that tree before which her sons and daughters had continued obeisance, and at no time more heartily than in the Renaissance. Milton had known the attractiveness of this "human or carnal wisdom," and he could now write out of a lifetime of experience as he presents Satan's distortion of the aim of the Son "to make perswasion do the work of fear":

> *Ruling them by perswasion as thou means't,*
> *Without thir learning how wilt thou with them,*
> *Or they with thee hold conversation meet?*
> *How wilt thou reason with them, how refute*
> *Thir Idolisms, Traditions, Paradoxes?* (IV, 230–234).

With eloquence Satan extols Greek poetry, oratory, and philosophy as means to this end. It is one of the great statements of the claims of classical learning as ancillary to the Renaissance ideal of humanism. We mistake the purpose, however, if we take it out of context to make the Son's reply a repudiation by Milton of the value of his years of study. Here it is presented as temptation to a Savior who had described his ideal king as "he who reigns within himself" and relies wholly upon knowing the will of God, wisdom, and doing that will, obedience. Satan is attempting to divert that aim by offering secular wisdom as necessary: "These rules will render thee a King compleat/ Within thy self, much more with Empire joyn'd" (IV, 283–284).

"To whom our Saviour sagely thus reply'd": once more the virtue is stressed through the adverb. "He who receives light from above" is contrasted, not with those conversant with classical literature but with those who rely on Greek philosophy from Socrates, "the first and wisest of them all," to the Stoic, whose virtuous man

> Wise, perfect in himself, and all possessing
> Equal to God, oft shames not to prefer,
> As fearing God nor man (IV, 302–304).

The indictment closes with the lines, "Who therefore seeks in these/ True wisdom, finds her not. . . ." Then follows the preference of Hebrew poetry and prophecy to the poetry and oratory of Greece and Rome, a theme not related to the contrast of a higher with a lower wisdom, but significantly expanding Milton's own preference expressed in *Paradise Lost* (III, 26–32).

The action shifts from the mount to the wilderness, to darkness, a tempest, ugly dreams and "grisly Spectres, which the Fiend had rais'd/ To tempt the Son of God with terrors dire" (IV, 430–431). A patient Son stands unshaken. Milton now illustrates the third group of virtues derived from self-esteem as from a fountain, those concerned with "the resistance to or patient endurance of external evil," fortitude and patience. In *Christian Doctrine,* after characterizing fortitude as "chiefly conspicuous in repelling evil, or in regarding its approach with equanimity," he had added: "The great pattern of Fortitude is our Saviour Jesus Christ . . ." (II, ii; CE, XVII, 249). Patience he defined as "the endurance of misfortunes and injuries." In answer to Satan's explanation that these terrors, voices, and prodigies had been sent to warn him, he contemns them "as false portents, sent not from God, but thee."

With this the temptations of all of the qualities comprehended as "consummate virtue" have been completed. At least, Satan said so, and I think that for once we may believe him. He had found the Savior "Proof against all temptation as a rock/ Of Adamant . . ." (IV, 533-534).

We must agree with Gilbert, Tillyard, Miss Pope, and others that Milton has represented the last temptation in *Luke* as something quite different from the first and second. The explanation of the Protestant commentators is at first glance attractive, that presumption is the sin which neatly balances the distrust in the desert. (Milton regarded both as opposites of trust.) The poem would thus achieve a kind of symmetry, with two temptations of trust enclosing the visions on the mount. It is also true that under "Overweening Presumption" in *Christian Doctrine* he had quoted "Tempt not the Lord thy God" among the proof-passages. It is more important to observe that the other scriptural citations under this heading refer only to the reprobate. For the poet to have regarded Jesus as susceptible to such a temptation is doubtful. For him to have regarded Satan in his rage as presumptuous is more likely. We may also reject as untenable the assumption of patristic writers that the Son in quoting "Tempt not the Lord thy God" was referring to himself. For Milton to have accepted this interpretation would have involved an amazing simplification of a problem to which he had devoted his longest chapter in Book I of *Christian Doctrine.*

It is better to accept Satan's assertion that he had found Jesus "firm/ To the utmost of meer man both wise and good" (IV, 534–535). "Desperate of better course, resolved to vent his rage," he would "know what more thou art than man/ Worth naming Son of God by voice from Heav'n . . ." (IV, 538–539). It is not the poet but Satan who undertakes the inquiry, and in an act of violence he catches up the Son and sets him upon the pinnacle of the temple:

> *There stand, if thou wilt stand; to stand upright*
> *Will ask thee skill. . . .*
> *. . . . . if not to stand,*
> *Cast thyself down; safely if Son of God* (IV, 551–555).

This is a surprising expansion of *Luke:* Satan here presents alternatives, to stand or to fall, and neither is a test of the divine rather than the human nature of Christ. The one "will ask thee skill," hardly a divine attribute, and the other requires complete trust of the Son as man in the promises of God. The theme of the tempting of virtues had been completed, and Satan has no knowledge by which to test the divine nature. This is no temptation.

It is, however, a highly effective end of the heroic encounter. "Tempt not the Lord thy God, he said and stood./ But Satan smitten with amazement fell . . ." (IV, 561–562). Milton may have had in mind Bullinger's comment in recording Satan's fall:

> Brevis est responsio, sed divinissima et iccirco validissima quoque, qua ita in gyrum contortus ac prostratus corruit satanas, ut in praesenti nihil habuerit quod opponeret, sed e palestra victus excederet protinus.[20]

The adoption of Luke's order provided the fitting climax of the combat in which the symbolic exaltation of the victor on the pinnacle is accompanied by the symbolic fall of the antagonist.

NOTES

1. Mark Pattison, *Milton* (London [1879], 1926), p. 191.

2. A. H. Gilbert, "The Temptation in *Paradise Regained,*" *JEGP,* XV (1916), 599–611.

3. Elizabeth M. Pope, *Paradise Regained: the Tradition and the Poem* (Baltimore, 1947).

4. See E. M. W. Tillyard, *Milton* (London, 1946), p. 323. He assigns 320 lines (I, 183–502) to the first temptation, 1081 (II, 242–IV, 393) to the second, and 187 (IV, 394–580) to the third. I would reduce all three, especially the first and third, making the disproportion greater.

5. *The Reason of Church Government,* in *The Works of John Milton,* ed. F. A. Patterson, 18 vols. (New York, 1932–1938), III, pt. 1, 237, hereafter cited in the text as CE.

6. *Faerie Queene,* Letter to Sir Walter Raleigh.

7. CE, IV, 311.

8. *Christian Doctrine,* I, viii; CE, XV, 87. Subsequent citations of the prose are to *Christian Doctrine* unless otherwise indicated.

9. CE, XV, 87.

10. See Tillyard, *op. cit.,* p. 305; ". . . for the plain fact is that Christ is no longer in the main the Redeemer of man. . . . The Pauline fabric of fall, grace, redemption and regeneration, seems to have crumbled."

11. A. O. Lovejoy, "Milton and the Paradox of the Fortunate Fall," in *ELH,* IV (1937), 161–179.

12. Tillyard (*op. cit.,* 317 fn.) commenting on R. L. Ramsay, "Morality Themes in Milton's Poetry," writes that "The debate between Christ and Satan could be compared with the struggle between the Virtues and the Vices." Unfortunately, the theme is never developed. Miss Pope (*op. cit.,* p. 29) denies to the temptations "an exemplary function." Subsequent studies such as that of Frank Kermode, "Milton's Hero" (*RES,* n.s. IV [1953], 317–330) and A. S. P. Woodhouse, "Theme and Pattern in *Paradise Regained*" (*UTQ,* XXV [1956], 167–182) mention virtues exemplified by Christ without attempting to set them against the pattern of *Christian Doctrine,* Book II. Northrop Frye, "The Typology of *Paradise Regained*" (*MP,* LIII [1953], 227–238) emphasizes virtues having their counterparts in classical and Biblical heroes; and this is in part the approach in the most recent volume dealing with the poem, Barbara Kiefer Lewalski, *Milton's Brief Epic* (Providence, R.I., 1966), henceforth indispensable. This approach to the virtues of Christ in Chapter IX, "Kingship over the Self," should be compared with that set forth here. Magnanimity may derive from Aristotle, patience from Job, and wisdom from

Socrates, but hardly Milton's temperance from "stoical apathy."

13. *The Reason of Church Government,* CE, III, pt. 1, 260.

14. See above, p. 205.

15. In PR, IV, 300–308, Stoicism is condemned, and in the poem up to IV, 499 Satan often exhibits "stoical apathy." There is no ground for the assumption of Christ's (or Milton's) Stoicism.

16. Italics mine. Cf. "sternly" (I, 406), "patiently" (II, 432), "Calmly" (III, 43), "fervently" (III, 121), "unmov'd" (III, 386 and IV, 109), and "sagely" (IV, 285).

17. Cf. M. Y. Hughes, "The Christ of *Paradise Regained* and the Renaissance Heroic Tradition," in *SP,* XXXV (1938), 254–277. This view of Christ as the magnanimous man, derived from Aristotle through Spenser, can stand, in a study of a poet such as Milton, side by side with this interpretation based on *CD.*

18. See my "Eve's Dream and the Temptation in *Paradise Lost,*" in *Research Studies of the State College of Washington,* X (1942), 280.

19. For zeal as the response to blasphemy see Heinrich Bullinger, *Novi testam, historia Evangelica* (Tiguri [Zurich], 1554), p. 44: "Principio abigit Satanam totus divino commotus zelo, dicens ὕπαγε Σατανᾶ, quod stomachum habet, perinde ac cum nos dicimus, *Heb dich Tüfel:* hoc ipso docens nunquam dissimulandam esse dei blasphemiam et ignominiam, tametsi ad privatem tuam iniuriam sis alias patientissimus.

20. Bullinger, *op. cit.,* p. 43.

Emmett L. Avery

୶ଽ ଽ୶

Rhetorical Patterns in
Restoration Prologues
and Epilogues

When the London theaters reopened in 1660, they inherited the conception of the prologue and epilogue as
proper frameworks for a dramatic performance, and both
soon became almost obligatory accompaniments to the day's
play. Theoretically, the prologue or epilogue might treat
any subject in any fashion, but traditionally the prologue,
especially that to a new play, urged the audience to receive it with a judicial air. As the Prologue to Aphra Behn's
The Amorous Prince (ca. 24 February 1670/1) stated:
"Well! you expect a Prologue to the Play,/ And you expect
it too Petition-way." The epilogue, under the handicap of
having been written before the verdict on the play was

EMMETT L. AVERY is Professor of English at Washington State University.

known, had the delicate problem of appealing to the audience for applause. In practice, although many approaches and devices were employed to relieve the tedium of the formal tradition, both prologue and epilogue retained these functions for many decades. These poems soon posed for dramatic authors genuine problems of attaining originality within a set form.

Had prologues and epilogues been confined to the first performance of a drama (some four hundred new plays were staged between 1660 and 1700), the strain upon the inventiveness of writers would perhaps have been only moderately severe, but the fact that audiences expected these poetic essays at old plays and upon special occasions obligated authors to seek freshness of theme or of approach. As is well known, authors varied the subject matter by making prologues and epilogues into forums for the discussion of literary topics (as Dryden often did) or topical events (as many authors did during the political disturbances of the 1680's); some authors varied the presentation by having the poems sung as ballads or recited by two or three speakers or by children.

It is with their primary functions, however—inviting the audience to welcome a play and wheedling a warm reception—that the prologue and epilogue in time created the most difficult rhetorical problems for their authors, for, as the Prologue to Settle's *Pastor Fido* (*ca.* December, 1676) lamented: "*Preface* and *Prologue,* are such modish Toys,/ Books ar'nt without *this,* nor without *that* Plays." In these circumstances, writers often emphasized the difficulty of attaining originality, a point stressed in the Prologue to Sir Robert Howard's *The Surprizal* (23 April 1662):

> *Since you expect a Prologue, we submit:*
> *But let me tell you, this Excise on Wit,*
> *Though undiscern'd, consumes the Stock so fast,*
> *That no new Phancy will be left at last.*[1]

The Epilogue to *Oroonoko,* November, 1695, summarized the general policy of the poets:

> *You see we try all Shapes, and Shifts, and Arts,*
> *To tempt your Favours, and regain your Hearts.*
> *We weep, and laugh, join Mirth and Grief together,*
> *Like Rain and Sunshine mixt, in April Weather.*
> *Your different Tasts divide our Poet's Cares:*
> *One Foot the Sock, t'other the Buskin wears.*

Faced with the problem of creating freshness within a formalized pattern, the poets sought variations within the rather loose form of the prologue and epilogue. In length the poems varied from fifteen lines to sixty or more and usually were written in heroic couplets (with a generous helping of triple rhymes); often, in imitation of colloquial speech, an occasional line might have only two to four syllables. These poems generally had no set pattern by which the ideas must necessarily be organized. Therefore, the poet often appealed to the spectators by rhetorical devices which would satisfy the traditional purpose but which would also offer a new and, hopefully, an engaging image or comparison. One pattern which proved most attractive to writers was a somewhat involved comparison between the poet (coupled with the actor who spoke the poem) and the audience.[2] If the author could create a witty, clever, and amusing comparison or figure of speech, he would entertain the audience while he sought a sympathetic response. From the almost infinite variety of occupations, professions, and human ventures, the poet sought a conceit which was apt but which was also witty, cogent, fanciful, and surprising. These comparisons, for example, might come from the military, legal, mercantile, or political realms. In this paper I wish to examine some of the principal rhetorical patterns which the writers of prologues and epilogues devised.

The poet or player introducing a new drama to an expectant but unpredictable audience bore, for example, a resemblance to a pilot, captain, or merchant-adventurer at sea. Because the dramatists often thought of themselves as facing a hostile audience (the wits, the critics, the young Templars), they visualized themselves as being at a gross disadvantage in the stormy tempests of the playhouse. The Epilogue to *The Squire of Alsatia*, May, 1688, characterized the plight of the poet in these terms:

> *Ye mighty scowrers [the critics] of these narrow Seas*
> *Who suffer not a Bark to sail in peace,*
> *But with your Tire of Culverins ye roar,*
> *Bring 'em by th' Lee, and Rummidge all their store;*
> *Our Poet duck'd, and look'd as if half dead,*
> *At every Shot that whistled o're his Head.*
> *Frequent Engagements ne're could make him bold.*

Staging *The Libertine*, June, 1675, Shadwell in the Prologue limited the comparison to the merchant-adventurer who, like the poet, hopes to salvage something from the wrath before him:

> *Remorsless as a Storm on us you fall:*
> *But as a Merchant, when by Storms distress'd,*
> *Flings out his bulkey Goods to save the rest,*
> *Hoping a Calm may come, he keeps the best.*
> *In this black Tempest which o'r us impends,*
> *Near Rocks and Quicksands, and no Ports of Friends,*
> *Our Poet gives this over to your rage.*[3]

In the Prologue to Mrs. Behn's *The Widow Ranter*, 20 November, 1689, the author used concreteness of detail in the play as parallels to merchandising from foreign lands:

> *Plays you will have; and to supply your Store,*
> *Our Poets trade to ev'ry Foreign Shore:*
> *This is the Product of Virginian Ground,*
> *And to the Port of Covent-Garden bound.*
> *Our Cargo is, or should at least, be Wit:*

Bless us from you damn'd Pyrates of the Pit;
And Vizard-Masks, those dreadful Apparitions;
She-Privateers, of Venomous Conditions,
That clap us oft aboard with French Commissions.

Another popular comparison was to the military. This figure of speech, also, was capable of considerable variation, for the poet might be like a soldier tested in battle, his prologue might be compared to the initial skirmish in a military engagement, or the poet and players might be considered brave or cowardly soldiers. One of these approaches was developed in the Prologue to Sir Robert Howard's *The Vestal Virgin, ca.* February, 1665: "Prologues, like Forlorn-Hopes, first face the Stage,/ Before the main Battalions do engage." Dryden, in the Prologue to *Secret Love,* February, 1667, developed a somewhat elaborate comparison of plays to fortified towns, poets to valiant defending soldiers, and the audience to a besieging force:

Plays are like Towns, which howe're fortifi'd
By Engineers, have still some weaker side
By the o'reseen Defendant uneaspy'd.

And with that Art you make approaches now;
Such skilful fury in Assaults you show,
That every Poet without shame may bow.

Ours therefore humbly would attend your doom,
If Souldier-like, he may have termes to come
With flying colours, and with beat of Drum.

The poet may be an individual, potentially brave or cowardly, as he advances with his play against the phalanxes of the audience, as in the Prologue to *Sertorius, ca.* March, 1679:

As Cowards pusht into a desperate fight
Move slowly forwards like their appetite;
Yet when they feel the blows, fill'd with despair,

> *Oft beat the brave, or battel with the Air;*
> *So our Gallant forc'd by his Friends to write,*
> *Now dreads his Fate which must be known this Night;*
> *Storm'd by his Friends they swore him into rage,*
> *And forc'd him fight the Hydra of the Stage.*

In a mock-heroic vein touching upon the political quarrels of the 1680's, the Prologue to D'Urfey's *The Commonwealth of Women* was spoken by Joe Haynes who, "with a Western Scyth in his Hand," came from the West "as Champion in defence of Wit,/ . . . to mow your Critticks of the Pit."

Somewhat closely related to the figure of the military is a comparison of the poet and player to components of the political society: sovereigns, subjects, the state. Sometimes the audience is the king, the poet a petitioning subject; the Prologue to Payne's *Fatal Jealousie,* 3 August 1672, compares the dramatists and actors to subjects before the "great Sovereign Wits . . . the Stages Kings." In the Prologue to *The Spanish Fryar,* ca. 1 November 1680, Dryden developed a similar comparison:

> *Honour is yours:*
> *And you, like Kings, at City Treats bestow it;*
> *The Writer kneels, and is bid rise a Poet:*
> *But you are fickle Sovereigns, to our Sorrow,*
> *You dubb to day, and hang a man tomorrow.*

In the Prologue to *The Loyal Brother,* 4 February 1682, Dryden reversed the comparison: "Poets, like Lawfull Monarchs, rul'd the Stage,/ Till Criticks, like Damn'd Whiggs, debauch'd our Age." Occasionally the subject matter of the play made the comparison doubly appropriate, as in John Caryll's Epilogue to *The English Princess,* 7 March 1666/7:

> *Richard is dead; and now begins your Reign:*
> *Let not the Tyrant live in you again. . . .*
> *First then, by Acts of Grace your Power declare:*

> *Newly install'd, all Princes gracious are;*
> *All lesser Crimes within their Pardon fall;*
> *And Poets Sins are not held Capital.*

As a variation on the theme of political power, the Prologue
to Dryden's *Love Triumphant, ca.* January, 1694, developed
at length a comparison between the poet leaving the stage
and an officer relinquishing his post in civil affairs:

> *As when some Treasurer lays down the Stick;*
> *Warrants are Sign'd for ready Mony thick:*
> *And many desperate Debentures paid;*
> *Which never had been, had his Lordship staid:*
> *So now, this Poet, who forsakes the Stage,*
> *Intends to gratifie the present Age.*
> *The Warrant shall be Sign'd for every Man;*
> *All shall be Wits that will; and Beaux that can:*
> *Provided still, this Warrant be not shown,*
> *And you be Wits, but to your selves alone.*

Similarly, the legal system offered parallels to the relationship between the dramatist and actor on the one hand
and the audience on the other. The figure of the poet-player
pleading as a prisoner before a jury of spectators, especially
at a premiere,[4] was a natural and popular one. In the
Epilogue to Dryden's *Sir Martin Marall,* 15 August 1667,
the poet faced a jury which determined his fate:

> *But when the Curtain's down we peep, and see*
> *A jury of the Wits who still stay late,*
> *And in their Club decree the poor Plays fate;*
> *Their verdict back is to the Boxes brought,*
> *Thence all the Town pronounces it their thought.*

Because the wits were often loud and vigorous in their con-
demnation of a play, the poet looked upon the critics' laws
as often extremely severe and the verdict an unjust one,
as suggested in the Epilogue to Settle's *Cambyses, ca.* January, 1671:

227

> *The Persian Laws now cease to seem severe;*
> *You have more cruel Laws that govern here:*
> *Your undisput'd pow'r, who Judges sit,*
> *To sentence all the trespasses of Wit,*
> *How can our Author then his doom recall?*
> *You know he must under your Justice fall;*
> *Being guilty of so capital a Crime,*
> *As shedding too much Humane blood in Rhime.*

The dramatists created many variations on this theme. In the Prologue to *The Comical Revenge*, March, 1664, several characters discuss the impending verdict of the judges (spectators). The Prologue to Wycherley's *Love in a Wood*, *ca.* March, 1671, compared the poet to the doomed criminal in the cart on the road to Tyburn:

> *Custom, which bids the Thief from Cart Harangue,*
> *All those that come to make, and see him hang,*
> *Wills the damn'd Poet (though he knows he's gone)*
> *To greet you, e're his Execution.*
> *Not having fear of Criticks 'fore his eyes,*
> *But still rejecting wholesome, good advice;*
> *He e'en is come to suffer here to day,*
> *For counterfeiting (as you judge) a Play,*
> *Which is against dread Phoebus highest treason,*
> *Damn'd damning Judges, therefore you have reason.*

In the Prologues to Sedley's *Mulberry Garden*, 18 May 1668, and Boothby's *Marcelia, ca.* August, 1669, the poet was sometimes thought of as a lawyer pleading his case, or asking that some of the spectators undertake his defense. In another variation, the Prologue to Stapylton's *Hero and Leander, ca.* 1668, suggested that the dramatist is like a citizen waylaid by a highwayman, more susceptible to assault than a banker traveling Shooter's Hill. In the Prologue to Shadwell's *The Royal Shepherdess*, 25 February 1669, the poet was accused of stealing the whole play but asked forgiveness on the ground that the spectators, having

pardoned other dramatic thieves, had caused him to steal.
In other legal terms, the Epilogue to *The Committee,* 27
November 1662, compared the poet to the holder of property, for his "small Estate," rates, and half-year's purchase
were now all represented in his play.

Another aspect of human concern to which the authors
turned for comparisons was religion. Like the prisoner
seeking a hopeful verdict from the jury, the poet was compared to a sinner repenting and hoping for forgiveness, as
in the Prologue to Shadwell's *Psyche,* 27 February 1674/5:

> *As a young Wanton when she first begins,*
> *With shame and with regret of Conscience sins;*
> *So fares our trembling Poet, the first time,*
> *He has committed the lewd sin of Rhime,*
> *While Custom hardens others in the Crime.*
> *It might in him that boldness too beget,*
> *To lay about him without Fear or Wit:*
> *But humbly he your pardon does implore;*
> *Already he repents, and says he'll sin no more.*

In another approach Dryden in the Epilogue to *Sir Martin
Marall,* 15 August 1667, compared the poet and player to
a vicar:

> *As Country Vicars, when the Sermon's done,*
> *Run hudling to the Benediction;*
> *Well knowing, though the better sort may stay,*
> *The Vulgar Rout will run unblest away:*
> *So we, when once our Play is done, make haste*
> *With a short Epilogue to close your taste.*

In the Prologue to *The Assignation, ca.* November, 1672,
Dryden related the poet and drama to the clergy and religious services:

> *Prologues, like Bells to Churches, toul you in*
> *With Chimeing Verse; till the dull Playes begin:*

> *With this sad difference though, of Pit and Pue;*
> *You damn the Poet, but the Priest damns you.*
> *But Priest can treat you at your own expence:*
> *And, gravely, call you Fooles, without offence.*
> *Poets, poor Devils, have ne'r your Folly shown*
> *But, to their cost, you prov'd it was their own.*

In the Prologue to Lacy's *The Dumb Lady, ca.* 1669, the author compared his presenting the audience with a second play to the clergy's preaching twice daily, but doubted that the dramatist could so easily secure applause by repeating himself.

Another comparison fruitfully employed described the poet as one preparing a feast, whether as cook or host; the play might hopefully appeal to the taste of the audience and the poet stressed the nature of the meal and his hospitality. Apologetically, the Prologue to Thomas Thomson's *The Life of Mother Shipton* issued an "invitation to a feast/ He hopes your stomacks will not ill digest," yet he could not, being a new poet, offer much "choice of dainties of the prime." In the Prologue to Dryden's *Sir Martin Marall*, 15 August 1667, the audience was invited to a "great Regalio's of a Play":

> *But such in Plays must be much thicker sown,*
> *Like yolks of Eggs, a dozen beat to one.*
> *Observing Poets all their walks invade,*
> *As Men watch Woodcocks gliding through a Glade:*
> *And when they have enough for Comedy,*
> *They stow their several Bodies in a Pye:*
> *The Poet's but the Cook to fashion it.*[5]

And in the spirit of Chaucer's hospitable Frankeleyn, the poet, as characterized in the Epilogue to John Crowne's *Andromache, ca.* August, 1674, offered hospitality and feasts to his friends:

As Country Gentlemen at Christmas Feasts,
Spare for no costs to entertain their Guests.
Keep open House for all that will but come,
And have a merry Crowd in every room:
But Friends departed, and the Good time past,
They then grow sparing and begin to cast,
How to live cheap, let prudence then prevail,
And manage well the small remain of Ale.
Yet will a dish for a chance Friend prepare,
But else will serve him with the usual care.
At such fond charge this House has been of Late,
But Friends all gone, must now their charge abate.

The taste of the times made another comparison palatable and popular: that of the poet and player to a young gallant (or husband or bridegroom or lover) wooing his beloved, or to a young woman (a bride, a woman with child, a wily mistress). In the Prologue to Dryden's *An Evening's Love, ca.* June, 1668, a poet with his first play was like a bridegroom, whereas the experienced dramatist was compared to a husband; their moods and techniques, therefore, differed. For a revival of *The Wild Gallant, ca.* 1668–1669, Dryden compared the poet with his first play to a young country squire, the experienced writer to the city-bred man. The Prologue to Mrs. Behn's *The Town-Fop* developed a similar comparison fully:

As Country Squire, who yet had never known
The long-expected Joy of being in Town;
Whose careful Parents scarce permitted Heir
To ride from home, unless to neighboring Fair;
. . . .
So a young Poet, who had never been
Dabling beyond the Height of Ballading;
Who in his brisk Essayes, durst ne'er excel
The lucky flight of Rhiming Dogerel,
Sets up with this sufficient Stock, on Stage,
And has, perchance, the luck to please the Age.

In the Prologue to Crowne's *Juliana, ca.* June, 1671, the poet was likened to a bashful country chap wooing the sophisticates of London:

> *Like Country Gallant just, whom Courtier brings*
> *To see fine dainty Miss—who playes and sings.*
> *Approaching to'r, poor Gallant falls a mumping,*
> *Scraping o'leggs, and feign he would say something;*
> *And round about the room he flings and skips,*
> *Whilst tongue lyes still i'th' scabbard of his Lips.*
> *Just so our Poet usher'd to the door*
> *To court coy Wits h'ad never seen before,*
> *Wits that have all the sparkish Gallants known,*
> *And tryed th'abilities of all the Town;*
> *Poor bashful Poet.*

In a similar vein in the Prologue to Sedley's *Antony and Cleopatra* the dramatist was characterized as a "brisk Gallant" admiring himself in a mirror as he tried various dance steps and imagined himself a fine figure of a man; so "Poet (with the like conceit) undone,/ Think that dull Verse which pleas'd 'em when alone,/ Must have the like effect on the whole Town." Or the author might be like a lover, who, in Dryden's Prologue to *Tyrannick Love, ca.* 1669, should "be bold and dare" and not "spoil [his] business with an over-care." He might even (as in a Prologue intended for *The Old Batchelor,* 9 March 1692/3) be like the inexperienced bridegroom of a widow and fear his ability to be the equal of his predecessor.

With equal frequency the dramatist compared himself to a woman, young or old, maid or mistress, bride or young mother. Davenant, for example, in the Prologue to *The Man's the Master,* 26 March 1668, developed in considerable detail a comparison in this vein:

> *No Country Lady ever yet did ask*
> *Such shrewd advice before a Ball or Masque*
> . . . .

As now young Poets doe, in this nice Age,

. . . .

The Muse, disdain'd, does as fond Women doe;
Instead of being courted she courts you:
But Women are less valu'd when they wooe.
And as young Poets, like young Ladies, fear
A Concourse, great as this Assembly here,
Till they seek counsell how they should appear,
So all old Poets, like old Ladies, may
Be more afraid to venture the survey
Of many apt to censure their decay.

In the Epilogue to *The Lancashire Witches,* Shadwell compared the "Skilful Mistress" and her "wondrous Art/ To keep a peevish crazy Lover's Heart" to the poet and players who must "try a thousand ways . . . your sickly Appetites to raise." In the Prologue to *The Mistaken Husband,* the poet was compared, in detail, to a young bride on her marriage night, whereas the Epilogue to Sedley's *Bellamira* compared the poet's uneasiness with his new play and what to do about it to a "young Wench" thinking of abandoning her illegitimate child.

This survey by no means exhausts the variety of conceits developed in prologues and epilogues. For example, the Epilogue to Sedley's *The Mulberry Garden* compared the poet to a physician, who, at the death of a patient, "shakes his head, and blames Mortality," whereas the "Poets their own faults must bear." In the Prologue to *Pompey the Great, ca.* January, 1664, the author, acknowledging his borrowing from the French, compared his play to fruit transplanted from a foreign land. And the Prologue to *The Double Dealer,* October, 1693, used a Moorish legend as a means of creating a new approach:

Moors have this way (as Story tells) to know
Whether their Brats are truly got, or no;
Into the Sea the new-born Babe is thrown,
There, as Instinct directs, to Swim or Drown.

233

A barbarous Device, to try if Spouse
Has kept Religiously her Nuptial Vows.
Such are the Tryals Poets make of Plays,
Only they trust no more Inconstant Seas;
So, does our Author, this his Child commit
To the Tempestuous Mercy of the Pit,
To know, if it be truly born of Wit.

As is obvious, the prologue and epilogue, almost an obligatory part of a theatrical performance, offered an author a pattern in which he could develop a fanciful image of himself in a variety of comparisons. Furthermore, because the poet and his alter ego, the player, faced an unknown response to the play, the dramatist tried a range of tone: amusing, ironic, serious, argumentative, plaintive. The knowing poet then depended upon a talented actor to speak the prologue and epilogue in precisely the right spirit.

Accompanying the variation in tone and comparisons, the playwright was also engaged in presenting to the audience a conception of himself as a creative artist. Although his play might well determine his ultimate reputation, a printed copy was not likely to be available until a month after the première; therefore, he had to rely upon securing a hearing for himself in the theater in the presence of a great diversity of spectators: wits, beaux, Templars, ladies of quality, royalty, citizens, members of Parliament, and a smattering of individuals from all walks of life. He could not very well praise himself or elevate his profession in a prologue or epilogue under these circumstances; to do so might make him seem arrogant, superior, or egotistic and endanger the warm reception for which he hoped. Although he might, as was often done in some of Dryden's prologues and epilogues, elevate the role of the writer by praising the great authors of a previous age (Shakespeare, Beaumont and Fletcher, and Ben Jonson), he had to try other tactics to enhance his own image.

By comparing himself with other men of skill and talent, such as the diplomat, the warrior, the sovereign, the hospitable man, or the lawyer, he might indirectly appeal for recognition of his stature and position. Tactically, it was also well to apologize, wheedle, amuse, and catch the attention of a potentially restless audience. He might well laugh at himself and let the audience laugh too, even speak cynically and bitterly of the province of the poet, as was done by the author of the Prologue to *Constantine the Great*, 1683, spoken by Cardell Goodman:

> *What think ye meant wise Providence, when first*
> *POETS were made? I'de tell you if I durst.*
> *That 'twas in Contradiction to Heaven's Word,*
> *That when its Spirit o're the Waters stir'd,*
> *When it saw All, and said that All was good,*
> *The Creative POET was not understood.*
> *For were it worth the pains of Six long Days,*
> *To Mould Retailers of dull Third-Day Plays,*
> *That starve out Three-score Years in Hopes of Bays.*
> *'Tis plain they ne're were of the First Creation,*
> *But came by meer Equiv'cal Generation.*
> *Like Rats in Ships, without Coition bred;*
> *As hated too, as they are, and unfed.*
> *Nature their Species sure must needs disown,*
> *Scarce knowing POETS, less by POETS known.*

Nevertheless, the playwright could, by means of his plays and especially by his cleverness in a prologue and an epilogue, disprove the self-denigrating pose he sometimes assumed. By being witty, inventive, fanciful in conception and tone, he might temper the harsh verdict that he feared and demonstrate by his cleverness the reverse of the characterization that he had drawn. If his play was well received, his ironic or amusing portrait of himself would still be applauded, for he had asked for tolerance and received more than he requested.

NOTES

1. Variations on these complaints often appeared. Dryden's Prologue to *The Rival Ladies* (ca. June, 1664) stated:

> *'Tis much Desir'd, you Judges of the Town*
> *Would pass a vote to put all* Prologues *down;*
> *For who can show me, since the first were Writ,*
> *They e'er Converted one hard-hearted Wit.*

Thomas Duffett's Prologue to *The Amorous Old Woman*, ca. March, 1674, asserted:

> *Poets in Prologue (to cajole the Age)*
> *Have spent such stocks of Wit upon the Stage,*
> *That 'tis become the hardest part o'th' Play,*
> *They've said so much, there's little left to say.*

And Thomas Shadwell, in *A Lenten Prologue Refus'd by the Players*, 1682, summed up the poet's dilemma: "Our Prologue-Wit grows flat: The Nap's worn off;/ And howsoe'er We turn, and trim the Stuff,/ The Gloss is gone."

2. It is not particularly useful to differentiate between the poet and the player in their relationship to the audience. Especially at the première of a drama, the author and actor stood in essentially the same position. Both introduced a new work and appealed for its success; both were uncertain of the reception of the play; both stood to gain or lose by its success or failure. The speaker might occasionally refer to the uneasiness or uncertainty of the poet, as though the actor was only mildly concerned with the play; but the difference in their moods was often one of degree, not kind.

3. In the Epilogue to *The Royal Shepherdess*, 25 February 1669, Shadwell varied the figure to compare the poet to the young merchant who has put all his wares in one vessel, now beset at sea. Other variations upon the nautical theme were utilized. After the King's Theater burned in the season of 1671–1672, the Prologue to *Wit Without Money*, the first play acted after a move to a temporary playhouse, compared the poet and company to shipwrecked passengers who try to survive on bare beaches. The Epilogue to Cartwright's *The Ordinary*, ca. January, 1671, refers to the "storme which hangs upon each brow" and remembers that those who were once bold in sea-fights but later took refuge in the hold now resemble the poet and players who seek refuge in the mercy of the audience. The Prologue to Banks' *The Unhappy Favourite*, ca. October, 1681, summarized the poet's predicament in nautical terms: "The Play's his Vessel, and his Venture, Wit:/ Hopes are his Indies, Rocks and Seas, the Pit." In another variation, the Prologue to *The Committee*, 27 November 1662, compared the poet's works to the wares offered by a tradesman, who by contrast is better able to cheat his customers.

4. When a play was given before the societies of the Inner or Middle Temples, the authors of prologues used the occasion for an emphasis on this relationship. The Prologue to a performance of *The Adventures of Five Hours at the Inner Temple* on 2 February 1662/3 stated:

> *As you were then [in the theaters] our Judge, so now we come,*
> *In yearly trial to receive our doom.*
> *If we be Pris'ners, yet there still is care,*
> *To make for Pris'ners room at every Bar.*

The Prologue to *The Impertinents* acted at the Middle Temple, 1 November 1672, developed a similar theme:

> *Th'ill-judging Town has favour'd what he writ*
> *Yet what so e're they do it is not fit,*
> *'Tshould pass for current 'till you licence it.*
> *Though they their Favour to him did allow,*
> *He may be found a Malefactor now;*
> *But to your Judgment he must humbly bow,*
> *He by your common law condemn'd must be,*
> *But for releif flies to your Chauncerie.*

5. In the Epilogue to Dover's *Roman Generals,* the author argued hopefully, that, just as at a feast one might by chance not like one dish yet not condemn the cook and the meal, so the audience should similarly respond "If not one Act prove good, throughout the Play." The audience should also be ready to appreciate a variety of feasts, and in the Prologue to Caryll's *The English Princess* should remember: "You must to day your Appetite prepare / For a plain English Treat of homely Fare."

Harry R. Warfel

ﻉ§ ﻉ

Image vs. Abstraction: Coleridge vs. Pope and the Tests of Poetry

Alexander Pope's writings have bulked large in all discussions of the evolution of the art of poetry since his own day. The perfection of his kind of crystallized and unforgettable statement in heroic couplets has made his poems a ready standard. A war of personalities, initiated by Pope and carried on belligerently by John Dennis and others, set the tone of criticism for two centuries, so that even now any mention of Pope arouses questions about the commentator's attitude toward the poet. After the publication of Warburton's edition of *The Works of Alexander Pope* (1751) new theories of aesthetics appeared; principles at variance with those of neo-classicism shifted emphasis in the criticism

HARRY R. WARFEL is Professor of English at the University of Florida.

of poetry toward the concepts of romanticism. "The change of accent was, generally speaking, from the apparent to the essential, from style to thought, from head to heart, from reason to emotion and imagination." [1] Joseph Warton in *An Essay on the Genius and Writings of Pope* (1757) raised questions about Pope as an artist and shifted attention to fundamentals of point of view and literary technique; to Warton, Pope was a second-rate poet, not to be classed with Spenser, Shakespeare, and Milton. Apparently Coleridge knew Warton's second edition of 1782, because Southey is said to have "agreed far more with Warton than with Johnson." [2] Coleridge and Wordsworth proceeded to supply a sound theoretical basis to Warton's ideas, even as they had given a practical demonstration of them in *Lyrical Ballads* (1798). Their new concepts altered the nature of poetry and established the essential tests of poetry which remain valid in our time. Taking their tone from the continuous military conflict associated with the Napoleonic wars, they saw themselves as embattled proponents for a new aesthetic to replace the one which Pope represented. Like Warton, they did not indulge in personalities but grounded their disapproval of Pope's poetry on their new view of a poet's essential duties and techniques. The effect of their example was to discredit Pope's poetic methods and his relevance as a model rather than to deny merit to his unique gift of aphoristic utterance. The starting point in the new revolution was the psychological basis of the communicative process.

There are two ways of reporting the world about us in language.[3] One is a kind of translation process in which sensory perceptions are transformed into our inherited or consciously learned abstract ideas. The primary business in the tutelage of infants and in school instruction is to provide youth with a body of concepts and a vocabulary whereby good and bad, true and false, beautiful and ugly, glory and shame, duty and pleasure, work and play—as well as thousands of other contrasts—can be handled. To this kind of elemental qualitative judgment system is added the systematic organization of abstract concepts; by these the chaos of the universe and of human behavior is reduced to systems of order and interpretation. By this handle of abstraction the scientist grasps all things. He talks of the world as having position, duration, distance, motion, liquid volume, number, and other abstractions. The grammarian imposes half a dozen different modes of analysis upon a single sentence. The literary critic employs a thousand terms like ideality, reality, aesthetic distance, unity, and symbolic form. In himself each person sees being, essence, soul, glory, hope, fear, love, and so on. By the power of abstraction has come the vast codification of the species, classes, and types of things. Possibly our most useful knowledge has resulted from man's capacity to employ reason through language to give orderly arrangement to the chaos which primitive man stumbled through and which modern man more or less has mastered. Man's dominance of his environment is obvious in his evasion of the weather by means of air conditioning, in his conquest of cosmic space, and in the mechanization and computerization of many of the processes once deemed to be the sole province of man's own brain. The chief tool of abstraction is analysis. It divides, arranges, and distributes the elements of any thing or idea. Its appropriate mode of statement is the essay.

The other way perceives the world as a set of pictures. These pictures may be separate and unrelated units, or they may form a sequence of images bound together by principles derived from, and in harmony with, logical conceptions of phenomena as organized by scientists. The world of thought is controlled ultimately by the rationalist, the reasoner. Yet it is interesting to note that he uses pictures and symbolic models as a means of shaping or interpreting his abstract data. The terms evolution, natural selection, and survival of the fit are now somewhat inert images, but they began as metaphors. The course of twentieth-century sociological thought from race suicide through birth control to planned parenthood is instructive of the manner in which an identical set of events about the declining birth rate in America could be given, successively, a pejorative, a scientifically neutral, and an affirmative connotation by imposing an image upon the statistical facts. These pictures are not photographs, because a photograph retains all the detail of chaos and does not necessarily highlight or give shaping definition to experience. Rather, these pictures are outlines like a mariner's compass, itself a two-dimensional symbolic model of our ever-turning three-dimensional planet. The origin of our mental picture making lies deep in human history. Primitive man saw animal and human images in the conformation of the stars. The Psalmist portrayed God as a Lord who had the quality of a shepherd. In 118 words and a half dozen related images are suggested the immeasurable providence, protection, sustaining helpfulness, benevolence, and other attributes of God. What the essayist says in many thousand of words, the picture-making Psalmist presents in less than six score of words. Still, the logic inherent in the 23rd Psalm is not that of the essayist, but the extent to which that poem has meaning derives from the reader's capacity to bring to it all the trains of thought devised by theological scholars. The interrelatedness of the abstract and picture-making modes of thinking is of primary importance to literary critics. There can be no disagreement about the significance of both. What has happened since 1798 is that picture making has not only become the essential duty of the literary artist but that it is the primary test of poetic merit.

It was Samuel Taylor Coleridge who had differentiated the two modes of writing which resulted from the two ways of examining the world. A metaphysician gifted with skill in analysis and image making, he understood and pointed out the chasmal difference between the versified essays of Alexander Pope and the poetry of William Wordsworth. Wordsworth was a revolutionary in poetry as well as in politics. But his new style in poetry was never really understood, even after Coleridge tried to explicate the matter. The discussion of the poems got bogged down in the morass called vocabulary, a swamp in which linguists still tend to get mired. It was Wordsworth's fault, no doubt, because he took too lofty a tone in his 1800 Preface.[4] He said that the subject was too large, that he did not want to discuss whether the public taste is healthy or depraved, that he did not desire to discuss the psychology of language, and that he did not intend to write a history of the revolutions of society and of the literature mirroring society (p. 5). His real faux pas was in saying that his purpose had been "to choose incidents and situations from common life, and to relate or describe them . . . in a selection of language really used by men" (p. 7). And he went on to say that farmers use a better language than city dwellers and court attendants whose poets "separate themselves from the sympathies of men, and indulge in arbitrary and capricious habits of expression, in order to furnish food for fickle tastes and fickle appetites" (p. 8).

Wordsworth the politician was thrusting hard at the opponents of the French Revolution. He went out of his way to preach new doctrines of the misdirection of poetry in a context of wrongly oriented social and political energies. The result, of course, was what might be expected from a people that was embroiled in a life-and-death struggle with France. They retaliated at the point that seemed easiest and that they best understood: vocabulary. And so Wordsworth's poetry was submerged in a sea of words about words.

It might have been different. Wordsworth used all the proper terms to put his poetic innovation into perspective. In the 1800 Preface he stated that his poems were an "experiment" (p. 3), that they were meant "to interest mankind permanently" (p. 4), that he would not by the act of writing verse "gratify certain known habits of association" (p. 5) which readers brought to metrical compositions nor utilize their "classes of ideas and expressions" (p. 5), especially "the gaudiness and inane phraseology of many modern writers" (p. 6), that readers no doubt would "frequently have to struggle with feelings of strangeness and awkwardness" (p. 6) while perusing his work, and that he sought above all else to evoke emotional responses in a context of moral ideas in harmony with "the primary laws of our nature" (p. 7). He undergirded this view of the purpose of poetry by giving his now-famous definition: "all good poetry is the spontaneous overflow of powerful feelings" and that "the feeling therein developed gives importance to the action and situation, and not the action and situation to the feeling" (p. 9).

But ever the social propagandist—"I am like a man fighting a battle" (p. 17)—Wordsworth turned to the subject matter of poetry. His writings were meant to counteract a vitiated taste that arose from "the great national events that are daily taking place, and the increasing accumulation of men in cities, where the uniformity of their occupations produces a craving for extraordinary incident" (p. 11), a craving that was being satisfied by Gothic novels and German melodramas (p. 11). In contrast he said that he had "a deep impression of certain inherent and indestructible qualities of the human mind, and likewise of certain powers in the great and permanent objects that act upon it, which are equally inherent and indestructible" (p. 11).

In short, he was proposing a new subject matter. Much like Whitman half a century later, Wordsworth was asking for a new set of metaphysical principles upon which Englishmen could frame a more just and more accurate estimate of their duties and worth. "I have wished," he wrote, "to keep the reader in the company of flesh and blood," and "I have at all times wished to look steadily at the object" (p. 12).

This emphasis upon the social basis of his subject matter informs the remainder of the 1800 Preface. Although the phrase "the real language used by men" is repeated again and again, the comments upon style, meter, and stanza structure center on Wordsworth's description of the poet as a picture maker, one who has faith in "the sanctity and truth of his pictures" (p. 24); he gives "the image of things" (p. 21); he finds truth as it is "carried alive into the heart by passion" (p. 20); and his thoughts will guide him "wheresoever he can find an atmosphere of sensation in which to move his wings" (p. 23). His subjects, therefore, will be the passions, thoughts, and feelings common to all mankind. They will be concerned with "our moral sentiments and animal sensations, and with the causes that excite these; with the operations of the elements, and the appearances of the visible universe; with storm and sunshine, with the revolutions of the seasons, with cold and heat, with loss of friends and kindred, with injuries and resentments, gratitude and hope, with fear and sorrow. These and the like are the sensations and objects which the Poet describes, as they are sensations of other men and the objects which interest them" (pp. 23–24). "There is still left open to me what confessedly constitutes the most valuable object of all writing, whether in prose or verse: the great and universal passions of men, the most general and interesting of their occupations, and the entire world of nature before me—to supply endless combinations of forms and imagery" (p. 27).

The radical newness of Wordsworth's poetry resulted, not from anything he said about vocabulary per se, but from his conception of the poet's character. He is a man "endowed with more lively sensibility, more enthusiasm and tenderness, who has a greater knowledge of human nature, and a more comprehensive soul than are supposed to be common among mankind" (p. 18). He looks into the actions of men and into the posture of nature to find moments symbolic of the moral and spiritual truth that is in all men. Profoundest of all human knowledge is the fact of man's essential goodness and high worth. His capabilities are limitless; his opportunities often are restricted. Wordsworth would loosen men from temporary political and social customs and principles, so that they might release their energies in ways productive of happiness. The joy of living, in a context of sorrows and disappointments, should inspirit all to strive toward the goal of happiness built of an inward contentment. The poet's task is to portray through pictures of man and nature the various steps toward this goal.

Samuel Taylor Coleridge, the friend, collaborator, and defender of Wordsworth, was also a revolutionary. A Priestleyan Unitarian, he was an iconoclast disdainful of the old ways of religious and political thought and friendly to the new. He welcomed the French Revolution in 1789. A year later he bitterly attacked the philistinism that allowed Chatterton, because of want and hunger, to commit suicide. In his sonnets on eminent characters he railed against governmental oppression and the mob violence that drove Priestley to America. He praised Lafayette's fighting for liberty and William Godwin's efforts in behalf of social justice. A similar strain of iconoclasm marks his participation in the Wordsworthian campaign to overthrow old concepts concerning the nature of poetry.

It was against Pope's rule over the realm of literature that Coleridge directed his first critical lance. "The writings

of Mr. Pope and his followers . . . gave me little pleasure.
. . . I saw that the excellence of this kind consisted in just
and acute observations on men and manners in an artificial
state of society, as its matter and substance: and in logic
of wit, conveyed in smooth and strong epigrammatic couplets, as its form. . . . A *point* was looked for at the end of
each second line, and the whole was (as it were) a sorites or,
if I may exchange a logical for a grammatical metaphor,
a conjunctive disjunctive of epigrams. Meantime the matter
and diction seemed to me characterized not so much by
poetic thoughts as by thoughts *translated* into the language
of poetry." [5] Throughout the discussion of poetry in *Biographia Literaria*, although Pope's name seldom appears,
the context makes clear the fact of Coleridge's feeling that
the enemy was Pope, that Pope had led poetry into a cul
de sac.

Like Wordsworth, Coleridge saw that poems must not
be a Popean "translation of prose thoughts into poetic language" (I, 60) but must have an organic unity built around
a central image or picture. Like Wordsworth, too, Coleridge
became mired in the swamp of talk about vocabulary and
also about the abstractions of imagination and fancy, in-
vention and originality. Yet the groundwork of his arguments lay in the fundamental proposition that Wordsworth's procedure was right while Pope's was wrong. A
just poem, he said, is not "a series of striking lines or
distichs, each of which, absorbing the whole attention of
the reader to itself, disjoins it from its context and makes
it a separate whole instead of a harmonizing part. . . . The
reader should be carried forward, nor merely or chiefly by
the mechanical impulse of curiosity or by a restless desire
to arrive at the final solution, but by the pleasurable activity
of the mind excited by the attractions of the journey itself"
(II, 10–11).

In the poems of Shakespeare and the early Italians, Coleridge found the formulas which contrasted with those at the basis of Pope's style. In *Venus and Adonis* was discerned "a series and never-broken chain of imagery, always vivid and, because unbroken, often minute . . . to provide a substitute for that visual language, that constant intervention and running comment by tone, look, and gesture . . . from the players" (II, 15). That is, *Venus and Adonis* transmits the same dramatic force as does a play on a stage; it does so because it is pictorial in presentation. Since the root word in imagination is image and the definition of the term is "the power of making or using images," it seems strange that commentators on Wordsworth and Coleridge have missed this essential doctrine in their poetic creed. Shelley, Keats, and Poe did not.

Alexander Pope apparently never wrote an extensive definition of poetry or described a poet or his duties. Although he was familiar with the theory of poetry from Aristotle to Dryden, he never discussed the fundamental principles upon which poetry is classified as a fine art. Though he unhesitatingly wrote about knotty philosophical problems relating to ethics, politics, and religion, he dealt only tangentially with the art of the poet.[6] To the heart of the matter he never went. It becomes necessary to construct from his writings any doctrine that he may have formulated. The line "What oft was thought but ne'er so well expressed" has usually served as Pope's criterion of poetry; yet the context of that statement is figures of speech as a form of wit rather than poetry as a whole. A poem, Pope seems to say, is a versified statement of general ideas whose merit lies in ornamented utterance. These ornaments include grammatical turns, imagery, and sound effects. As Edith Sitwell pointed out in her *Alexander Pope* (New York, 1962, p. 20), an interest in Pope must derive from a delight in the texture of his poetry rather than in any composition as a whole. Since any one idea is of no more significance than another as far as poetry is concerned, subject matter being chiefly valuable as the means of exhibiting an artist's command over the malleable materials of his medium, Pope could demonstrate in any work about the same degree of competence. Some subjects are more attractive than others; hence the longer essays are deemed memorable, while the shorter pieces have fallen into oblivion, because the latter cannot stand comparison with similar writings of the Elizabethans and the romantics. Let us make a test. Here is a short one by Pope.

ON A CERTAIN LADY AT COURT

I know the thing that's most uncommon
  (Envy, be silent and attend!)
I know a reasonable woman,
  Handsome and witty, yet, a friend.

Not warped by passion, awed by rumour,
  Not grave through pride, or gay through folly;
An equal mixture of good-humour,
  And sensible soft melancholy.

"Has she no faults then," Envy says, "Sir?"
  Yes, she has one, I must aver;
When all the world conspires to praise her,
  The woman's deaf and does not hear.

Here is an essay, a statement that ascribes certain qualities of mind and heart to a lady. Here are adroitly turned sentences, a satisfactory formal verse pattern in meter and rhyme, and internal maneuvering of word and sound that is praiseworthy. But there is no imagery except the personification of Envy, and therefore imaginative lift is missing. By comparison with Shelley's "I arise from dreams of thee" and Poe's "Helen, thy beauty is to me," Pope's statement is as prosily abstract and unimaginative as an article in any biographical encyclopedia.

In "A Discourse on Pastoral Poetry" prefacing his youthful *Pastoral Poems* Pope laid down his program as a poet. Each subject, he wrote, must contain "some particular beauty in itself" and each scene should have variety. "This variety is obtained in a great degree by frequent comparisons, drawn from the most agreeable subjects in the country; by interrogations to things inanimate; by beautiful digressions, but those short; . . . and lastly by elegant turns on the words, which render the numbers extremely sweet and pleasing. As for the numbers themselves, . . . they should be the smoothest, the most easy and flowing imaginable. It is by rules like these that we ought to judge the pastoral." [7] Except that scene dropped from Pope's procedure in later poems, his statement contains his theory of poetics. To Spence he said later, "The three great *tours* of poetry are the design, the language, and the versification." [8]

Pope was a word man, a devotee of the handbooks of rhetoric and a precursor of Dr. Johnson as a student of words.[9] What a difference there might have been if Nathaniel Bailey had issued a dictionary before 1721! Pope antedated the mid-eighteenth-century preoccupation with rhetoric and style. Yet his thinking was a throwback to Lyly's euphuism and even to Thomas Wilson's and George Puttenham's books on the art of rhetoric. Pope invented nothing, took no new direction, and perceived nothing about language that had not been known before. Where the metaphysical poets had widened the scope of imagery and had enriched the musical range of poetry, Pope narrowed both imagery and verbal music. His ticking iambics halted progress in metrics for nearly a century. Compared with Poe and Whitman, Pope may be said to have had a metronome rather than the sounds of English or music as his guide. Adroit as was his syntax, his rhymes forced inversions and transpositions. His progress through a poem, his design, was made less by a logic of progression than by the fortuitous and accidental requirement to move on to new topics that rhyme words indicated.

It is instructive, therefore, that commentators on Pope have rarely attempted to reconstruct his theory of poetry or to define poetry in terms of his achievement. Words of praise for his verse usually state that it is quotable, that it manipulates language adeptly, and that it made, in Wimsatt's words, "the universal as brilliantly particular as it could be." [10] The usual commentary on Pope is limited to a species of footnotes on the historical backgrounds and sources of his writings, his word choice, and his rhetorical skill. His verse has been made an object of study, not a source of delight or inspiration having relevance to our day.

With Wordsworth and later poets it is different. Their revolution, grounded upon philosophical principles, was as necessary as it was useful, just as with the American political revolution. All great writers, of course, have rebelled against the customs and techniques of their predecessors. Everyone makes progress, it seems, by discontentment with the past. A new order of poetry was born in 1798 with the publication of *Lyrical Ballads*. With the new-style poetry came the tests for excellence which remain valid today.

The great innovation of Wordsworth was the use of a picture as the focus of his statement. This picture does not necessarily appear in a description of scenery and action. But whatever thoughts and feelings are evoked arise from the picture. The difference between Wordsworth and Pope is that Pope began with an abstract idea and occasionally embellished it with a figure of speech; Wordsworth at his best managed not only to visualize his idea but also to add further imagery to the initial description. The lowest level of image making is in "My Heart Leaps Up," wherein a single image of delight in nature gives the basis for meditation.

MY HEART LEAPS UP

My heart leaps up when I behold
A rainbow in the sky:
So was it when my life began;
So is it now I am a man;
So be it when I shall grow old,
Or let me die!
The Child is father of the Man;
And I could wish my days to be
Bound each to each in natural piety.

More dense is "She Dwelt among the Untrodden Ways," which has in its second stanza two figures that enrich the initial picture.

SHE DWELT AMONG THE UNTRODDEN WAYS

She dwelt among the untrodden ways
Beside the springs of Dove,
A Maid whom there was none to praise
And very few to love.

A violet by a mossy stone
Half hidden from the eye!—
Fair as a star, when only one
Is shining in the sky.

She lived unknown, and few could know
When Lucy ceased to be;
But she is in her grave, and, oh,
The difference to me!

Poems thus organized can be said to have re-established the poetic tradition which Dryden and Pope interrupted. All modern lyric poetry of any merit contains this mode of viewing life. Out of an image comes the meaning which the poet wishes to express; the picture may stand by itself,

or it may be interpreted. Wordsworth kept his moral reflections largely within the area of emotional response.
Thus there is a hope expressed in "My Heart Leaps Up"
that a joy experienced in childhood and young manhood
can be retained in old age. In "She Dwelt among the Untrodden Ways" there is a feeling of grief at the death of a
beautiful country maiden who never knew the social life of
a city or the court. The contrast between the warm content
of Wordsworth's poems and the cold abstractionism of
Pope's "On a Certain Lady at Court" requires no analysis.
One needs to say only that an essay is not a lyric poem;
rhyme, meter, and intricate syntax, however commendable
in texture, do not in themselves do more than give a decora-
tive element to a prose statement.[11] The first test of poetry,
therefore, is the quality, extent, and appropriateness of the
image material in any given composition.

The second test is, as Coleridge explained, that "A continuous undercurrent of feeling . . . [must be] everywhere
present, but seldom anywhere as a separate excitement"
(I, 15). A comparison between Pope's "Argus" and Tennyson's "Ulysses" can clarify the distinction.

ARGUS

When wise Ulysses, from his native coasts
Long kept by wars, and long by tempests tossed,
Arrived at last, poor, old, disguised, alone,
To all his friends and even his Queen unknown;
Changed as he was, with age, and toils, and cares,
Furrow'd his rev'rend face, and white his hairs,
In his own palace forced to ask his bread,
Scorned by those slaves his former bounty fed,
Forgot by all his own domestic crew;
The faithful dog alone his rightful master knew!
Unfed, unhoused, neglected, on the clay,
Like an old servant, now cashiered, he lay;
Touched with resentment of ungrateful man,
And longing to behold his ancient lord again.

Him when he saw—he rose, and crawled to meet,
('Twas all he could) and fawned, and kissed his feet,
Seized with dumb joy—then falling by his side,
Owned his returning lord, looked up, and died!

ULYSSES

It little profits that an idle king,
By this still hearth, among these barren crags,
Matched with an agéd wife, I mete and dole
Unequal laws unto a savage race,
That hoard, and sleep, and feed, and know not me.
I cannot rest from travel; I will drink
Life to the lees. . . .

In Pope's lines the characterization is excellent as a prose statement. In "Ulysses" the emotional coloration begins in the first line and runs through the seventy lines of the poem; the imagery of "still hearth," "barren crags," and "I will drink life to the lees" supplies the vividness and imaginative richness which lifts Tennyson's statement into the realms of poetry. If it be said that Pope's verse evokes an emotion, it may be said to be of our creation as a result of a transference of his intellectualized content into feeling. In "Ulysses" the poet has established the emotion and made it run, in Coleridge's image, as an undercurrent throughout the entire poem.

The third test of poetry established by Coleridge is that the new vocabulary mentioned by Wordsworth is not so much a set of new words (Wordsworth specifically said that there is no difference between the vocabulary of poetry and prose) as a new logic in the use of words in poetry. Pope relied wholly upon the literal dictionary meaning for almost all his words; he seldom gave them an imaginative twist beyond the denotations and connotations already present. Wordsworth made "a violet by a mossy stone" carry all the old associative values plus the new one that the image contains. Pope's words can be altered without any

loss and possibly some gain, as in the first two lines of
"Argus":

> *When wise Ulysses, from his native* shore
> *Long kept by wars, and long* in tempests' roar.

Coleridge, therefore, was correct in asserting that "lines
that can be translated into other words of the same language, without diminution of their significance, either in
sense or association or in any worthy feeling, are so far
vicious in the diction" (I, 14).[12] That is, the imagery must
be so chosen that necessity dictates its absolute appropriateness both to the meaning and to the rhetorical structure.
A poem like Poe's "To Helen" illustrates the impossibility
of translation as described by Coleridge.

TO HELEN

> *Helen, thy beauty is to me*
>   *Like those Nicéan barks of yore*
> *That gently, o'er a perfumed sea,*
>   *The weary, way-worn wanderer bore*
>   *To his own native shore.*
>
> *On desperate seas long wont to roam,*
>   *Thy hyacinth hair, thy classic face,*
> *Thy Naiad airs have brought me home*
>   *To the glory that was Greece*
>   *And the grandeur that was Rome.*
>
> *Lo! in yon brilliant window-niche*
>   *How statue-like I see thee stand,*
> *The agate lamp within thy hand!*
>   *Ah, Psyche, from the regions which*
>   *Are Holy-Land!*

In these three stanzas Poe has told of a mariner who has
returned to his home community after a long absence. He
has gone to his sweetheart's dwelling at night, and there
he sees a light in her window and, between the light and

the window shade, her silhouette. He speaks in the form of a serenade. The first stanza tells of her physical beauty, the second of her intellectual beauty, and the third of her spiritual beauty. The unified imagery is drawn from the Mediterranean area of ancient Greece and Rome. It would be impossible, I think, to alter any of the words or lines and still maintain the harmony of imagery and the fullness of thought. Poe omitted the abstract terms about which the poetry discourses; here is a sample of the new logic of poetry. The words except *Nicéan* are old, but the meanings are not merely those found in a dictionary.

The fourth Coleridgean test of poetry was the elimination of the stock vocabulary and image-making devices of Pope. The tin-plated, shiny verbiage of the eighteenth century needs no exemplification here; Coleridge gave as an example (I, 13) of "rag-tag finery" for the simple statement "I will remember thee" the following:

> *Thy image on her wing*
> *Before my Fancy's eye shall Memory bring.*

Nor need there be comment upon Pope's fondness for classical invocations and personification. Wrote Coleridge: "One great distinction, I appeared to myself to see plainly, between the characteristic faults of our elder poets and the false beauty of the moderns. In the former, from Donne to Cowley, we find the most fantastic out-of-the-way [statements] but in the most pure and genuine mother English; in the latter [Pope and his followers], the most obvious thoughts in language the most fantastic and arbitrary. Our faulty elder poets sacrificed the passion and the passionate flow of poetry to the subtleties of intellect and to the starts of wit; the moderns to the glare and glitter of a perpetual yet broken and heterogeneous imagery, or rather to an amphibious something made up of half of image and half of abstract meaning. The one sacrificed the heart to the

head; the other both heart and head to point and drapery"
(I, 15). Wordsworth's plea for "the real language of men"
included a rejection of poetic diction and personification.
This is not to say that personification is now out of place
and improper; rather the overuse and misuse of personification is now thoroughly frowned upon.

The fifth Coleridgean test is that the versification shall
be appropriate to the subject and treatment of the poem
(II, 9–10). Particularly, of course, heroic couplets had become associated with bad poetry, and naturally any form
would be better than that one, just as in the American
Revolution any form of government was deemed better than
a monarchy. Coleridge liked Wordsworth's blank verse, as
in "Tintern Abbey," and was favorably impressed with
enjambed or run-on lines. Coleridge wanted a reunion of
music and poetry (II, 14, 24), so that there could be variations in structure paralleling the inventiveness of the great
musical composers. It was not until Poe that the relationship between syntax and sound was discovered; it took Poe,
Whitman, and Lanier to extend the reaches of music in
poetry.[13] Later Gerard Manley Hopkins, Vachel Lindsay,
Carl Sandburg, and Archibald MacLeish carried forward
experiments of significant value. Novelty is the rule today,
in poetry as in music and the other fine arts.

The sixth test of poetry is that the syntax must be natural
and unforced (II, 115). Rhyme has always created problems
for the poet, so that inversion in metrical verse is commonplace, as in Pope's "Argus": "Him when he saw." In the
nineteenth century, inversion was a common procedure;
many satisfying effects were gained from moving the units
out of the normal order. Yet Swinburne's complexity, as
in "Ave atque Vale," caused his younger contemporaries
to seek simplicity and directness. Whitman created a wholly
new concept of syntax by exploiting apposition and com-
pounding; his immensely long sentences (and nonsentences,

as in "We Two Boys") gave a new awareness of the significance of syntax. Possibly less study has been made of this area of style than of any other, for the whole field of the relationship of syntax to outward form, both of lines and stanzas, has yet to be worked out. For example, what is the difference in the syntax of rhymed and unrhymed passages in the works of Shakespeare or Milton?

Once upon a time there were tests based upon subject matter. Today any topic is freely available, provided that it does not violate the ordinary canons of taste, libel, or treason. What has happened is that the poet has lost his one-time position as a formulator of public opinion. Long before a poet can hope to have completed a poem on a topic of immediate importance, a thousand journalists will have written and published editorials, columns, and essays in newspapers and magazines. Just as painting moved away from representation to abstract art, the photograph having replaced portrait and scenic painting, so poetry has sought new areas of technique to exploit. Contemporary poetry has been so varied that no one can easily define the present period. No artist or critic since the ascendancy of T. S. Eliot has established a mode or theory which has gained wide acceptance. Graeco-Roman metric theorizing is still dominant despite Whitman's example; free verse, the characteristic prosody of the first half of the twentieth century, still lacks a rationale. New tests of poetry doubtless are needed.

The tests of poetry which remain valid are those which relate to the artistic manipulation of material. Of these tests the primary one is that a poem must focus upon a picture or be a picture. Abstraction must be replaced by imagery. The language must exploit the procedures of syntax as well as the resources of the dictionary. Until more is known about the rhythms available in English and about the relationship among metrics, subject matter, and form, there is little to be said about the comparative merits of regular and free verse.[14] A capacity to present and to evoke emotion must continue to distinguish poetry from prose. The revolution started by Wordsworth and Coleridge was won by 1815. Our new age with its altered conditions will bring new theories of poetry, because poets are exemplifying the new methods of artistic presentation that are matching the new modes of music, painting, and sculpture.

NOTES

1. W. L. MacDonald, *Pope and His Critics* (London, 1951), p. 233.

2. *Biographia Literaria of S. T. Coleridge*, ed. J. Shawcross, 2 vols (London, 1907), I, 40.

3. A fundamental concept in grammar makes a distinction between abstract and concrete words, and between these two classes of words and a third class called relational or structure words. If there are only two classes of meaning-carrying words, there can be only two major kinds of verbal reports. See my *Language: A Science of Human Behavior* (Cleveland, Ohio, 1962), pp. 89–120.

4. *The Complete Poetical Works of William Wordsworth*, 10 vols. (Boston and New York, 1904), X, 3–38. Further citations to pages will be given in the text.

   Wordsworth mentioned Pope on p. 6. In the "Appendix to the Preface" he wrote: "Perhaps in no way, by positive example, could more easily be given a notion of what I mean by the phrase *poetic diction* than by referring to a comparison between the metrical paraphrase which we have of passages in the Old and New Testament, and those passages as they exist in our common Translation. See Pope's 'Messiah' throughout" (pp. 42–43). Other references to the style of Pope and his followers include "capricious habits of expression" (p. 8), "the present outcry against the triviality and meanness, both of thought and language, which some of my contemporaries have introduced into their metrical compositions" (p. 8), "personifications of abstract ideas . . . are utterly rejected [by me] as an ordinary device to elevate style and raise it above prose" (p. 12), "There will also be found [in my writings] little of what is usually called poetic diction" (p. 12), "little falsehood of description" (p. 13), "phrases and figures of speech which . . . have long been regarded as the common inheritance of poets" (p. 13), "poetic diction, arbitrary and subject to infinite caprices" (p. 27), "adulterated phraseology" (p. 41), and "extravagant and absurd diction" (p. 42).

5. *Biographia Literaria*, I, 11. Further citations will be given in the text.
   Cf. "His translation of Homer . . . [is] the main source of our pseudo-poetic diction" (I, 33n). In Pope's version of Achilles' shield

"the whole *visual* likeness is lost" (I, 33n). "The language [of] Pope's 'Translation of Homer' . . . may . . . be too faithfully characterized, as claiming to be poetical for no better reason, than that it would be intolerable in conversation or prose" (II, 21).

6. Robert Kilburn Root, *The Poetical Career of Alexander Pope* (Princeton, 1938), pp. 20–33: "The *Essay on Criticism* contains little that is Pope's own except its felicity of expression. . . . It is not an 'art of poetry' but an 'art of criticism'—or rather an 'essay' towards such a treatise."

7. *Alexander Pope: Selected Poetry and Prose,* ed. William K. Wimsatt, Jr. (New York, 1951), p. x.

8. *Ibid.,* p. xxviii.

9. *Ibid.,* pp. xxv–li. Cf. "Pope's career was devoted to the creative power of the word" (p. 1).

10. *Ibid.,* p. xxv.

11. *Biographia Literaria,* II, 8–9. Further citations will be given in the text.

12. Cf., also, "I have ventured to propose as the infallible test of a blameless style: its *untranslatableness* in words of the same language without injury to the meaning" (II, 115).

13. See my "Mystic Vision in 'The Marshes of Glynn,' " *The Mississippi Quarterly,* XIX (Winter, 1965–1966), 34–40.

14. Seymour Chatman in *A Theory of Meter* (The Hague, 1965), after dismissing as untenable some of the "fanciful qualities that have been attributed to it," concludes that "meter most clearly collaborates with meaning. . . . The meter is a sign of the poet's control; it signals propriety of formalization and generalization" (p. 224). "Meter, then, is a sign of a certain kind of discourse" (p. 221).

See also, Paul Fussell, Jr., *Poetic Meter and Poetic Form* (New York, 1965), p. 24: "ascending rhythm does not, in itself, transmit a feeling of aspiration, levity, or cheer, nor does descending rhythm . . . necessarily transmit illusions of falling nor emotions of depression or gloom."

Lionel Stevenson

❧ ❦

The Key Poem of
the Victorian Age

So much major poetry has been written in the past century
and a quarter, and poets are still so profuse at the present
moment, that it is almost impossible for us to realize that
about the year 1825 poetry was suddenly faced with an
ideological assault that gravely menaced its survival.

Never until then had there been a serious challenge to
the primacy of poetry in the field of literature. When Shakespeare wrote,

> *So long as men can breathe, or eyes can see,*
> *So long lives this, and this gives life to thee,*

he was not egotistically bragging, but uttering a universally
accepted axiom. As late as 1800, Wordsworth did not feel

LIONEL STEVENSON is Professor of English at Duke University.

impelled to apologize for setting out to write on an epic scale about "the growth of a poet's mind." But within the next twenty years strange and disquieting phenomena appeared. Coleridge wrote virtually no poetry after 1805, Southey and Scott after 1815—though those two had been the most popular poets of their era. Landor shifted to his *Imaginary Conversations* by 1820. Even Wordsworth withheld *The Prelude* from publication and abandoned his project of the colossal *Recluse* which it had been intended to introduce.

A blight had fallen upon the creative energy of the poets and the perceptive response of the reading public alike. The younger poets, it is true, kept on until the untimely close of their lives; but Byron's later poems achieved mainly *un succès de scandale;* and besides, *Don Juan* was so like prose fiction in every respect except rhyme and meter that I feel convinced Byron would soon have followed Scott out of poetry and—had he lived out a normal span—would have become the leading Early Victorian novelist. One cannot feel altogether certain that even the visionary dedication of Shelley and Keats could have withstood the vituperation of the critics and the neglect of the public.

It was not long until critical theory formulated reasons for poetry's decline from its traditional eminence. The harshest antagonism came, as might be expected, from the Utilitarians. Jeremy Bentham's contemptuous remarks occurred in "The Rationale of Reward" (1825):

> Prejudice apart, the game of push-pin is of equal value with the arts and sciences of music and poetry. If the game of push-pin furnish more pleasure, it is more valuable than either. Everybody can play at push-pin: poetry and music are relished only by a few. The game of push-pin is always innocent: it were well could the same be always asserted of poetry. Indeed, between poetry and truth there is a natural opposition: false morals, fictitious nature. The poet always stands in need of

something false. When he pretends to lay his foundations in truth, the ornaments of his superstructure are fictions; his business consists in stimulating our passions, and exciting our prejudices. Truth, exactitude of every kind, is fatal to poetry.

More stridently, in the same year, a reviewer in the chief Utilitarian journal, the *Westminster Review*, declared:

> To be literary . . . is the disease of the age. But ledgers do not keep well in rhyme, nor are three-deckers [warships] built by songs as towns were of yore. . . . Literature is a seducer; we had almost said a harlot. She may do to trifle with; but woe be to the state whose statesmen write verses, and whose lawyers read more in Tom Moore than in Bracton.

It was in conformity with this Utilitarian gospel that James Mill educated his son:

> There was another kind of composition which was [compulsory], namely, writing verses, and it was one of the most disagreeable of my tasks. . . . My father . . . gave me, for this, two reasons highly characteristic of him: one was, that some things could be expressed better and more forcibly in verse than in prose; this, he said, was a real advantage. The other was, that people in general attached more value to verse than it deserved, and the power of writing it was, on this account, worth acquiring. . . . The poetry of the present century he saw scarcely any merit in, and I hardly became acquainted with any of it till I was grown to manhood. . . . The whole course of my intellectual cultivation had made precocious and premature analysis the inveterate habit of my mind.

Eventually, to be sure, the psychological horrors of this anti-poetic bias were gruesomely displayed; but it was not until 1854 that Dickens lambasted the educational, methods of Gradgrind in *Hard Times*, and John Stuart Mill's *Autobiography* remained unpublished until 1873.

The Utilitarians were formidable enemies enough, for

their pragmatism and rationalism represented the most dynamic tendency of the time; but they were not the only vilifiers of poetry. The Whig intellectuals were almost as severe. Henry Brougham, who gave currency to the phrase that "the schoolmaster is abroad," in 1827 organized the Society for the Diffusion of Useful Knowledge, which provided sixpenny books of a strictly informative nature as the only reading matter needful for the newly-literate masses. The first volume of the series was Brougham's own treatise on "The Pleasures and Advantages of Science." Even Macaulay, though a lover of great poetry and himself a writer of vigorous verse, was reluctantly obliged to assume that poetry had no role to play in the modern world. In a famous passage in his essay on Milton (also written in 1825) he mourned:

> We think that, as civilisation advances, poetry almost necessarily declines. . . . Language, the machine of the poet, is best fitted for his purpose in its rudest state. Nations, like individuals, first perceive, and then abstract. They advance from particular images to general terms. Hence the vocabulary of an enlightened society is philosophical, that of a half-civilised people is poetical. . . . Perhaps no person can be a poet, or can even enjoy poetry, without a certain unsoundness of mind, if anything which gives so much pleasure can be called unsoundness. . . . He who, in an enlightened and literary society, aspires to be a great poet, must first become a little child. He must take to pieces the whole web of his mind. He must unlearn much of that knowledge which has perhaps constituted hitherto his chief title to superiority. His very talents will be a hindrance to him. His difficulties will be proportioned to his proficiency in the pursuits which are fashionable among his contemporaries; and that proficiency will in general be proportioned to the vigour and activity of his mind. And it is well if, after all his sacrifices and exertions, his works do not resemble a lisping man or a modern ruin. We have seen in our own time great talents, intense labour, and long meditation, employed in this struggle against the spirit of the age, and employed, we will not say absolutely in vain, but with dubious success and feeble applause.

Macaulay's condescending pity was, if anything, more lethal than Bentham's open disdain.

It is not particularly surprising that the rationalism of the Utilitarians and the smug materialism of the Whigs united them in antagonism to the imaginative and impractical art of poetry. The truly amazing fact is that this unholy alliance won the adherence of a more potent writer who was the implacable foe of materialists and rationalists on every other issue. Thomas Carlyle, with his Calvinistic earnestness and his penchant for physics and mathematics, eyed poetry with dyspeptic sourness. His friend John Sterling termed him "a gigantic anti-poet." In this crucial year of 1825 he wrote to Jane Welsh:

> I swear to you I had rather be a substantial peasant that ate my bread in peace and loved my fellow mortals, tho' I scarcely knew that my own parish was not all the universe, than one of these same miserable metre ballad-mongers, whose heart is dead or worse, for whom creation is but a mirror to reflect the image of his own sorry self and still sorrier doings!

Seventeen years later he told Varnhagen von Ense, "There is now for me very little speculation and almost nothing of the so-called Poetry that I can bear to read at all." When Elizabeth Barrett sent him some of her poems, he infuriated her (as she reported to Miss Mitford) by replying that "a person of my 'insight and veracity' ought to use 'speech' rather than 'song' in these days of crisis." Months later, still fuming, she wrote to Browning: "And does Mr Carlyle tell you that he has forbidden all 'singing' to this perverse and froward generation, which should work and not sing?"

Nor did Carlyle confine his anti-poetic sentiments to his letters and conversations. It is true that in *Heroes and Hero Worship* he devoted one lecture to "The Hero as Poet," and declared firmly, "it is a man's sincerity and depth of vision that makes him a Poet. See deep enough, and you see musically; the heart of Nature *being* everywhere music, if you can only reach it." But he immediately proceeded:

> The *Vates* Poet, with his melodious Apocalypse of Nature, seems to hold a poor rank among us, in comparison with the *Vates* Prophet; his function, and our esteem of him for his function, alike slight. . . . Dante and Shakespeare are a peculiar Two. They dwell apart, in a kind of royal solitude; none equal, none second to them; in the general feeling of the world, a certain transcendentalism, a glory as of complete perfection, invests these two. . . . Such, in spite of every perverting influence, in the most unheroic times, is still our indestructible reverence for heroism.

Having thus relegated great poetry to the past, Carlyle went on to deal with modern literature in a separate lecture on "The Hero as Man of Letters"; "a product of these new ages . . . he has hardly lasted above a century in the world as yet." Of the three authors selected to typify this new phenomenon, only one is a poet; and the inclusion of Burns is obviously dictated less by the fact of his having written in verse than by his having been a defiant Scottish farm lad and therefore supplying (along with Samuel Johnson and Rousseau) a necessary ingredient in the composite portrait of what the author was not quite bumptious enough to offer openly as his ideal of the Hero as Man of Letters—namely, Thomas Carlyle himself. In the body of this lecture he mentioned poetry seldom and grudgingly, making clear that in his view influential modern literature was primarily identified with prose.

The significance of the foregoing evidence is not merely that such an array of eminent writers were unanimous in their belief that poetry no longer wielded any real power, but also that they were unquestionably spokesmen for a wide and otherwise diversified segment of public opinion. Moreover, as well as this articulate and plausible campaign, there was another and more material force working against poetry, though probably neither the critics nor the poets were as yet fully aware of it. This was the rapid emergence of prose fiction as the most enjoyable form of creative literature. The new reading public, for whom Brougham was so solicitously offering "useful information," did not lack a taste for imaginative and emotional fare; but they could not readily grasp the complexities of poetry, which hitherto had been the principal medium for purveying those delights. The unprecedented fame and profits of the Waverley novels initiated the new era, and by 1825 the torrent of popular fiction was nearing full spate. Publishers and circulating libraries had been readily seduced by the fresh commodity; and, thus encouraged, the writers of prose fiction extended the range and quality of their themes and techniques, so that the novel was soon on the verge of acceptance as the major form of creative literature.

Needless to say, the antagonism to poetry was based upon doubtful premises, and the rivalry of the novel was far from disastrous. But for young people growing up in the 1820's and feeling an impulse to become poets, the adversaries were too formidable to be ignored. As never before, a poet was obliged to justify his choice of vocation, first of all to himself and thereafter to the readers with whom he hoped to communicate. Speaking about modern literature as a whole, Arnold remarked later that "the dialogue of the mind with itself had begun"; in my narrower context I may say that about 1830 the dialogue of the poet with himself had begun. No longer could he serenely follow traditional methods, themes, and values. He was compelled to re-examine every presupposition in order to determine its validity in the competitive situation that had developed, and to experiment in the hope of discovering new techniques that might prove more effectual in demonstrating poetry's unique function.

There were two main alternatives that a poet might choose if he wished to repel the strictures of the rationalists and to defy the challenge of the novelists. One way was frankly to admit the utilitarian premise that poetry existed solely to give pleasure, and then to endow sheer aesthetic delight with the highest value in human experience and to assert that poetry could achieve it more fully than any other medium. It was for this reason that young poets were drawn to Keats, with his reveling in sensuous detail and his easily quoted doctrines that "a thing of beauty is a joy for ever" and "beauty is truth, truth beauty—that is all ye know on earth and all ye need to know." Tennyson's undergraduate volume of 1830 is full of Keatsian melody and word-painting. But overt hedonism did not find an encouraging climate in the morally earnest Early Victorian age, and the young poets lacked the fervor and self-confidence to fight for it. The most promising disciples of Keats were destroyed in the effort: Beddoes lapsed into morbid grotesquerie and eventual madness, Tom Hood took refuge in hack-written facetiousness. And Tennyson, of course, the most gifted of them all, turned to the other alternative.

This was to demonstrate that poetry was neither emptily aesthetic nor primitive and archaic, but that it could apply its unique power to themes of contemporary life with such subtlety, vividness, compression, and emotional intensity that it was more than a match for prose. If the aesthetic alternative is to be regarded as the legacy of Keats, this other may be identified as the legacy of Shelley, with his recurrent depictions of

> *a poet hidden*
> *In the light of thought,*
> *Singing songs unbidden*
> *Till the world is wrought*
> *To sympathy with hopes and fears it heeded not.*

This ideal of the poet's social responsibility was formulated by Tennyson in his naive early piece, "The Poet":

> *So many minds did gird their orbs with beams,*
> *Tho' one did fling the fire,*
> *Heaven flow'd upon the soul in many dreams*
> *Of high desire.*
>
> *Thus truth was multiplied on truth, the world*
> *Like one great garden show'd. . . .*

Though Tennyson soon lost this sublime assurance, the poem indicated which fork of the road he was about to choose.

Within the general alternative there were several specific methods by which the poet might hope to attain his ends. One, obviously, was to write poems about strictly contemporary life, to be as realistic as the novelists in portraying the houses and the costumes and the conversations that readers would immediately recognize as identical with those of themselves and their neighbors. Tennyson undertook this in dozens of poems, ranging from studies of psychological crisis in "Locksley Hall" and *Maud* to Wordsworthian episodes of rural life such as "Enoch Arden" and "Dora" and playful scenes of country-house elegance like "Audley Court" and "Edwin Morris." Other poets of considerable talents followed the same mode. Arthur Clough employed it in all his long poems—*The Bothie of Tober-na-Vuolich,* "Amours de Voyage," and "Mari Magno." Elizabeth Barrett produced a plushy society melodrama in "Lady Geraldine's Courtship" and followed it with her full-scale "novel in verse," *Aurora Leigh.* The *genre* reached its *reductio ad absurdum* in Owen Meredith's pretentious *Lucile* (1860), though at almost the same moment its potentiality was startlingly proved by the other Meredith with *Modern Love.* In spite of occasional successes, however, the *genre* was handicapped by one fatal weakness: in adopting the

full technique of realism from prose fiction, the poets sur-
rendered the initiative to the novelists, and the poems
tended to verify rather than to disprove the assumption
that the novel in prose was the only medium adequate for
reproducing the complexities and the trivialities of modern
life. Arnold put his finger on the crucial defect when he
said in the preface to his 1853 volume:

> A great human action of a thousand years ago is more interest-
> ing to [the elementary part of our nature] than a smaller human
> action of today, even though upon the representation of this
> last the most consummate skill may have been expended, and
> though it has the advantage of appealing by its modern lan-
> guage, familiar manners, and contemporary allusions, to all our
> transient feelings and interests. . . . We have the domestic epic
> dealing with the details of modern life which pass daily under
> our eyes: we have poems representing modern personages in
> contact with the problems of modern life, moral, intellectual,
> and social; these works have been produced by poets the most
> distinguished of their nation and time; yet I fearlessly assert
> that [they] leave the reader cold in comparison with the effect
> produced upon him by the latter books of the Iliad, by the
> Oresteia, and by the episode of Dido. And why is this? Simply
> because in the three last-named cases the action is greater, the
> personages nobler, the situations more intense.

A second alternative for the modern poets was to dis-
regard narrative and scene altogether, and to write reflective
poems upon the topics of grave debate that were impinging
so insistently upon the consciousness of thoughtful people.
The danger of didacticism and abstractness in such poems
would be avoided only by the richest possible importation
of specific imagery and personal feeling. If these were in-
adequate, the poem would be as dry and rigid as "The
Two Voices"; and all Tennyson's unsurpassed powers of
word-painting scarcely sufficed to compensate for the pon-
derous allegorizing in "The Palace of Art." In the most
effective poems of this category—"In Memoriam," "Christ-

mas-Eve and Easter-Day," "Dipsychus," "The Scholar-Gipsy"—there is sufficient tension between the philosophical argument and the author's emotional involvement to arouse even a modern reader's response. But most of the other poems of exposition and debate, whether by Tennyson or Clough or Arnold, are now read more as documents in the intellectual history of Victorianism than as masterpieces of sheer poetry; and it is difficult to defend them against the complaint that the same ideas might be expressed as well, if not better, in prose. It was apparently a recognition of this fact that impelled Arnold to abandon poetry almost entirely in favor of essays in literary and social criticism.

There remained one other alternative, by which the poet could hope to avoid both the abstractness of reflective discussion and the triviality of contemporary settings. This was to use the familiar material of history and legend, with its greatness of action, its nobility of personages, its intensity of situations, but to reinterpret it in such a way as to convert it into a commentary upon contemporary conditions and problems.

This method also was adopted by Tennyson at an early stage and retained throughout his career. He expanded episodes from Homer in "Oenone," "The Lotos Eaters," and "Ulysses"; he portrayed other classical figures, mythical or historical, in "Tithonus," "Tiresias," and "Lucretius"; and most notable of all was his life-long fidelity to the Arthurian theme, which started with "The Lady of Shalott" and "Sir Launcelot and Queen Guinevere" in the early thirties and persisted until "Merlin and the Gleam" nearly sixty years later. The major instance, of course, is the *Idylls of the King,* Tennyson's longest work, and this poem itself took forty years to grow, from the experimental fragment, "Morte d'Arthur," written before 1835, to the last idyll, "Balin and Balan," written in 1874.

Later critics are prone to condemn these poems for distorting their ancient material in order to introduce modern significance; and Tennyson undoubtedly supplied ammunition for such assailants by several unguarded comments that too openly equated King Arthur with both Arthur Henry Hallam and Albert the Prince Consort. But, after all, Tennyson was doing nothing unusual. The romances of chivalry had transformed the primitive British chief and his henchmen to fit the feudal ideal; Spenser remodeled them again as exponents of the Renaissance and the Reformation; if Milton had pursued his project of an Arthurian epic he would certainly have proclaimed good Puritan doctrine in it, as he did through the figures of Samson and the Archangel Gabriel. The fetish of historical authenticity is a very modern development.

Tennyson's difference from his poetical predecessors lay in his greater anxiety to justify his procedure and to interpret his techniques to the reader. This explanatory habit betrays his awareness of the skeptical view of poetry that was so widely disseminated at the time. Also, I think, Tennyson was hoping to captivate readers of the new type that was not thoroughly conditioned to the subtleties of poetic communication, and therefore he was trying to train their comprehension, even at the cost of belaboring what would be obvious to more sophisticated readers.

It was for this reason, I believe, that he began "Oenone" and "The Lotos Eaters" with passages of straight narrative before shifting to dramatic monologue, which demands more imaginative adaptability in the reader. Even more gratuitously, he prefaced the already over-explicit "Palace of Art" with a dedicatory poem summarizing the allegorical meaning. Similarly, his graceful retelling of the Sleeping Beauty legend, in "The Day Dream," opens with a prologue explaining how the theme occurred to him and closes with a separately-headed "Moral" and then "L'Envoi" and then an "Epilogue," encrusting the fragile tale in a solid shell of self-consciously playful exposition. He insists that occasionally a poem need have no purpose beyond giving pleasure, though every reader is apt to find his own personal meaning in it:

> *Oh, to what uses shall we put*
> *The wildweed flower that simply blows?*
> *And is there any moral shut*
> *Within the bosom of the rose?*
> *But any man that walks the mead,*
> *In bud or blade, or bloom, may find,*
> *According as his humours lead,*
> *A meaning suited to his mind.*
> *And liberal applications lie*
> *In Art, like Nature, dearest friend;*
> *So 'twere to cramp its use if I*
> *Should hook it to some useful end.*

Yet after this declaration of independence, Tennyson goes on with several stanzas proposing possible modern applications of the tale. Nowadays the ambiguity of poetic suggestion is perfectly respectable critical doctrine; but in 1842 Tennyson was forced into the absurd position of writing an explicit poem to assert that a poem does not need to be explicit.

Two of Tennyson's explanatory disquisitions are especially extensive and significant. When his fascination with the Arthurian material first led him, about 1832, to consider the possibility of narrating it on an epic scale, he wrote a trial passage of 270 lines depicting the climactic event, the death of the king. Some ten years later, when he was ready to publish his next volume of poems, he was apparently doubtful as to how this piece would be received, not only for its fragmentary condition but also because the king's farewell speech injected a modern concept into Malory's archaic scene. Accordingly the poet provided introductory

272

and concluding passages, totaling almost one-third as many lines as the fragment itself, and couched in whimsical, colloquial blank verse that contrasts sharply with the sonorous music of the "Morte d'Arthur" passage. By an ingenious device, the narrator of the frame-portions is not a poet, and thus Tennyson is free to depict himself—the author of the epic fragment—as Everard Hall, seen through the friendly but mildly scornful eyes of a representative of the uninitiated public. The group of former college friends, reunited for a Christmas house party, are bored by the local rector's interminable monologue on the evils of contemporary life, and it is in a desperate effort to change the subject that the guest brings up Everard Hall's undergraduate scheme for an Arthurian epic. The poet, it appears, burned it in a mood of disgust because

> *"He thought that nothing new was said, or else*
> *Something so said 'twas nothing—that a truth*
> *Looks freshest in the fashion of the day."*

These words of the host are amplified by the poet himself:

> *"Why take the style of those heroic times?*
> *For nature brings not back the Mastodon,*
> *Nor we those times; and why should any man*
> *Remodel models? these twelve books of mine*
> *Were faint Homeric echoes, nothing worth,*
> *Mere chaff and draff, much better burnt."*

The reading of the epic fragment serves to send the tedious rector fast asleep, but the other auditors are strangely impressed:

> *It was the tone with which he read,*
> *Perhaps some modern touches here and there*
> *Redeem'd it from the charge of nothingness—*
> *Or else we lov'd the man, and prized his work;*
> *I know not.*

And the nonpoetic narrator is further astonished to find that its theme reappears that night in his dreams, with Arthur coming back to life "like a modern gentleman/ Of stateliest port."

By the frame device Tennyson achieved several protective results: he explained the purpose of mingling modern implications with the materials of traditional heroic romance; he forestalled adverse criticism by showing the poet's own contempt for the experiment; and yet he implied that it might have some value, since an uncommitted listener was strongly affected by it.

Even more significant are the prologue and conclusion that Tennyson wrote for his more ambitious poem, *The Princess*. In it he was undertaking a highly topical theme, the controversy over women's rights and—in particular—the higher education of women, which suddenly emerged in the 1840's as a corollary to the general movements in favor of human equality and educational opportunity. The subject was obviously inappropriate for embodiment in a Homeric or medieval fable; and yet its very topicality made the poet anxious to handle it with a degree of imaginative perspective, so that it would be dissociated from the immediate pressures of a current argument. Besides, he wanted to propose an eminently sensible approach to a potentially explosive topic, and one of the best ways to maintain an unbiased attitude is by an admixture of humor. These desiderata led him to adopt the mode of fantasy.

Through his interest in the romances of chivalry he selected a vaguely feudal setting and story, unidentifiable as to geographical region or historical century; but the feminist institution established by the Princess Ida and the Lady Psyche would be unthinkable in any medieval context, and the actual curriculum of the college was more advanced than anything that Oxbridge was offering undergraduates in the mid-nineteenth century. The incongruities and anachronisms contribute, of course, to the prevailing mood of comedy; and the poem annoyed extremists of both camps: ultra-feminists accused the poet of ridiculing their crusade, while reactionaries held that he was altogether too sympathetic toward the mania of women's rights. From an aesthetic point of view, too, the poem was open to objection as an inept mixing of modes: the basically serious theme and climax conflict with such almost farcical episodes as the disguise of three brawny young men as bashful maidens. Nevertheless, the poem is an interesting experiment as an attempt to find another solution to the predicament of bringing poetic imagination and emotion into meaningful relationship with the contemporary world.

Well aware that many readers would find the poem either distasteful or downright incomprehensible, Tennyson provided a prologue with the same sort of country-house setting as that of "The Epic." Problems of progress and social responsibility are suggested by the great annual picnic that the rich squire, Sir Walter Vivian, gives for his tenants and "The neighboring borough with their Institute/ Of which he was the patron." The historical ruins on the estate and the associated heroic legends are neatly contrasted with the up-to-date scientific demonstrations that the Institute instructors are conducting for their earnest students.

The house party includes seven undergraduates on vacation and also the host's coquettish daughter Lilia, who playfully challenges the boys to prove that women are not the equal of men:

> "O, I wish
> That I were some great princess, I would build
> Far off from men a college like a man's,
> And I would teach them all that men are taught;
> We are twice as quick!"

The outcome of the subsequent argument is that the young

people decide to make this the theme for "a tale from mouth to mouth," a game they have already played in the winter vacation:

> "He began,
> The rest would follow, each in turn; and so
> We forged a seven-fold story. Kind? what kind?
> Chimeras, crotchets, Christmas solecisms,
> Seven-headed monsters only made to kill
> Time by the fire in winter."

Thus the reader is warned in advance that the story will be unrealistic and incoherent, since each narrator must improvise from the point where the previous one leaves off. In the "Conclusion," when Tennyson is requested to make a unified poem out of the disparate items, he laments the inconsistency of tone:

> How to bind the scatter'd scheme of seven
> Together in one sheaf? What style could suit?
> The men required that I should give throughout
> The sort of mock-heroic gigantesque,
> With which we banter'd little Lilia first:
> The women—and perhaps they felt their power
> For something in the ballads which they sang,
> Or in their solemn influence as they sat,
> Had ever seem'd to wrestle with burlesque,
> And drove us, last, to quite a solemn close—
> They hated banter, wish'd for something real,
> A gallant fight, a noble princess—why
> Not make her true-heroic—true-sublime?
> Or all, they said, as earnest as the close?
> Which yet with such a framework scarce could be.
> Then rose a little feud betwixt the two,
> Betwixt the mockers and the realists;
> And I, betwixt them both, to please them both,
> And yet to give the story as it rose,
> I moved as in a strange diagonal,
> And maybe neither pleased myself nor them.

Just as in the introduction and conclusion to the "Morte d'Arthur" fragment, Tennyson has anticipated unfavorable critics by belittling his own poem; and also, as in the previous instance, he uses the dramatic frame to suggest the poem's serious significance:

> *But we went back to the Abbey, and sat on,*
> *So much the gathering darkness charm'd; we sat*
> *But spoke not, rapt in nameless reverie,*
> *Perchance upon the future man.*

Possibly my readers are wondering how much longer I can delay the revelation of my mysterious title, and perhaps they are beginning to suspect that I am planning a climax like that of "The Lady or the Tiger," leaving them to select "the key poem of the Victorian period" for themselves. But their patience will be imposed upon only a little while longer. I have felt the necessity of demonstrating in some detail the extent of the antagonism toward poetry, and I have used various poems of Tennyson as my principal illustrations of how the conditions affected young poets in the thirties and forties because he was so responsive to the ideas and pressures of the time and because his methods were so transparently explicit. Indeed, "The Princess" has some claim to be regarded as *one* of the key poems of the era. But Tennyson's debates about the function of poetry are too consciously defensive and too artificially extraneous to the main poems to be fully effective. The key poem has to be something more confident—even aggressive—and more complex and subtle in its uniting of the central theme with the aesthetic problem. Only one poem fully meets these conditions, and it is *Sordello*.

I have not chosen this notoriously abstruse poem in order to achieve surprise or to imply any intellectual superiority on my part. I am prepared to concede that *Sordello* was a failure, since it won neither the praise of the critics nor the comprehension of the public. But some other highly significant works of literature, both past and recent, were failures on similar terms. *The Excursion* was a failure, *Sartor Resartus* was a failure, *Finnegans Wake* was a failure, Mr. Pound's *Cantos* have been a failure. After decades of intermittent struggle with *Sordello*, I confess that much of it remains opaque to me. I am not one of the modern pundits who assign a poem's merit in direct ratio to its obscurity. I find myself returning to *Sordello* again and again, always infuriated by its seemingly willful obliquity, and yet always fascinated by its insights.

I consider *Sordello* important, then, because it was essentially a new undertaking. It is a poem about a poet writing a poem about a poet writing poems. A moment ago I put *Sordello* into the same category with *Sartor Resartus;* and in this respect the two works have a specific resemblance. Carlyle's treatise is about a philosopher writing a treatise about a philosopher writing a treatise. The public was pardonably confused in trying to distinguish Thomas Carlyle (the actual author) from the unnamed "editor and translator" who is struggling with a mass of German documents, and both of them from the learned Professor Teufelsdröckh, the ostensible topic of the whole study. In just the same way, Browning's poem is apparently concerned with a half-forgotten medieval minstrel involved in complicated feudal intrigues; but the narrative is repeatedly suspended in favor of direct statements by the poet himself, in London and Venice, from 1833 to 1838, explaining his choice of topic, his technical devices, and the inner significance of the events narrated. And just as Teufelsdröckh, underneath his fictitious Teutonic trappings, is primarily a portrait of Thomas Carlyle, so Sordello, underneath his historical Italian habiliments, is something like a portrait of Robert Browning.

Sordello is described in his childhood as having the temperament that foredooms him to be a poet:

> *a soul fit to receive*
> *Delight at every sense; you can believe*
> *Sordello foremost in the regal class*
> *Nature has broadly severed from her mass*
> *Of men, and framed for pleasure.*

Browning immediately raises the question as to which of the two basic types of poet the boy will eventually become. One type is endowed with negative capability:

> *they are fain invest*
> *The lifeless thing with life from their own soul,*
> *Availing it to purpose, to control,*
> *To dwell distinct and have peculiar joy*
> *And separate interests that may employ*
> *That beauty fitly, for its proper sake . . .*
> *One character*
> *Denotes them through the progress and the stir,—*
> *A need to blend with each external charm,*
> *Bury themselves, the whole heart wide and warm,—*
> *In something not themselves.*

The other type is essentially introspective, with the dangerous tendency to withdraw from the world:

> *For there's a class that eagerly looks, too,*
> *On beauty, but, unlike the gentler crew,*
> *Proclaims each new revealment born a twin*
> *With a distinctest consciousness within,*
> *Referring still the quality, now first*
> *Revealed, to their own soul—its instinct nursed*
> *In silence, now remembered better, shown*
> *More thoroughly, but not the less their own.*

In his boyish dreams Sordello visualizes himself as a great hero, uniting in his own person the attributes of all those whom he idolizes most, "half minstrel and half emperor." Abruptly transported from his solitude at Goito to the court at Mantua, he arrives just in time to listen contemptuously to a performance by the champion troubadour Eglamor, who smoothly tosses off a conventional ballad to general applause. Impulsively the young poet snatches the lute and retells the same story with strict fidelity to truth:

> *the true lay with the true end,*
> *Taking the other's names and time and place*
> *For his. On flew the song, a giddy race,*
> *After the flying story; word made leap*
> *Out word, rhyme—rhyme; the lay could barely keep*
> *Pace with the action visibly rushing past.*

After winning the prize with this impromptu performance, the youth begins to ponder for the first time upon his poetic vocation. The defeated Eglamor, meanwhile, has died of humiliation, even while generously admitting that Sordello's song was greater than his. Eglamor represents the purely aesthetic concept of poetry:

> *For him indeed was . . .*
> *. . . verse a temple-worship vague and vast,*
> *A ceremony that withdrew the last*
> *Opposing bolt, looped back the lingering veil*
> *Which hid the holy place; should one so frail*
> *Stand there without such effort? or repine*
> *If much was blank, uncertain at the shrine*
> *He knelt before, till, soothed by many a rite,*
> *The power responded, and some sound or sight*
> *Grew up, his own forever, to be fixed*
> *In rhyme, the beautiful, forever! . . .*
> *He, no genius rare,*
> *Transfiguring in fire or wave or air*
> *At will, but a poor gnome that, cloistered up*
> *In some rock-chamber with his agate cup,*
> *His topaz rod, his seed-pearl, in these few*

> *And their arrangement finds enough to do*
> *For his best art. Then, how he loved that art!*

Meanwhile, Sordello's easy triumph gratifies his love of admiration, but his creative spirit soon rebels against the mere reiterating of conventional lyrics in the same manner as Eglamor's. He becomes dissatisfied with the medieval allegorizing that gratifies his audience:

> *Virtue took form, nor vice refused a shape;*
> *Here heaven opened, there was hell agape,*
> *As Saint This simpered past in sanctity,*
> *Sinner the Other flared portentous by*
> *A greedy people. Then why stop, surprised*
> *At his success?*

Sordello's ambition is to depict actuality rather than oversimplified types, and he foolishly imagines that he has trained his auditors to appreciate something superior, saying to himself,

> *"These lays of yours, in brief*
> *Cannot men bear, now, something better?—fly*
> *A pitch beyond this unreal pageantry*
> *Of essences? the period sure has ceased*
> *For such: present us with ourselves, at least,*
> *Not portions of ourselves, mere loves and hates*
> *Made flesh: wait not!"*

This objective, however, bogs down in problems of vocabulary and technique, and eventually he succumbs to the temptation of continuing to accept easy popularity:

> *"Are those*
> *I sing to, over-likely to suppose*
> *A higher than the highest I present*
> *Now, which they praise already? Be content."*

Even on this basis, however, he is disillusioned in his hope of establishing genuine communication with the audience and winning their recognition of his inner power and genius:

> He set to celebrating the exploits
> Of Montfort o'er the Mountaineers.
> Then came
> The world's revenge: their pleasure, now his aim
> Merely—what was it? "Not to play the fool
> So much as learn our lesson in your school!"
> Replied the world. He found that, every time
> He gained applause by any ballad-rhyme,
> His auditory recognized no jot
> As he intended, and, mistaking not
> Him for his meanest hero, ne'er was dunce
> Sufficient to believe him—all, at once.
> His will . . . conceive it caring for his will!
> —Mantuans, the main of them, admiring still
> How a mere singer, ugly, stunted, weak,
> Had Montfort at completely (so to speak)
> His fingers' ends; while past the praise-tide swept
> To Montfort, either's share distinctly kept:
> The true meed for true merit! his abates
> Into a sort he most repudiates,
> And on them angrily he turns. Who were
> The Mantuans, after all, that he should care
> About their recognition, ay or no?

With this bitter discovery that a poet can never be a hero in the eyes of the insensate public, he enters a schizophrenic period in which he is

> Sundered in twain,—each spectral part at strife
> With each; one jarred against another life;
> The Poet thwarting hopelessly the Man.

Like Teufelsdröckh in his cynical "Center of Indifference," Sordello mechanically continues to grind out trite verses, while arguing with the common-sense critic Naddo as to the true function of poetry. When Sordello demands, "How

should externals satisfy my soul?" his friend quotes another
critic to bolster his own position:

> *"Why that's precise the error Squarchialupe"*
> *(Hazarded Naddo) "finds; 'the man can't stoop*
> *To sing us out,' quoth he, 'a mere romance;*
> *He'd fain do better than the best, enhance*
> *The subjects' rarity, work problems out*
> *Therewith.' Now, you're a bard, a bard past doubt,*
> *And no philosopher; why introduce*
> *Crotchets like these? fine, surely, but no use*
> *In poetry—which still must be, to strike,*
> *Based upon common sense; there's nothing like*
> *Appealing to our nature! what beside*
> *Was your first poetry? No tricks were tried*
> *In that, no hollow thrills, affected throes!*
> *'The man,' said we, 'tells his own joys and woes;*
> *We'll trust him.' Would you have your songs endure?*
> *Build on the human heart! why, to be sure*
> *Yours is one sort of heart—but I mean theirs,*
> *Ours, every one's, the healthy heart one cares*
> *To build on!"*

Finally, at the end of the second book, Sordello reaches
his first great decision when he finds himself unable to com-
pose a conventional ode of welcome for the return of the
military hero Salinguerra; he flees to his childhood home
and flings away his laureate's crown. For a year he abandons
ambition, and lives in the sensuous dream-world of his
youth until he seems to have lost all his gift for song. Then,
in a long and difficult internal debate, his will reasserts itself. He goes to Verona to immerse himself in the power-
struggle under the guidance of Palma, the Ghibellin princess whom he adores. Gradually he realizes that his visions
of personal renown through poetry were egotistical and
delusory, and that he must seek to fulfill his true duty
through the slow and discouraging process of initiating
ideals that may eventually result in some improvement of

the human condition. Having thus decided to write the kind of poetry that is bound to be difficult and unpopular because it deals seriously with contemporary problems, Sordello still has to decide what his attitude is to be. And like any good nineteenth-century liberal he elects to promote the cause of the populace against that of the autocratic nobles. In the climax of the poem, this decision leads him into an excruciating moral dilemma, when wealth and authority come to him unexpectedly as the heir to the ruthless Ghibellin leader Salinguerra. Sordello feels that he must relinquish all this eminence, such as he had once ardently desired, and align himself with the opposing faction because it is more sympathetic toward the democratic cause. The emotional conflict precipitates his death, much as Tennyson's Lady of Shalott incurred her death by turning her back upon the formal, second-hand art of her tapestry weaving and accepting the genuine emotions of real experience.

By Browning's life-long doctrine, of course, Sordello has achieved more by his abortive effort to create the great democratic manifesto than he ever could have achieved by composing facile lyrics:

> For thence,—a paradox
> Which comforts while it mocks,—
> Shall life succeed in that it seems to fail:
> What I aspired to be,
> And was not, comforts me.

Dante provided Browning's authority, by classifying Sordello in Purgatory among the dilatory souls who died before their repentance was complete; but Browning is certainly not prepared to admit that Sordello was merely a procrastinator. Rather he insists that the minstrel was slowly surmounting apparently insuperable obstacles to the fulfillment of a great purpose. To be sure, Browning has the advantage of historical hindsight, by which he can assert that Sordello's bold use of the vernacular in serious poetry paved the way for Dante's achievement half a century later; but even this is not the full extent of the triumph that is claimed for the hero. Browning depicts the thirteenth-century troubadour as a mid-Victorian "gentleman of stateliest port" just as clearly as Tennyson depicts King Arthur in the same role; Sordello is merely a little further left of center in his social views. Both heroes die in apparent failure because their ideals are so far above the comprehension of their contemporaries; but in both instances the poet implies that the heroes' visions are well on the way to fulfillment in the nineteenth century, if only poets will recognize their duty as shapers of the public conscience.

So much for the ostensible topic of the poem—the *Bildungs roman* of a young poet who gradually discovers the frustrations and the responsibilities of his vocation. It is not merely by implication, however, that Sordello's experiences mirror Browning's own. Again and again he injects himself overtly into the poem in order to expatiate upon the development of his poetic theory. These passages form an intimate and convincing record of how Browning arrived at the objectives and the techniques that were to characterize all his poetry.

The two most essential passages occur at the beginning and near the middle, in the latter part of the third book. The first one expounds Browning's preference for dramatic monologue and his reason for deciding on this one occasion to use third-personal narrative:

> *Never,—I should warn you first,—*
> *Of my own choice had this, if not the worst*
> *Yet not the best expedient, served to tell*
> *A story I could body forth so well*
> *By making speak, myself kept out of view,*

> *The very man as he was wont to do,*
> *And leaving you to say the rest for him. . . .*
> *But it seems*
> *Your setters-forth of unexampled themes,*
> *Makers of quite new men, producing them,*
> *Would best chalk broadly on each vesture's hem*
> *The wearer's quality; or take their stand,*
> *Motley on back and pointing pole in hand,*
> *Beside them. So, for once I face ye, friends.*

The other, and longer, passage, in the third book, describes in detail how Browning became discouraged with the poem and set it aside after several years of experiment and revision. On a visit to Venice he acquires a new perspective toward the theme. He realizes that a good poem cannot be a perfect artifact, unrelated to the author's inner life:

> *Note,*
> *In just such songs as Eglamor (say) wrote*
> *With heart and soul and strength, for he believed*
> *Himself achieving all to be achieved*
> *By singer—in such songs you find alone*
> *Completeness, judge the song and singer one,*
> *And either purpose answered, his in it*
> *Or its in him: while from true works (to wit*
> *Sordello's dream- performances that will*
> *Never be more than dreamed) escapes there still*
> *Some proof, the singer's proper life was 'neath*
> *The life his song exhibits, this a sheath*
> *To that.*

Looking at the tattered peasantry around him on the canal bank, Browning decides that henceforth his inner objective must be dedicated to people of this sort, and that therefore his poetry must deal with vice and ugliness as much as with virtue and beauty:

> *As good you sought*
> *To spare me the Piazza's slippery stone*

> *Or keep me to the unchoked canals alone*
> *As hinder life the evil with the good*
> *Which make up Living, rightly understood . . .*
> > *Beside, care-bit erased*
> *Broken-up beauties ever took my taste*
> *Supremely.*

From this he proceeds to his other revelation: that every human being is justified in his own eyes:

> *Ask moreover, when they prate*
> *Of evil men past hope, "Don't each contrive,*
> *Despite the evil you abuse, to live?—*
> *Keeping, each losel, through a maze of lies,*
> *His own conceit of truth? to which he hies*
> *By obscure windings, tortuous, if you will,*
> *But to himself not inaccessible.*

Such subject matter is bound to be repulsive to the average reader: it will be rejected as ugly, as incomprehensibly subtle, as morally ambiguous. Accepting all this disfavor, Browning defiantly identifies himself with Moses, leading the thirsty Israelites through the desert while their popular poet chants his aesthetic songs:

> *"Meantime, just meditate my madrigal*
> *O' the mugwort that conceals a dewdrop safe!"*
> *What, dullard? we and you in smothery chafe,*
> *Babes, baldheads, stumbling thus far into Zin*
> *The Horrid, getting neither out nor in,*
> *A hungry sun above us, sands that bung*
> *Our throats, . . .*
> *And you, 'twixt tales of Potiphar's mishap,*
> *And sonnets on the earliest ass that spoke,*
> *—Remark, you wonder any one needs choke*
> *With founts about! Potsherd him, Gibeonites!*
> *While awkwardly enough your Moses smites*
> *The rock, though he forego his promised land*
> *Thereby, have Satan claim his carcass, and*
> *Figure as Metaphysic Poet.*

This last is one of the most notable implications of *Sordello*. It marks the first occasion in two centuries when a poet was frankly prepared to be incomprehensible to the majority of readers. This is what Browning meant by the much-ridiculed first and last lines of the poem: "Who will, may hear Sordello's story told," and "Who would has heard Sordello's story told." The phrases "who *will*" and "who *would*" do not signify the mere passive attention that neoclassical and romantic poets assumed to be the normal attitude of their readers. Browning intends to emphasize that there is a strenuous co-operative relationship between the author and the reader, and that a continuous act of volition is necessary if the reader is to grasp the unfamiliar and perhaps unpalatable fare that is being offered to him. The final authorial comment, in the closing lines, resorts to a vulgar metaphor to describe this new sort of response:

> *The ghost's gone, and the story ends*
> *I'd fain hope, sweetly; seeing, peri or ghoul,*
> *That spirits are conjectured fair or foul,*
> *Evil or good, judicious authors think,*
> *According as they vanish in a stink*
> *Or in a perfume. Friends, be frank! ye snuff*
> *Civet, I warrant. Really? Like enough!*
> *Merely the savour's rareness; any nose*
> *May ravage with impunity a rose:*
> *Rifle a musk-pod and 'twill ache like yours!*
> *I'd tell you that same pungency ensures*
> *An after-gust, but that were overbold.*

As a devotee of Shelley, Browning will admit to no mistrust in the supreme and eternal importance of poetry; and his robust assertiveness is more impressive than Tennyson's deprecatory modesty; but it is evidence that he was just as acutely aware of the campaign against poetry and of the need for every poet to strengthen his defenses and to take stock of his equipment. The agonizing reappraisal was conducted so thoroughly in *Sordello* that the poem is not merely a manifesto for Browning's life work, nor even merely the key poem of the Victorian era; as a survey of the functions and responsibilities of poetry, it still remains vitally applicable.

Matthew Arnold, in his essay on "The Function of Criticism at the Present Time," insisted that "the creation of a modern poet, to be worth much, implies a great critical effort behind it." Tennyson and Browning, as well as Arnold himself, made the critical effort so strenuously that it sometimes showed in the texture of the resultant poem, and nowhere more clearly than in *Sordello.*

Frederic E. Faverty

❧ ❧

Browning's Debt to Meredith in *James Lee's Wife*

For *James Lee's Wife,* the poem which opens *Dramatis Personae* and sets the disconsolate mood for much of the volume, no sources have thus far been discovered. The most convincing suggestion as to origin is that by Herford, who believes that the poem grew out of Browning's dejection over the loss of his wife and out of his residence on the "bitter coast of France," where he spent his late summer vacations in 1862 and 1863. The problem confronting James Lee's wife was, like Browning's own, "how to live when the answering love was gone." [1] Unquestionably, these elements enter into the composition, yet they explain only the generating mood and the landscape. The theme itself, the

FREDERIC E. FAVERTY is Morrison Professor of English at Northwestern University.

method of developing the theme, the imagery, the phraseology, the philosophical import, all these still await investigation. In the case of houses not made with hands it is often difficult to determine the quarries whence the stones were drawn. Browning as a builder is notorious for wandering into far places in search of strange materials. In the case of *James Lee's Wife,* however, I believe it can be shown that he did not wander so far afield as was his custom, no farther, in fact, than to Meredith, his contemporary and fellow-Englishman. For the foundation, and for parts of the super-structure itself he drew upon *Modern Love* and *Ode to the Spirit of Earth in Autumn* which appeared in *Modern Love, and Poems of the English Roadside, with Poems and Ballads,* published on April 28, 1862.

Browning read Meredith's volume of poems shortly after its publication and complimented the author highly upon the performance. Of this commendation Meredith boasts in a letter to Captain Maxse,

> I hope, by the way, your review won't be written before you see the book. One poem, new to you (Ode to the Spirit of Earth in Autumn), will please you better than all—please you specially. It will suffice for me if you tell me what you think of it, and not the public. The notices that have appeared fix favourably on the Roadside poems, but discard "Modern Love," which, I admit, requires thought, and discernment, and reading more than once. The Saturday R. has not yet spoken. One paper calls me a genius—one, a meretricious, clever, bold man. I find, to my annoyance, that I am susceptible to remarks on my poems, and criticisms from whipsters or women absolutely make me wince and flush. I saw Robert Browning the other day, and he expressed himself "astounded at the originality, delighted with the naturalness and beauty."—Pardon my egotism—I write to please you! [2]

Toward the close of the summer of 1862 Browning went for a vacation to the coast of Brittany, the coast described with such detail in *James Lee's Wife*. In view of his enthusiastic approval of Meredith's recently published work, it is not impossible that he took the volume with him for vacation reading. In a letter to Isa Blagden, from Ste. Marie, Pornic, Loire Inférieure, August 18, he says, "The place is much to my mind; I have brought books and write." [3] For the purpose of proving Meredith's influence, however, it is not necessary to assume that Browning had the book with him in Brittany. [4] If *James Lee's Wife* was written during this vacation, it may well have arisen partly out of the earlier reading of Meredith's work.

Although Browning's poem was not published until 1864, the evidence indicates that it was probably written in Brittany during the vacation of 1862. As DeVane suggests, "the mood of Browning at this time, as may be seen in his letters, is the mood of James Lee's wife." [5] The details of the picture of Ste. Marie which Browning gives in his letter to Isa Blagden, August 18, are reproduced in the poem:

> This is a wild little place in Brittany something like that village where we stayed last year, close to the sea, a hamlet of a dozen houses, perfectly lonely, one may walk on the edge of the low rocks by the sea for miles, or go into the country at the back . . . If I could, I would stay just as I am for many a day. I feel out of the very earth sometimes, as I sit here, at the window, with the little church, a field, a few houses, and the sea . . . Such a soft sea and such a mournful wind! I wrote a poem yesterday of 120 lines, and mean to keep writing, whether I like it or no. [6]

The "window" of the letter, as Mrs. Orr has pointed out, [7] is the "Doorway" of the poem, and from it the fig tree, as well as the field and the sea of section III of the poem was visible. It is not possible to identify definitely the poem "of 120 lines." Of the poems published in *Dramatis Personae* none is of this exact length, and the reference may possibly be to a part of *James Lee's Wife*. The poem was probably written by sections, and the first four form a unit of 121 lines.[8]

If, then, the poem was composed at this time, the memory of Meredith's work would still have been fresh in Browning's mind.

Modern Love is the title poem of Meredith's 1862 volume. It is also the best, being distinguished particularly for "originality," "naturalness," and "beauty," the qualities that "astounded" and "delighted" Browning. The title itself is suggestive, and may have given Browning an idea for his next volume of poems.[9] At any rate, *Dramatis Personae* differs from Browning's usual work in that it is concerned primarily with contemporary subjects. Love when it is treated is modern love, not that of the Renaissance or of the *ancien régime.* The very title in one case is indicative: *Dîs aliter Visum; or, Le Byron de nos Jours.* Whether or not this general influence is granted, however, the following comparisons will show, I believe, that Meredith supplied Browning with some of the ideas, imagery, and even phraseology used in *James Lee's Wife.*

1. *Similarity in theme.* The subject of both poems is the same, a dying love, a study in alienation. Since Meredith's work is more than twice as long as Browning's, some aspects of the subject are developed with which Browning does not deal at all. The fundamental situation, however, is the same in both poems—the realization by a wedded lover that love is no longer returned. The fundamental problem is also the same—the determination of the course to be pursued by the injured spouse. In both poems the wronged lover is the speaker: in *Modern Love* the husband,[10] in Browning's poem the wife. The husband of *Modern Love* finds his wife unfaithful. In *James Lee's Wife,* the husband's love, evidently light to begin with, has flown at

"suspicion of a bond." Too shallow to appreciate the deeper spiritual attributes of his wife, and finding her "harsh, ill-favoured," he is ready to find his pleasure

> *in a laughing eye,*
> *And why should you look beyond?*

The problem, as can be seen from the account thus far, is basically the same in both poems. The solutions of the difficulty differ. The husband of *Modern Love* repays infidelity with infidelity, a course which leads to jealousies, "deep questioning," "endless dole," indeed, the suicide of the wife. Meredith's lovers are indecisive, vacillating, and in their indecision they enmesh themselves more and more in deceit and despair, with fatal result. For such indecision in love, as in most other matters, Browning had little patience. The sin he would impute to all those who fail through inability to come to a decision and act upon it

> *Is—the unlit lamp and the ungirt loin,*
> *Though the end in sight was a vice, I say.*[11]

James Lee's wife, therefore, solves her problem in a quicker, more decisive, and for these reasons more humane fashion. Like the husband of *Modern Love,* she tries "parley," and with as little effect. Realizing the futility of all her efforts, she takes refuge in renunciation and departure. Such a course, it is important to note, is suggested in *Modern Love* and rejected: husband and wife are engaged in a discussion of their dilemma; she implies that he is happy while she is miserable.

> *"Take ship!*
> *For happiness is somewhere to be had."*

is his advice. The wife, however, chooses to remain and act out the "wedded lie." James Lee's wife, on the other hand, does depart, does literally "take ship." The last section of the poem is devoted to her soliloquy as she stands *On Deck*.

It would seem, therefore, that Browning took the problem in human relationships dealt with so brilliantly by Meredith and provided a different, and to his mind a better solution. Such a procedure is not foreign to Browning's general method. In the same volume, *Dramatis Personae*, *Rabbi Ben Ezra* develops the metaphor of the Potter's wheel in an extended refutation of the philosophy stated by Fitz-Gerald in the *Rubáiyát*. It was in all likelihood his meditations upon Arnold's *Empedocles* that led Browning to the composition of *Cleon* (1855).[12] And in *The Glove* (1845) Browning revises Leigh Hunt's account as given in *The Glove and the Lions* to accord with his own observations upon feminine psychology.

2. *Similarity in setting, in development of theme, in imagery, and in phraseology.* The major part of the action in *Modern Love* takes place along the seashore, where husband and wife are guests in a "country house." It is on the seashore that they "dig Love's grave." The seashore also provides the setting for *James Lee's Wife*. To be sure, the argument for Meredith's influence in this case is none too strong, for Browning here describes the actual coast of Brittany where he was spending his vacation. But the similarity at least deserves mention.

The themes of both poems are developed in much the same fashion—through the soliloquies of the speaker at various intervals of time, each soliloquy being given a different setting. To list a few examples from *Modern Love:* the speaker comments upon the changing relationships between the lovers as they wander—in the "yellow meadows" (sonnet XI), on the lawn (sonnet XXI), "Along the garden terrace" (sonnet XXXVII), along the seashore (sonnet XLIII), in the wood (sonnet XLVI), and "by the ocean's moaning verge" (sonnet XLIX). James Lee's wife meditates:

"At the Window" (section I), "By the Fireside" (section II), "In the Doorway" (section III), "Along the Beach" (section IV), "On the Cliff" (section V), "Under the Cliff" (section VI), "Among the Rocks" (section VII), "Beside the Drawing Board" (section VIII), "On Deck" (section IX).

In one instance, *Modern Love* (sonnet XVI), the setting and the development of the theme are strikingly similar:

> *In our old shipwrecked days there was an hour,*
> *When in the firelight steadily aglow,*
> *Joined slackly, we beheld the red chasm grow*
> *Among the clicking coals.*

The idea of shipwreck had been stressed earlier in sonnet IV. The second section of *James Lee's Wife* is called "By the Fireside." And the figure of the shipwreck runs through the whole section:

> *Is all our fire of shipwreck wood,*
>   *Oak and pine?*
> *Oh, for the ills half-understood,*
>   *The dim, dead woe*
>   *Long ago*
> *Befallen this bitter coast of France!*
> *Well, poor sailors took their chance; I take mine.*
> . . . .
> *God help you, sailors, at your need!*
>   *Spare the curse!*
> *For some ships, safe in port indeed,*
>   *Rot and rust,*
>   *Run to dust,*
> *All through worms i' the wood, which crept,*
> *Gnawed our hearts out while we slept:*
>   *That is worse!*
>
> *Who lived here before us two?*
>   *Old-world pairs!*
> *Did a woman ever—would I knew!—*
>   *Watch the man*
>   *With whom began*

Love's voyage full-sail,—(now, gnash your teeth!)
When planks start, open hell beneath
   Unawares?

One must remember, of course, that Browning had written a poem called *By the Fireside* which antedated Meredith's. As Herford says: "The second section of *James Lee's Wife, By the Fireside,* cannot have been written without a conscious, and therefore significant, reference to the like-named poem in *Men and Women,* which so exquisitely plays with the intimate scenery of his home life." [13] The earlier poem depicts the domestic bliss which Browning anticipates for himself and his wife. The hopelessness and desolation of the later poem show the sad outcome of that expectation. To enforce the contrast Browning used Meredith's figure of the shipwreck. The very fact that he himself had written a poem with a like setting would have increased his interest in Meredith's picture, and the idea of shipwreck would have struck him with emphasis as an all too exact description of his own state. Meredith's poem may thus have served to call his own earlier one to mind, and out of the coalescence of the two impressions the third poem might have been formed.

Another case displays a striking similarity in subject, imagery, and even phraseology. In sonnet XXIX of *Modern Love,* the husband describes the "spiritual splendour" with which love should endow the object of affection, a consecration which he finds impossible for the "Lady" whom he has chosen as a rival for his wife.

   "Am I failing? For no longer can I cast
   A glory round about this head of gold.
   Glory she wears, but springing from the mould;
   Not like that consecration of the Past!
   Is my soul beggared? Something more than earth
   I cry for still: I cannot be at peace
   In having Love upon a mortal lease.

I cannot take the woman at her worth!
Where is the ancient wealth wherewith I cloathed
Our human nakedness, and could endow
With spiritual splendour a white brow
That else had grinned at me the fact I loathed?" [14]

Browning also describes the glory with which love greatens
and glorifies what was *mere earth* before. And he does so
in language similar to that of Meredith's poem. James Lee's
wife expostulates with her husband, pointing out that her
love has been great enough to glorify him in spite of his
obvious deficiencies (section IV):

> *I took you—how could I otherwise?*
> *For a world to me, and more;*
> *For all, love greatens and glorifies*
> *Till God's a-glow, to the loving eyes,*
> *In what was mere earth before.*
>
> Yes, earth—yes, mere ignoble earth!
> *Now did I mis-state, mistake?*
> *Do I wrong your weakness and call it worth?*
> *Expect all harvest, dread no dearth,*
> *Seal my sense up for your sake?*
>
> *Oh, love, love, no, love! not so, indeed!*
> You were just weak earth, *I knew:*
> *With much in you waste, with many a weed,*
> *And plenty of passions run to seed,*
> *But a little good grain too.*
>
> *And such as you were, I took you for mine:*
> . . . .   [15]

3. *Similarity in philosophical idea.* In one of the most famous of the fifty sonnets in *Modern Love,* number XIII,
Meredith plays upon the theme that all things are subject
to nature's inexorable change—the rose however beautiful
must die; nature bears "here, a seed-bag—there, an urn."

Love, the human rose, like all else, is subject to the law. This is the lesson we must teach our foolish hearts to learn. It is a lesson which the husband finds altogether unconsoling. For the human rose, "fair surpassingly," he would ask exemption, but he knows, of course, that his plaint is vain.

> *"I play for Seasons; not Eternities!"*
> *Says Nature, laughing on her way. "So must*
> *All those whose stake is nothing more than dust!"*
> *And lo, she wins, and of her harmonies*
> *She is full sure! Upon the dying rose*
> *She drops a look of fondness, and goes by,*
> *Scarce any retrospection in her eye;*
> *For she the laws of growth most deeply knows,*
> *Whose hands bear, here, a seed-bag—there, an urn.*
> *Pledged she herself to aught,'twould mark her end!*
> *This lesson of our only visible friend*
> *Can we not teach our foolish hearts to learn?*
> *Yes! yes!—but, oh, our human rose is fair*
> *Surpassingly! Lose calmly Love's great bliss,*
> *When the renewed for ever of a kiss*
> *Whirls life within the shower of loosened hair!*

James Lee's wife is as deeply disillusioned. Through her lips Browning voices a criticism of six stanzas of his own published twenty-eight years before, stanzas in which he had interpreted too lightly and optimistically the wailing of the wind. To the mature mind nature brings a sterner doctrine: that "nothing endures," that man is swept "From change to change unceasingly." Like the husband of *Modern Love*, James Lee's wife laments that we cannot

> *. . . draw one beauty into our heart's core,*
> *And keep it changeless.*

To love, as to all things, time assigns a limit.

> *Then, when the wind begins among the vines,*
> *So low, so low, what shall it mean but this?*

299

"*Here is the change beginning, here the lines*
 Circumscribe beauty, set to bliss
The limit time assigns."

Nothing can be as it has been before;
 Better, so call it, only not the same.
To draw one beauty into our heart's core,
 And keep it changeless! such our claim;
So answered,—Never more!

Simple? Why this is the old woe o' the world;
 Tune, to whose rise and fall we live and die.
Rise with it, then. Rejoice that man is hurled
 From change to change unceasingly.
His soul's wings never furled!

That's a new question; still replies the fact,
 Nothing endures: the wind moans, saying so;
We moan in acquiescence: there's life's pact,
 Perhaps probation—do I know?
God does: endure His act!

Only, for man, how bitter not to grave
 On his soul's hands' palms, one fair, good, wise thing
Just as he grasped it! For himself, death's wave;
 While time first washes—ah, the sting!—
O'er all he'd sink to save.

After *Modern Love,* the *Ode to the Spirit of Earth in Autumn* is perhaps the most remarkable poem in Meredith's 1862 volume. The *Ode* begins with an arresting picture,

  Fair Mother Earth lay on her back last night
  To gaze her fill on Autumn's sunset skies.

Then follows a long description of the natural phenomena of autumn, and at the tumultuous change nature *laughs* since of her eventual harmonies she is "full sure."

For once, good souls, we'll not pretend
To be aught better than her who bore us,
And is our only visible friend.
Hark to her laughter! who laughs like this,
Can she be dead, or rooted in pain?
She has been slain by the narrow brain,
But for us who love her she lives again.

And after another description of the "riotous companies"
of autumn, the lesson is drawn,

Great Mother Nature! teach me, like thee,
To kiss the season and shun regrets.
And am I more than the mother who bore,
Mock me not with thy harmony!
    Teach me to blot regrets,
    Great Mother! me inspire
    With faith that forward sets
    But feeds the living fire,
    Faith that never frets
    For vagueness in the form.
    In life, O keep me warm!
    For, what is human grief?
    And what do men desire?

In section VII of *James Lee's Wife*, Browning draws a picture of the earth in autumn which closely resembles the one
which opens the *Ode:* the "brown old earth" basks his
bones in the sun, his knees and feet thrust into the sea for
the ripple to run over. He wears a "good gigantic smile."
And, as in the *Ode*, he has a doctrine to teach.

Among the Rocks

Oh, good gigantic smile o' the brown old earth,
    This autumn morning! How he sets his bones
To bask i' the sun, and thrusts out knees and feet
For the ripple to run over in its mirth;
    Listening the while, where on the heap of stones
The white breast of the sea-lark twitters sweet.

301

That is the doctrine, simple, ancient, true;
  Such is life's trial, as old earth smiles and knows.
If you loved only what were worth your love,
Love were clear gain, and wholly well for you:
  Make the low nature better by your throes!
Give earth yourself, go up for gain above.

The picture—autumn; earth lying on his back; the smile —I believe it will be granted is very similar to that in the *Ode.* The doctrine which nature teaches is a fusion of that to be found in *Modern Love* (sonnet XIII), and that given in the *Ode,* to which Browning adds an element of his own. To the stern philosophy of renunciation (*Modern Love*) is added the doctrine (the *Ode*) that one must give oneself unselfishly to the earth and its processes. To some such philosophy Browning in his deep dejection over the loss of his wife must have been brought, and as certainly he must have found some comfort in Meredith's beautiful expression of it. But unmodified it would have proved cold comfort, and in accepting it, Browning adds his familiar injunction: "go up for gain above." Renunciation and the submergence of one's being in the larger cycle of earth's change, nature's teaching, to a philosophical acceptance of which neither betrayed husband (*Modern Love,* sonnet XIII) nor dejected wife (*James Lee's Wife,* section VI) could rise, here finds a more persuasive advocate in "the brown old earth." His smile is fraught with sympathetic pathos, revealing an understanding of "life's trial." Browning is able to follow Meredith part way upon the philosophical path of the *Ode.* "Give earth yourself" is part of the doctrine as finally enunciated, but the mood remains somber. His is no glad acceptance, like Meredith's. It is not a *laugh* that he discovers in the world of nature, but a *smile,* sober, reflective, even compassionate. That nature did provide even this much comfort is worthy of notice, for at this source Browning seldom finds balm for the hurt spirit. He

finds it often in art, but seldom in nature. Indeed, such
ministration by art is also provided in *James Lee's Wife*.
The doctrine taught by nature is supplemented in the next
section by advice from Da Vinci, who says that life may
still have its uses though love be denied. It is unusual for
Browning to sit at the feet of nature for lessons in philosophy. The ideas expressed in section XXV of another of his
poems, *Easter Day,* inform most of his works.

> *"What though my trust were gone*
> *From natural things? Henceforth my part*
> *Be less with Nature than with Art!*
> *For Art supplants, gives mainly worth*
> *To Nature; 'tis Man stamps the earth—*
> *And I will seek his impress, seek*
> *The statuary of the Greek,*
> *Italy's painting—there my choice*
> *Shall fix!"*

For support, if any is required, in this opinion on Browning's general attitude toward nature one may turn to J. W.
Beach, "Browning was, if possible, even less of a 'naturalist'
than Tennyson. By nature he means for the most part, like
Tennyson, the world of science. . . . And he was at least
as insistent as Tennyson on the necessity of finding man's
destiny and the meaning of the world outside the frame of
nature." [16] That nature in *James Lee's Wife* has so dominant a function, plays so philosophical a role, may be
credited in part to Meredith's influence.

The foregoing evidences in their cumulative effect indicate, I think, that Browning's poem had a threefold
genesis: the somber mood induced by his loss, the bleak
landscape of the coast of Brittany, and his recollections of
Meredith's tragic theme. He takes himself to task for the
easy faith and buoyant optimism of his early manhood, for
in this poem he speaks *de profundis.* That from these

depths he is able to rise to the half-way station of stoicism, that for once he is willing to lend an attentive ear to the kindly, if stern, teaching of earth, he owes in part to Meredith. A poignant theme that at once enlisted Browning's interest, a few apt and striking images, a pregnant phrase or two, and a source of philosophic healing in a new reading of earth—these Meredith may have contributed. Browning's imagination was stirred and he mounted to the middle altitude of renunciation. The heights of assurance and hope that earlier he had arrived at "by the happy, prompt, instinctive way of youth," he did not reach until some while later when solitude and time had performed their beneficent offices. Then other and more congenial teachers whispered him in the ear. At best, Meredith presented a vision of the "broken arcs"; Abt Vogler and others, the "perfect round."

NOTES

1. C. H. Herford, *Robert Browning* (Edinburgh and London, 1905), pp. 153–155.
2. *Letters of George Meredith*, ed. W. M. Meredith, 2 vols. (New York, 1912), I, 72, 73.
3. *Dearest Isa: Robert Browning's Letters to Isabella Blagden*, ed. E. C. McAleer (Austin, Texas, 1951), p. 116.
4. Browning owned a presentation copy: *Catalogue of Pictures, Drawings and Engravings; Autograph Letters and Manuscripts; Books and Works of Art, the Property of R. W. Barrett Browning, Esq. (Deceased)* (London: Sotheby, Wilkinson and Hodge, 1913), Item 916.
5. W. C. DeVane, *A Browning Handbook* (New York, 1955), p. 285. DeVane also mentions the possibility of Meredith's influence, since *Modern Love* and *James Lee's Wife* depict "the same kind of tragic event."
6. *Dearest Isa . . .* , pp. 116, 119.
7. Mrs. Sutherland Orr, *Life and Letters of Robert Browning*, 2 vols. (Boston and New York, 1892), II, 387.
8. W. C. DeVane, *op. cit.*, p. 285, believes that "the conditions fit better with *Gold Hair*." He offers no explanation, however, and the poem as it appeared in the first edition of *Dramatis Personae* consisted of 135 lines.

9. In *Dramatis Personae* Browning for the first time in his career made a considerable concession to his critics. He had failed of popularity partly because of his deliberate choice of themes dealing with past ages and with countries other than England. By the reviewers he had been repeatedly taken to task on these counts, and the 1864 volume was a conscious attempt at greater conformity. Its comparative popularity with critics and with public was due in part to this fact.

10. In those sonnets of the sequence in which the husband is not the speaker, the poet himself comments upon the psychological entanglements.

11. It is the frustrate ghosts of *The Statue and the Bust* who are thus found wanting. The speaker in *Too Late* is guilty of the same sin. *The Flight of the Duchess* and *The Ring and the Book* furnish examples of the more vigorous action which Browning would approve.

12. A. W. Crawford, "Browning's 'Cleon,' " *JEGP*, XXVI (1927), 485ff.

13. C. H. Herford, *op. cit.*, p. 154.

14. Italics are mine.

15. Italics are mine.

16. J. W. Beach, *The Concept of Nature in Nineteenth-Century English Poetry* (New York, 1936), p. 435.

Carl J. Weber

❧ ☙

Two Fires at
Max Gate

In 1791, by what was then a brilliant innovation, James Boswell demonstrated the value of letters to a biographer, and since the publication of the *Life of Johnson* no biographer has failed to acclaim, by his own use of letters, the soundness of Boswell's conviction that this "mode of biography is the most perfect than can be conceived." Bruce R. McElderry was well aware of this fact while writing his biography of Thomas Wolfe. "I have derived much help," he remarks on page viii, "from Elizabeth Nowell's edition of Wolfe's *Letters*," and on page 23 he points out the significance of Wolfe's letter to his mother: "Mama, in the name of God, guard Papa's letters to me with you life. . . .

CARL J. WEBER, who died 17 December 1966, was Professor Emeritus of English at Colby College.

Watch them like a hawk. . . . There has never been anybody like Papa. . . . He is headed straight not for one of my plays but for a series. . . . Save those letters!"

Alas for the biographer, people are not always eager to "save those letters." When, only a few weeks ago, the first volume of the Pilgrim Edition of *The Letters of Charles Dickens* appeared, a London reviewer remarked: "Letters . . . are primary sources. . . . They are revealing, often to a degree that might astonish or disconcert their writer. . . . It is sad for the reader, and a mixed tragedy for the editors, that Dickens made more than one bonfire at Gad's Hill of his incoming mail. . . . Letters . . . could have helped to keep the record straight." [1]

Tossing letters into a bonfire is not the only way by which authors have sometimes constructed road blocks in the path of future biographers. Willa Cather lit no bonfire, but "her will contains an unqualified prohibition of the publication 'in any form whatsoever of the whole, or any part, of any letter or letters by me.' This may be regarded . . . as a loss. . . . George F. Whicher has expressed the belief that, as a result of the novelist's restriction upon her personal papers 'even a judicious examination of her career' is made difficult 'if not impossible.' " [2]

In his attitude toward the legitimate use of letters, Thomas Hardy was more inclined to agree with Willa Cather or with Charles Dickens than with Thomas Wolfe. That is to say, he was a lighter of bonfires rather than a wholesale preserver of letters. One cannot imagine Hardy writing to his mother: "Mama, in the name of God, . . . save those letters!" On the contrary, like Willa Cather, he "believed intensely in the artist's right to a private life." His private papers, in so far as they have survived, do not include a single letter to or from his father or his mother, and their absence is the result of Hardy's imitation of Dickens' performance at Gad's Hill. He lit a bonfire.

Hardy himself enables us to date the first of the great conflagrations at Max Gate, for on 7 May 1919 he wrote to Sir George Douglas: "I have not been doing much—mainly destroying papers of the last thirty or forty years." [3] We know, too, what was the occasion of their destruction. Hardy had decided to write his autobiography and was going to use letters from his files to guide him in his work.

He had been urged to write an autobiography many times, but he had always disliked the idea and had declined the suggestion every time it was made to him. Ten years previously, Henry M. Alden, editor of *Harper's Magazine,* had written Hardy from New York to invite him to "prepare for publication in the *Magazine* some papers of a reminiscent or autobiographical sort which might ultimately be gathered together into a book," but Hardy had not accepted the invitation; and when, in April, 1910, the proposal was repeated, it was again declined. Hardy had replied that he "could not appear in a better place" than in *Harper's Magazine,* "but it is absolutely unlikely that I shall ever change my present intention not to produce my reminiscences to the world." [4] But after April, 1910, several things happened to make Hardy change his mind. He had had some correspondence with Frank A. Hedgcock (the Max Gate files preserve letters from Hedgcock dated 12 August 1907, 2 December 1907, and 19 July 1910), but Hardy was not at all prepared for what he found in Hedgcock's book, *Thomas Hardy, Penseur et Artiste,* when it was published in Paris in 1911. There he came upon "many erroneous and grotesque statements advanced as his [own] experiences," [5] and he reluctantly came to the conclusion that the only way to protect himself from the future publication of such "erroneous statements" was to prepare a truthful account himself.

Unfortunately, this was not an easy thing to do, for Hardy had not kept a systematic day-by-day record, and his "entries of his doings were always of a fitful and irregular kind." [6] "He had kept, at casual times, a record of his experiences in social life, though it had always been a drudgery to him." [7] He had, however, preserved letters and to them he now turned for help. "His memoranda," so he later reported, get "more and more meagre as the years go on, until we are almost entirely dependent on letter-references." [8] So to his unassorted stacks of old letters he turned and, as Mrs. Hardy afterwards described the process, the "letters were sorted and tied in bundles by years." On 6 February 1919 she wrote to Sydney Cockerell at Cambridge: "The letter sorting is still going on—nineteen years more to do." Mrs. Hardy then added: "When they are all sorted, I am going to arrange them under initials, instead of dates." The letters which Hardy planned to use in the autobiography were put aside for preservation, and a few others were salvaged, but great quantities of letters were then burned, prior to Hardy's writing Sir George Douglas on 7 May 1919 about "destroying papers of the last thirty or forty years."

Hardy's plan was to conceal his authorship of the biographical narrative by delaying its publication until after his death (an event which he felt could not be far off, for he was approaching his seventy-ninth birthday when he wrote Douglas), and to have the work published as if it had been written by his wife. This plan was kept a carefully guarded secret, but news of it leaked out. "Only five people . . . know of it," wrote T. E. Lawrence,[9] but five were enough to render it impossible to keep the secret forever inviolate. The five who were "in the know" may now be identified as Lascelles Abercrombie, James M. Barrie, Cyril Clemens (Mark Twain's nephew), Sydney Cockerell, and Lawrence himself. When, shortly after Hardy's death on 11 January 1928, Abercrombie was invited to prepare a new article about Hardy for the fourteenth edition of the *Encyclopaedia Britannica,* he responded with alacrity, ending his article with a bibliographical statement which clearly shows that Abercrombie was one of those to whom Hardy had disclosed the secret about the autobiography; for the *Britannica* article stated that "In 1928 appeared his *Memoirs,* written in the third person." Unfortunately, in his eagerness to meet the *Britannica* deadline, Abercrombie wrote this note before the publication of *The Early Life of Thomas Hardy* on 2 November 1928 and thus deprived himself of the opportunity to refer to the book by title.

Tucked into a bibliographical note as this statement was, it passed unobserved by most readers; and when Abercrombie was later asked (as he was by the present writer) about his reference to "*Memoirs* written in the third person," he decided to give loyal support to the myth of Mrs. Hardy's authorship of *The Early Life* and fell back first on evasive replies and then on noncommittal silence. This refusal to explain his reference to *Memoirs* opened the door to later claims of priority (whatever they may be worth) regarding the earliest disclosure of Hardy's secret. Cyril Clemens, for example, reported in 1944 that on "an October day in the year 1925" Hardy had told him, "in confidence," that he was then engaged in the business of writing his autobiography, but that the plan was "to have the work appear after my death as a biography of myself written by my wife." [10] And in 1960 the claim was made that "the first disclosure of Hardy's authorship of *The Early Life* . . .— apart from the *New York Times* account [in 1940 of a lecture delivered at the Grolier Club in New York City] . . .—was made in *Thomas Hardy, A Bibliographical Study*" in 1954.[11] Despite these rival claims, however, the 1929 *Britannica* shows that Hardy's secret was not only out but even in print long before the "disclosures" of 1944 and 1954.

Mrs. Hardy's letter of 6 February 1919 to Sydney Cockerell, telling him of her intention to rearrange the letters "under initials, instead of dates," offers a partial explanation of the condition in which the Max Gate letters were finally found when they came to the Dorset County Museum in Dorchester where they are now housed. For many of the letters are not grouped by dates, but are assembled in stout manila envelopes "under initials"—an "M" envelope, for example, contains letters from Macmillan, Maitland, Masefield, Morley, Morris, Murray, and others—but before Mrs. Hardy had gone very far in her rearranging she ran into the difficulties with which every cataloguer and every bibliographer is familiar. One example will suffice. Lady Hester Pinney wrote Hardy a letter, 16 January 1926, in which she discussed the facts of a true story about a public execution that had taken place in Dorchester when Hardy was a boy—an event which he had recalled when he was engaged in writing *Tess of the D'Urbervilles.* How should one file such a letter? Under "P" for Pinney? Under "T" for *Tess?* Or leave it in a bundle marked "1926"? The letter finally landed in an envelope marked "B". Why? "B" for Martha Brown, the name of the woman whose public execution Hardy remembered; and in the "B" envelope Lady Pinney's letter of 1926 is now a close neighbor of one written on 8 May 1888 by Robert Browning, thanking Hardy for the gift of a copy of *Wessex Tales.*

Hardy's work on the autobiography occupied him during the years 1919 to 1926, and throughout that period letters continued to arrive at Max Gate. Unlike Charles Dickens at Gad's Hill, Hardy (in these later years) allowed the incoming mail to accumulate; and when, after his death, Mrs. Hardy had the task of trying to cope with the accumulation, she decided to follow her husband's earlier example and light a fire. The Max Gate gardener has recently described what happened:

> Within a week or so . . . , there was a grand clearance of . . . letters and other papers from his [Hardy's] study. I was given the task of burning . . . bundles of newspapers on a bonfire in

the garden. Mrs. Hardy stood by . . . to ensure that nothing escaped the flames. . . . Mrs. Hardy herself burnt, on another bonfire, baskets full of the letters and private papers that I had carried down from the study to the garden under her supervision and watchful eye. She would not let me burn these, but insisted upon doing it herself, and after all the papers had been destroyed, she raked the ashes to be sure that not a single scrap or word remained. . . . My impression was she did not want any of the letters . . . to be seen by anyone. . . . Whether she was destroying them on her own initiative or carrying out the wishes of her late husband I never knew, and the world will never learn what went up in flames on that "bonfire day".[12]

The two conflagrations at Max Gate, one in 1919 and the other in 1928, have doubtless deprived the reader and the future biographer of much that would have been helpful. To quote the *Times Literary Supplement* once again: "Letters would have helped to keep the record straight." Even so, enough has remained to serve many useful purposes, some of which the present report aims at suggesting.

Mrs. Hardy died in October, 1937, providing in her will for the construction of a Hardy Memorial Room in the Dorset County Museum. This Room was opened to the public on 10 May 1939 by the Poet Laureate, John Masefield. At that time it was expected that the Room would shortly house all the books, papers, letters, and other surviving memorabilia which had been removed from Max Gate, but the outbreak of World War II soon thereafter delayed the transfer. As a result the letters preserved by Hardy were not deposited in the Memorial Room until some years later, after the war had ended. By that date, various other things had happened. When Mrs. Hardy discovered, after the 1928 bonfire which she had supervised, that there still remained a mountainous quantity of salvaged letters, she invited Miss Kitty Inglis of Weymouth to assist her in sorting and classifying the letters. This led at times to decisions at variance with those that had previously been made. Next, when some of the major groups of letters seemed important enough to give rise to thoughts of publication, they were extracted from the files, and Mrs. Dorothy M. Meech was hired to come to Max Gate with a portable typewriter and make copies of these letters.[13] Mrs. Meech accordingly made "numerous daily visits lasting for some weeks," in the course of which she typed a number of the transcripts (not all of them) which are now present in the Museum.

The plan to publish never materialized. Mrs. Hardy's ill health, and various other considerations, interfered with the plan; but the 1928 preparation of typescript copies has in some cases resulted in our possession of information that might otherwise not have become available to us. One illustration may here be cited. In 1923 the Honorable Mrs. Arthur Henniker died, and shortly thereafter 150 of the letters Thomas Hardy had written to her were returned to Max Gate, where their preservation has been generally assumed to be by Hardy's own decision. He had, we now know, preserved thirty-eight of her letters to him, but had preserved none written by her prior to 30 May 1910.[14]

Hardy had met Florence Henniker in May, 1893, and in the course of the next six months he wrote her no fewer than twenty-four letters. It has been commonly assumed that such a statement as Purdy's, that "Hardy's letters to Mrs. Henniker were returned at her death in 1923," [15] means that they were returned *to him;* but Mrs. Hardy's handwritten note, at the end of the typescript made by Mrs. Meech, indicates that this was not so. Florence Hardy wrote: "There must have been other letters [and there certainly were; the evidence on this point is conclusive], but these are all that were sent me. F. H." Sent *me.* The Henniker letters were sent to Mrs. Hardy because her long and intimate friendship with Mrs. Henniker was well known. Florence Henniker was the one who, in 1904, first brought Florence Dugdale to call at Max Gate, and Florence Henniker was among the first to whom Hardy wrote to announce his marriage in 1914 to Florence Dugdale. Mrs. Hardy's note that the letters "were sent *me*" (my italics) indicates the probability that their survival, and certainly their being copied in typescript, are due to decisions made by Mrs. Hardy and not by her husband.

No matter which one of the two made the decision to save or to burn, the important fact is that more than five thousand items have been allowed to survive. They are *there*—uncatalogued, it is true, unsystematically arranged, and at times illogically "sorted" by Miss Inglis—but there they are. The letters survive, not only to show us what use Hardy made of them in writing his autobiography—for example, his use of Robert Louis Stevenson's letter in 1886 written in praise of *The Mayor of Casterbridge*—but also to show us two other aspects of the autobiography: its occasional errors and its frequent omissions.

An example of error may be given by calling attention to page 127 of *The Early Life,* where (near the bottom of the page) Hardy reports the arrangements he made with Leslie Stephen for the serialization of *Far from the Madding Crowd* in *The Cornhill Magazine.* Hardy states: "At the end of October [1873] an unexpected note from the *Cornhill* editor asked if, supposing he were to start *Far from the Madding Crowd* in the January number (which would be out the third week in December) instead of the spring, as [previously] intended, Hardy could keep in front of the printers with his copy." The letters from Stephen, now preserved in the Museum at Dorchester, make it clear that in writing this sentence Hardy confused several letters and garbled the dates. When Leslie Stephen wrote on 20 October 1873 (not "at the *end* of October"), he expected to begin the serialization of the novel in the February, 1874, number of the *Cornhill* (not in "the spring"), and it was

314

not until 18 November 1873 that he wrote his "unexpected note" proposing to start the novel in the January number. The truth is therefore much more startling than Hardy's report of it. The first installment of the novel was actually in print within one month of Stephen's "unexpected" advancement of the date for beginning.

There are other instances of such slips on Hardy's part. In *Later Years* he reports (page 134) that the University of Virginia invited him "in the following January (1909) . . . to attend the celebration of the 100th anniversary of the birth of Edgar Allan Poe"; the letter from the University is, however, dated 12 December 1908. On page 133 of *The Later Years* Hardy states that "The remainder of the month [of July, 1908] was spent in Dorset." Hardy's correspondence shows, however, that this was not so. After attending the Milton Tercentenary Celebration at Cambridge on 10 and 11 July, Hardy sat in London to Sir Hubert von Herkomer for a portrait, he attended in Kensington the wedding of Edmund Gosse's son, when Philip married (on 14 July) Miss Gertrude Agnes Hay, he made a trip out to Bushey, and he accepted an invitation to have lunch on the 17th at the House of Commons.[16] None of this was "in Dorset."

Such slips are, of course, not very important, but there are other instances where the autobiographical account falsifies the facts. In such instances we can be grateful for letters that set the record straight. In *The Later Years,* for example, Hardy tries to pass off his "Satires of Circumstance" as "humorous productions which had been issued [by him] with a light heart before the war" (page 164). The twelve "Satires" had originally appeared in the *Fortnightly Review* in April, 1911, but they had *not* been issued "with a light heart": Hardy's correspondence shows this. The poems had, in fact, been written in great bitterness of spirit —Edmund Gosse's way of describing them was to remark that "the wells of human hope have been poisoned for him

[Hardy]"—and when the poems were collected in *Satires . . . , Lyrics and Reveries* (1914) Hardy wrote Gosse that "The little group of satires cost me much sadness in having to reprint them in the volume." [17] But *did* he have to reprint them? And *was* it done with much sadness? The letters that survive say "No" to both these questions. On 28 August Hardy wrote to Sydney Cockerell: "What I care most about just now is that the poems entitled *Satires of Circumstance* (they are by no means all satires, but the title seems as good as any) should be brought out by the Macmillans. . . . The manuscript is already in their hands." [18]

Even more helpful than the letters that serve as correctives are those that help to fill in the numerous gaps in *The Early Life* and *The Later Years*. Some of these gaps are instances of modest reticence on Hardy's part; others, of more significant silence. Let me give examples of both kinds.

Hardy himself says nothing in the autobiography about his having been offered a knighthood. One reads rumors about such an offer, but are the rumors true? On Sunday, 24 November 1912, when Hardy's American admirer Rebekah Owen called on Mr. and Mrs. Albert Bankes at Wolfeton House, near Dorchester, Mr. Bankes lamented to Miss Owen that Hardy "had three times refused a knighthood." [19] Was the report true or false? The autobiography does not say. But the Max Gate files contain a letter from the Right Honorable H. H. Asquith, dated 2 November 1908, asking "if I could persuade you to accept a Knighthood." Four days later the Prime Minister wrote again to say that he fully understood Hardy's "desire to have fuller time to consider." Asquith had apparently told his wife about the offer made to Hardy, but failed to tell her about Hardy's refusal of the offer. As a result Margot Asquith addressed him as "Dear Sir Thomas" and continued to write to "Dear Sir Thomas" long after she ought to have known that Thomas had decided not to become a "Sir."

In the Max Gate files, gap-filling letters are not always found where one might expect to find them. A good illustration of this fact may be given by citing letters that deal with Hardy's debut as a London author—an event the centenary of which passed unobserved only a few months ago. Hardy's sketch "How I Built Myself a House" was published anonymously in *Chambers's Journal* for 18 March 1865, but the Max Gate files retain no contemporary letters about that publication. Hardy's bonfire in 1919 was, in fact, so drastically carried out that only eighteen letters have survived from the 1860's. But there are other pertinent letters of later date. On 27 June 1891 John Lane, the London publisher, wrote to Hardy to propose the preparation of a bibliography of his works: it appeared in print three years later as part of Lionel Johnson's pioneer book *The Art of Thomas Hardy*. In the course of lending assistance to Lane in the preparation of this bibliography, Hardy could unostentatiously disclose his authorship of the anonymous sketch published in 1865.

Lane's "Bibliography," appearing only three years after the date when *Tess of the D'Urbervilles* had successfully carried Hardy's name all over the world, proved a great boon to the book collectors who were beginning to crop up in all sorts of unexpected places. In Cleveland, Ohio, for example. There one Paul Lemperly tried to find a copy of *Chambers's Journal* and, failing to find it, eventually wrote Hardy in December, 1909, to propose a reissue of "How I Built Myself a House." Hardy deliberated for several weeks but on 3 January 1910 wrote Lemperly as follows: "I have considered the suggestion you make . . . for reprinting . . . 'How I Built Myself a House.' The idea does not commend itself to me, the sketch being unrepresentative, and having arisen out of an incident that had no connection with my literary pursuits at the time." Ten years later, when Hardy set to work to write his autobiography, he was even more depreciatory in his attitude toward the sketch in *Chambers's* than he had been when he wrote to the Cleveland book collector. In *The Early Life* he called the sketch "a trifle . . . written to amuse the pupils of Blomfield."

However, further exploration of the Max Gate files reveals the fact that Hardy had not always regarded "How I Built Myself a House" as a trifle. On the contrary, there was a time when he regarded it as quite momentous. We learn this when we come upon a letter Hardy received (18 April 1878) from the editor of *The Literary World* in Boston, Massachusetts, asking for biographical information about the author of *The Return of the Native*, then being serialized in *Belgravia* in London and in *Harper's Magazine* in New York. The novelist promptly responded to the request from Boston, and his autobiographical thumbnail portrait appeared in *The Literary World* for 1 August 1878. There, on page 46, Hardy reported, among other things, that he had "sent a first attempt in fiction to a London magazine. It was at once accepted, and his career was determined." That is to say, the prompt acceptance of "How I Built Myself a House" by the editor of *Chambers's Journal* in 1865 "determined" Hardy's readiness to forsake the career as an architect on which he had embarked three years previously, and to risk shifting to a precarious literary career, one which led eventually to burial in Poets' Corner, Westminster Abbey.

Paul Lemperly in Cleveland, Ohio, was not the only one to show an interest in the 1865 work. The editor of the London *Review of Reviews* reprinted the sketch in the issue of that magazine for 15 May 1922, and two weeks later Mrs. Florence Henniker wrote Hardy to express her pleasure in "your story about the house." A year later, in a new edition of Lionel Johnson's *The Art of Thomas Hardy*, John Lane published "A Bibliography of First Edi-

tions of Thomas Hardy" in which the priority of the sketch
was again emphasized. A graduate student at Columbia
University hunted up the anonymous work and eventually
reprinted it in 1925 in a book entitled *Life and Art by
Thomas Hardy,* edited by Ernest Brennecke.

On Hardy's eighty-third birthday, an inquirer named
Margaret Shewring wrote from Bristol to ask the editor of
Chambers's Journal whether he too was planning to reprint
"How I Built Myself a House." The editor of the *Journal*
at this date was Charles Chambers, son of the Robert Cham-
bers who was the nephew of William Chambers who
founded the *Journal* in 1832. (William was the older
brother of Robert Chambers, author of the *Vestiges of the
Natural History of Creation* which Tennyson had studied
before writing about "scarpèd cliff and quarried stone" in
In Memoriam.) Charles Chambers deliberated, but on 21
June 1924 he wrote Hardy about "the approach of the
Diamond Jubilee of your reign" and indicated the readiness
of *Chambers's Journal* to celebrate the occasion. Hardy responded on 27 June; Chambers wrote again on 11 and 30
July, and in the final outcome "How I Built Myself a
House" was again reprinted in the January, 1925, issue of
Chambers's Journal, together with an editorial comment on
the occasion headed " 'Tis Sixty Years Since." Hardy soon
had reason to see that in the eyes of readers his sketch was
not "a trifle," for on the first day of the New Year, 1925,
one William S. Dixon wrote Hardy to express pleasure in
the story, and Dixon's letter was *not* one of those tossed
into the flames by Mrs. Hardy three years later.

Hardy may have had little to say in the autobiography
about his London debut, but he had even less to say about
his first appearance as an author in New York; in fact, he
never mentions it. It is interesting, therefore, to discover
that two letters which escaped the two fires at Max Gate,
two letters written fifty-one years apart, both point to the

effectiveness of the voluntary and unpaid aid rendered to Hardy in New York by a young man who is never mentioned in *The Early Life* at all, one whose services as impresario for the New York debut were never heralded and perhaps never appreciated by the novelist. Those two letters were, however, retained by Hardy in his files and both serve to contradict the bitter statement in *Jude the Obscure* (I, iv) that "Somebody might have come along . . . who . . . might have cheered him. . . . But nobody did come, because nobody does." It is clear to *us* that at times somebody does come along, and in 1873 that somebody was Frederick Macmillan, nephew of Alexander Macmillan, the London publisher who had rejected Hardy's first three offerings.

Fred was then twenty-two years old. He had been sent from London to learn about the business of the New York branch of the publishing house, and he obviously brought with him a copy of *Under the Greenwood Tree,* the recently published London novel. In 1873 there was doubtless no one in New York other than Frederick Macmillan who knew that the author of this anonymous work was Thomas Hardy, and the identity of the author was known to young Macmillan solely by reason of the fact that, before the publication of the novel by Tinsley, it had been offered to Fred's uncle, Alexander Macmillan.

Fred arrived in New York in 1872 and spent five years there. Upon his return to London in 1876 he took an American wife home with him. In 1874 he had married Miss Georgiana Elizabeth Warrin, of Newton, Long Island. In the course of his wooing Miss Warrin, Fred had told her about Hardy's novel and had lent her his copy to read. Fifty years later, after Hardy had been admitted to the Order of Merit, and after Fred had become Sir Frederick and Georgiana had become Lady Macmillan, she wrote to Hardy (18 April 1924) as follows: "I made your acquaintance through *Under the Greenwood Tree* before I was married and have been a constant follower and admirer ever since. . . . Believe me ever to be one of the many to whom you have given many hours of happiness."

In addition to telling his future bride about Hardy, young Fred also talked about the unknown English novelist to Henry Holt, a young publisher in New York who was just setting out on what was to be a long and successful career. On 29 May 1873, before Hardy's name had as yet appeared upon the title page of any book, Holt wrote to Hardy as follows: "My friend Mr. Frederick Macmillan has directed my attention to your writings with a favourable criticism which, coming from him [Fred was then twenty-two!], predisposed my own. I have [accordingly] caused *Under the Greenwood Tree* to be prepared for publication, which will soon take place." [20] It did. The book was out within a week of Holt's writing; its publication marks the beginning of what was destined to be a most profitable side of Hardy's career as a novelist. Of that fact he came in time to be well aware. In one of the letters in the Max Gate files (5 December 1890), he speaks of "the passing of the Copyright Bill by the American House of Representatives" and of his thereby saving (i.e., profiting by) "the Copyright of *Tess* in America" and of "how fortunate" that piece of good luck will be.[21]

It has sometimes been assumed—and asserted—that what Hardy preserved in his letter files was chiefly, if not exclusively, his business correspondence. This assumption is ill-founded. He did, it is true, preserve at least some of his business letters, some (for example) from Smith, Elder & Co. in London and from Harper & Brothers in New York. But in 1877, when H. S. King & Co. published a new edition of *A Pair of Blue Eyes,* Hardy retained no letters from this publishing house. In 1889 he corresponded with Ward & Downey about the publication of a new edition of *Desper-*

ate Remedies. His letters *to* this firm have survived (they are now in the Colby College Library), but there are no letters *from* Ward & Downey in the Max Gate files. In 1892 Heinemann published a third edition of *Desperate Remedies,* but there is nothing from Heinemann among the Max Gate letters. On 3 March 1896 Harper & Brothers acknowledged their receipt of letters from Hardy dated 9, 11, 14, and 21 February 1896; Hardy had kept copies of two of these letters but not of the other two.

He was equally inconsistent and unsystematic in his handling of personal letters. In June, 1893, he had been entertained at lunch by General George B. Milman, who was Major of Her Majesty's Tower of London. At this time Hardy met the General's daughter, Lena. On Friday, 9 June, he took her to Toole's Theatre to see Barrie's play, *Walker, London,* and in the six months that followed, Hardy wrote to Lena Milman at least five times. He sent her his photograph and asked for hers in return. When he failed to receive it, he wrote and asked again. She kept all his letters; he destroyed all of hers—all except one. On 17 August 1908 Lena Milman wrote Hardy: "I am engaged to be married."

Hardy retained the letter of Stuart J. Reid (27 July 1892), asking whether the novelist would care to receive a call from "a young lady, charming and intellectual," who was eager to meet him. She was a Miss Rebekah Owen from New York City. With Hardy's permission, she came to Dorchester and, in the company of her sister Catharine, called at Max Gate on 5 August 1892. She so captivated the novelist that, in the preface to a new edition of *The Mayor of Casterbridge* (1895) he referred to her and her sister as "some good judges across the Atlantic." From that date on, Rebekah Owen continued to write to Hardy; she corresponded also with both of his wives. On 14 December 1915 Mrs. Florence Hardy addressed her as "Best and Belovedest

Betty" (Rebekah did not like to be called Becky), and in the year 1916 alone, Florence wrote no fewer than thirty-three letters to "Betty," who by this time had left New York and was living in England. But not a single communication *from* Rebekah Owen survives among the Max Gate letters.

Professor William Lyon Phelps of Yale called on Hardy in September, 1900, and began writing to him soon thereafter. Phelps's *Autobiography* quotes letters the Yale professor received from Max Gate, but only one letter from Phelps was preserved by Hardy, a letter of 9 December 1919 inviting Hardy (at the age of seventy-nine!) to come to Yale to deliver two lectures. Hardy replied that such a thing was "out of my power."

Hardy and Henry James were acquainted for nearly forty years and often sat side by side on various occasions in London—at meetings of the Rabelais Club, for example, at Tennyson's funeral, at Philip Gosse's wedding, and the like. If, knowing of this long acquaintance, Professor McElderry had gone to Dorchester, in the course of preparing to write his critical biography of Henry James, and had looked into the Max Gate files for letters from James, he would probably have been disappointed. For there are only four such letters there: one dated 13 July 1889 inviting Hardy to dinner—"a modest cutlet"—and then, after a gap of twenty-six years, two letters in July, 1915, soliciting a contribution from Hardy to Mrs. Wharton's war-time compilation, *The Book of the Homeless;* and finally a letter of 10 August 1915 in which James tells Hardy that his "fine strong stanzas" in the "Cry of the Homeless" (a poem eventually printed in Mrs. Wharton's book, London, 1916, page 16) made James "so dreadfully aware of *my* mere flapping voluminous verbiage."

If a search for James letters would have disappointed Professor McElderry, there would have been compensations. For the Max Gate files contain surprises of the sort described by Hardy's old editor in the *Cornhill* office. Leslie Stephen once declared that "no one is a real reading enthusiast until he is sensible of the pleasure of turning over [the pages of] some miscellaneous collection, lying like a trout in a stream, snapping up with the added charm of unexpectedness any of the queer little morsels of oddity or pathos that may drift past him." The visitor who turns over the pages of the collection of letters in the Hardy Memorial Room will have abundant opportunity to snap up little morsels of one kind or another as they drift past. From Ellen Terry, for example, comes sincere appreciation of *Jude the Obscure* as "better than *Tess*: far finer than your finest," whereas Mrs. Humphry Ward feels moved to confess "I am not going to pretend that I liked *Jude*." Virginia Woolf tells Hardy that, in her opinion, his *Satires, Lyrics and Reveries* is "the most remarkable book to appear in my lifetime." Champ Clark, for more than a quarter of a century a Member of Congress and from 1911 to 1919 Speaker of the House of Representatives, considered (so we learn from a letter of 20 June 1910) that *The Mayor of Casterbridge* is "the greatest novel in the English language." A future Poet Laureate, John Masefield, declares (2 November 1911): "I should be very proud, if you, the greatest of living English poets, would accept from me this little English poem." And Edmund Gosse, calling Hardy his "most admired of friends," thanks him in 1919 "for the unbroken record of nearly forty-five years of precious intercourse" and expresses the hope that they may both live "to celebrate our Jubilee of Friendship."

There are surprises, too, of another sort. Florence Henniker explodes (on 10 March 1922): "I think it is *absurd* to have given the 'O.M.' to Sir James Barrie. It might as well have been bestowed on Arthur Bouchier or Fay Compton!" On 26 October 1923 a frivolous girl in Yonkers, New York, wrote to ask Hardy, "with your eyes shut," to draw her a pig and send the drawing to her.

On 2 March 1918 Gosse wrote to Hardy: "Why does it make you so indignant to be called a 'pessimist'?" Hardy's reply to a question of this sort would open the door to a discussion of what was obviously, to Hardy, the most interesting subject of all, one's philosophy of life, a subject far more interesting than any discussion of literary techniques or of metrical theories. But that would carry us far beyond the limits of a *Festschrift* contribution.

As early as 25 February 1876 Hardy received an inquiry about the possibility of a German translation of *Far from the Madding Crowd,* and a letter of 20 March 1876 inquires about a Danish translation. From this modest beginning, when Hardy was only thirty-five years old, his fame spread until it reached every corner of the world. One of the surprising discoveries that await the researcher among the thousands of letters that survived the two great bonfires at Max Gate is the evidence that Hardy's grim message came eventually to appeal to readers all over the earth. Edwin Arlington Robinson, of Gardiner, Maine, once wrote a sonnet in which he spoke of "seeing the cottage lights of Wessex beam" in Maine. Obviously, those lights have been seen beaming in many far more distant places, for the letters now in the Museum at Dorchester came to Hardy from no fewer than thirty-eight countries outside of England. We can sense the reason for this wide appeal. On 4 March 1886 Hardy wrote in his notebook: "The human race . . . [is] one great network or tissue which quivers in every part when one point is shaken, like a spider's web if touched." This attitude toward mankind is clearly the idea which eventually led to the establishment of the United Nations, and the all-inclusiveness of Hardy's sympathy with suffering men and women everywhere goes far toward explaining the warm, world-wide reception his writings have enjoyed.

NOTES

1. *TLS*, February 11, 1965, pp. 97, 99.
2. Leon Edel, in *Willa Cather: a Critical Biography* by E. K. Brown (New York, 1953), p. xxiii.
3. See Sir George Douglas, "Thomas Hardy: Some Recollections and Reflections," *Hibbert Journal*, XXVI (April, 1928), 385–398.
4. Carl J. Weber, *Hardy in America* (Waterville, Maine, 1946), p. 103.
5. Florence Emily Hardy, *The Early Life of Thomas Hardy* (London, 1928), p. vii.
6. Florence Emily Hardy, *The Later Years of Thomas Hardy* (London, 1930), p. 37.
7. *The Later Years*, p. 66.
8. *The Later Years*, p. 108.
9. *Letters of T. E. Lawrence*, ed. David Garnett (London, 1938), p. 475.
10. Cyril Clemens, *My Chat with Thomas Hardy* (Webster Groves, Missouri, 1944), pp. 15, 26.
11. R. L. Purdy, in a letter entitled "Authorship of Hardy's Biography," *TLS*, December 20, 1960.
12. Bertie Norman Stephens, *Thomas Hardy in His Garden* (Beaminster, Dorset, 1963), pp. 15–16.
13. See Dorothy M. Meech, *Memories of Mr and Mrs Thomas Hardy* (Beaminster, Dorset, 1963).
14. R. L. Purdy states, *Thomas Hardy, A Bibliographical Study* (New York, 1954), p. 344: "A few of Mrs. Henniker's letters, 1910–1922, are . . . among the Max Gate papers." Actually, there are more than "a few"—thirty-six, to be exact.
15. Purdy, *Thomas Hardy*, p. 344.
16. See *"Dearest Emmie"*: Hardy's Letters to His First Wife, ed. Carl J. Weber (London, 1963), pp. 71–72.
17. See *Hardy's Love Poems*, ed. Carl J. Weber (London, 1963), p. 68.
18. *Letters of Thomas Hardy*, ed. Carl J. Weber (Waterville, Maine, 1954), p. 99.
19. Carl J. Weber, *Hardy and the Lady from Madison Square* (Waterville, Maine, 1952), p. 163.
20. Weber, *Hardy in America*, p. 15.
21. *"Dearest Emmie,"* pp. 8–9.

Selected List of the Publications of Bruce Robert McElderry, Jr.

Compiled by Max F. Schulz

Excluded from this list are approximately one hundred book and theater reviews published in *The Personalist* and newspapers.

I. AMERICAN LITERATURE

BOOKS

Thomas Wolfe. New York: Twayne Publishing Company, 1964.
Henry James. New York: Twayne Publishing Company, 1965.

EDITIONS

Hamlin Garland. *Main-Travelled Roads.* New York: Harper & Brothers, 1956. Reissued in the Perennial Classics Series by Harper and Row, 1965.
Hamlin Garland. *Boy Life on the Prairie.* Lincoln, Nebraska: University of Nebraska Press, 1961. Bison Books Series.
A. B. Longstreet. *Georgia Scenes.* New York: Sagamore Press, 1957.

Bibliography

Contributions to the Galaxy, 1868–1871, by Mark Twain. Gainesville, Florida: Scholars' Facsimiles and Reprints, 1961.

Owen Chase. *A Narrative of the Whale-Ship Essex.* New York: Corinth Books, 1963.

The Realistic Movement in American Writing. New York: The Odyssey Press, 1965.

ARTICLES AND REVIEWS

POE

"The Edgar Allan Poe Collection," *The Library Bulletin,* University of Southern California (1948).

"Poe's Concept of the Soul," *N & Q,* II (1955), 173–174.

LOWELL

"J. R. Lowell and 'Richard III'—A Bibliographical Error," *N & Q,* V (1958), 179–180.

EMERSON

"Emerson's Second Address on the American Scholar," *The Personalist,* XXXIX (1958), 361–372.

"Emerson Resurgent," *The Personalist,* XLIII (1962), 127–130.

THOREAU

"An Early Review [in *National Era*] of *Walden,*" *Thoreau Society Booklet,* No. 14 (1959).

Review of James Lyndon Shanley: *The Making of* Walden. Chicago: The University of Chicago Press, 1957. In *The Personalist,* XL (1959), 91.

HAWTHORNE

"The Transcendental Hawthorne," *The Midwest Quarterly,* II (1961), 307–323.

Review of Hyatt H. Waggoner: *Hawthorne, A Critical Study.* Cambridge, Massachusetts: Harvard University Press, 1955. In *The Personalist,* XXXVII (1956), 316–318.

MELVILLE

"Three Earlier Treatments of the *Billy Budd* Theme," *AL,* XXVII (1955), 251–257.

"The *National Era* Review of *White Jacket,*" *Melville Society Newsletter,* XV (1960).

Review of Dorothee Metlitsky Finkelstein: *Melville's Orienda.* New Haven: Yale University Press, 1961. In *The Personalist,* XLIII (1962), 419.

Review of Hugh W. Hetherington: *Melville's Reviewers British and American 1846–1891.* Chapel Hill: University of North Carolina Press, 1961. In *The Personalist,* XLIII (1962), 419–420.

DICKINSON

"Emily Dickinson: A Viable Transcendentalist," *Emerson Society Quarterly*, No. 44 (1966), 17–21.

TWAIN

"Tom Sawyer's Fence—Original Illustrations," *CE*, XIX (1958), 370.

"Who Was Sarah Findlay?" *The Twainian*, September-October, 1961, p. 3.

Review of Albert E. Stone, Jr.: *The Innocent Eye: Childhood in Mark Twain's Imagination.* New Haven: Yale University Press, 1961. In *The Personalist*, XLIII (1962), 421.

Review of Roger B. Salomen: *Twain and the Image of History.* New Haven: Yale University Press, 1961. In *The Personalist*, XLIII (1962), 421–422.

GARLAND

"Hamlin Garland's View of Whitman," *The Personalist*, XXXVI (1955), 369–378.

"Boy Life on the Prairie: Hamlin Garland's Best Reminiscence," *The Educational Leader*, XXII (1959), 5–16.

"Introduction" to *Hamlin Garland: Centennial Tributes and a Checklist of the Hamlin Garland Papers in the University of Southern California Library*, ed. Lloyd A. Arvidson. Los Angeles: University of Southern California Library Bulletin, No. 9, 1962. Pp. xiii–xvi.

WHITMAN

"The Inception of 'Passage to India,'" *PMLA*, LXXI (1956), 837–839.

"Poetry and Religion: A Parallel in Whitman and Arnold," *Walt Whitman Review*, VIII (1962), 80–83.

"Robert Penn Warren and Whitman," *Walt Whitman Review*, VIII (1962), 91.

Review of Walter J. Slatoff: *Quest for Failure: A Study of William Faulkner.* Ithaca, New York: Cornell University Press, 1960. In *The Personalist*, XLII (1961), 427.

Review of Milton Hindus (editor): Leaves of Grass *One Hundred Years After.* Palo Alto: Stanford University Press, 1955. In *The Personalist*, XXXVI (1955), 431–432.

Review of Horace Traubel: *With Walt Whitman in Camden.* Philadelphia: University of Pennsylvania Press, 1953. In *The Personalist*, XXXVI (1955), 432–433.

JAMES

"The Uncollected Stories of Henry James," *AL*, XXI (1949), 279–291.

"Henry James and *The Whole Family*," *The Pacific Spectator*, IV (1950), 352–360.

"Hamlin Garland and Henry James," *AL*, XXIII (1952), 433–446.

"The Published Letters of Henry James: A Survey," *Bulletin of Bibliography*, XX (1952), 165–171, 187.

"James's Revision of *Watch and Ward*," *MLN*, LXVIII (1952), 457–461.

"Henry James's Neglected Thriller: *The Other House*," *Arizona Quarterly*, VIII (1952), 328–332.

Bibliography

768# Bibliography

"Gertrude Atherton and Henry James," *Colby Library Quarterly,* Series III (1954), 269–272.

"The 'Shy Incongruous Charm' of Daisy Miller," *NCF,* X (1955), 162–165.

"Henry James's 'The Art of Fiction,' " *Research Studies,* State College of Washington, XXV (1957), 91–100.

"Henry James," *American Literary Scholarship: An Annual/ 1963,* ed. James Woodress, Duke University Press, 1965. Pp. 64–71.

"Henry James," *American Literary Scholarship: An Annual/ 1964,* ed. James Woodress, Duke University Press, 1966. Pp. 62–72.

Review of Leon Edel (editor): *The Complete Plays of Henry James.* Philadelphia: J. B. Lippincott Co., 1949. In *AL,* XXII (1950), 205–207.

Review of Leon Edel and Gordon N. Ray (editors): *Henry James and H. G. Wells: A Record of Their Friendship, Their Debate on the Art of Fiction, and Their Quarrel.* Urbana: University of Illinois Press, 1958. In *NCF,* XIII (1958), 260–263.

Review of Leon Edel and Dan H. Laurence: *A Bibliography of Henry James.* London: Rupert Hart-Davis, 1957. In *NCF,* XIII (1958), 263–264.

Review of Richard Poirier: *The Comic Sense of Henry James: A Study of the Early Novels.* New York: Oxford University Press, 1960. In *SAQ,* LX (1961), 243–244.

Review of Oscar Cargill: *The Novels of Henry James.* New York: Macmillan, 1961. In *The Personalist,* XLIII (1962), 420–421.

Review of Walter F. Wright: *The Madness of Art: A Study of Henry James.* Lincoln, Nebraska: University of Nebraska Press, 1962. In *The Personalist,* XLIV (1963), 560–561.

Review of Krishna Baldev Vaid: *Technique in the Tales of Henry James.* Cambridge, Massachusetts: Harvard University Press, 1964. In *NCF,* XIX (1965), 413–414.

Review of Edward Stone: *The Battle and the Books: Some Aspects of Henry James.* Athens, Ohio: Ohio University Press, 1964. In *AL,* XXXVII (1965), 336–337.

ELIOT

"Eliot's 'Shakespeherian Rag,' " *American Quarterly,* IX (1957), 185–186.

"Santayana's and Eliot's 'Objective Correlative,' " *Boston University Studies in English,* III (1957), 179–181.

WOLFE

"The Autobiographical Problem in Thomas Wolfe's Novels," *Arizona Quarterly,* IV (1948), 315–324.

"Thomas Wolfe's *Look Homeward, Angel*—Twenty-five Years After," *Arizona Quarterly,* XI (1955), 123–128.

"Wolfe and Emerson on 'Flow,' " *MFS,* II (1956), 77–78.

"Thomas Wolfe: Dramatist," *Modern Drama,* VI (1963), 1–11.

STEINBECK

"*The Grapes of Wrath:* In the Light of Modern Critical Theory," *CE,* V (1944), 308–313. Reprinted in Warren French, *A Companion to*

332

the Grapes of Wrath. New York: The Viking Press, 1963. Pp. 199–208.

FAULKNER

"The Narrative Structure of Faulkner's *Light in August,*" *CE,* XIX (1958), 200–207. Reprinted in *Mississippi Quarterly,* XI (1958), 177–187.

WOUK

"The Conservative as Novelist: Herman Wouk," *Arizona Quarterly,* XV (1959), 128–136.

II. ENGLISH LITERATURE

EDITIONS

Shelley's Critical Prose. Lincoln, Nebraska: University of Nebraska Press, 1967.

ARTICLES AND REVIEWS

SPENSER

"Archaism and Innovation in Spenser's Poetic Diction," *PMLA,* XLVII (1932), 144–170.

BOSWELL

"Boswell in 1790–91: Two Unpublished Comments," *N & Q,* IX (1962), 266–268.

COLERIDGE

"Coleridge's Revision of 'The Ancient Mariner,'" *SP,* XXIX (1932), 68–94.

"Coleridge's Plan for Completing *Christabel,*" *SP,* XXXIII (1936), 437–455.

"Walton's *Lives* and Gillman's *Life of Coleridge,*" *PMLA,* LII (1937), 412–422.

"Coleridge's 'Preface' to *Christabel,*" *Wordsworth and Coleridge, Studies in Honor of George McLean Harper,* ed. Earl Leslie Griggs. Princeton: Princeton University Press, 1939. Pp. 166–172.

"*Christabel,* Coleridge, and the Commentators," *Research Studies,* State College of Washington, IX (1941), 206–212.

"Coleridge on Blake's Songs," *MLQ,* IX (1948), 298–302.

"Lowes as Critic," *TLS,* February 22, 1957, p. 113.

Review of Kathleen Coburn (editor): *The Philosophical Lectures of Samuel Taylor Coleridge.* New York: Philosophical Library, 1949. In *The Personalist,* XXXI (1950), 425–427.

WORDSWORTH *et al*

"Common Elements in Wordsworth's 'Preface' and Shelley's *Defence of Poetry,*" *MLQ,* V (1944), 175–181.

"Southey, and Wordsworth's 'The Idiot Boy,'" *N & Q,* II (1955), 490–491.

Bibliography

Review of Mary Moorman: *William Wordsworth, A Biography: The Early Years, 1770–1803.* Oxford: At the Clarendon Press, 1957. In *The Personalist,* XXXIX (1958), 321–322.

Review of Earl R. Wasserman: *Shelley's* Prometheus Unbound. Baltimore: The Johns Hopkins University Press, 1965. In *The Personalist,* XLVII (1966), 435.

BYRON

"Byron's Interest in the Americas," *Research Studies,* State College of Washington, V (1937), 145–178.
"Byron's Epitaph on Boatswain," *MLN,* LVIII (1943), 553–554.

BROWNING

"Browning and the Victorian Public in 1868–1869," *Research Studies,* State College of Washington, V (1937), 193–203.
"Victorian Evaluation of *The Ring and the Book,*" *Research Studies,* State College of Washington, VII (1939), 75–89.
"Narrative Structure of *The Ring and the Book,*" *Research Studies,* State College of Washington, XI (1943), 193–233.

THACKERAY

"Thackeray on Swift and Macaulay on Chatham," *N & Q,* I (1954), 32.

III. GENERAL TOPICS

ARTICLES AND REVIEWS

"The Philosophy of Fear," *The Personalist,* XXXV (1954), 293–299.
"The Semantics of Conservatism," *The Personalist,* XXXVI (1955), 274–280.
"Literature and Philosophy: A Vital Relationship," *Centennial Review of Arts and Science,* II (1958), 48–66.
Review of Charles Feidelson, Jr.: *Symbolism and American Literature.* Chicago: The Chicago University Press, 1954. In *The Personalist,* XXXVI (1955), 309–311.
Review of Wayne C. Booth: *The Rhetoric of Fiction.* Chicago: The University of Chicago Press, 1961. In *The Personalist,* XLIV (1963), 263–264.
Review of Ihab Hassan: *Radical Innocence: The Contemporary Novel.* Princeton: Princeton University Press, 1961. In *The Personalist,* XLIII (1962), 572–573.
Review of Richard Ellmann and Charles Feidelson, Jr. (editors): *The Modern Tradition: Backgrounds of Modern Literature.* New York: Oxford University Press, 1965. In *The Personalist,* XLVI (1965), 563.